Thirty Tomorrows

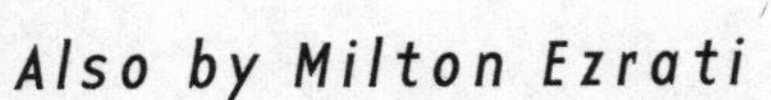

Also by Milton Ezrati

Kawari
How Japan's Economic and Cultural Transformation Will Alter the Balance of Power Among Nations.

Thirty Tomorrows

THE NEXT THREE DECADES OF GLOBALIZATION, DEMOGRAPHICS, AND HOW WE WILL LIVE

Milton Ezrati

Thomas Dunne Books
St. Martin's Press
New York

THOMAS DUNNE BOOKS.
An imprint of St. Martin's Press.

 Printed in the United States of America. For information, address St. Martin's Press, 175 Fifth Avenue, New York, N.Y. 10010.

www.thomasdunnebooks.com
www.stmartins.com

Library of Congress Cataloging-in-Publication Data

Ezrati, Milton.
Thirty tomorrows : the next three decades of globalization, demographics, and how we will live / Milton Ezrati.
pages cm
Includes bibliographical references and index.
ISBN 978-1-250-04255-2 (hardcover)
ISBN 978-1-4668-4107-9 (e-book)
1. Aging—Social aspects—United States. 2. Social prediction—United States. 3. United States—Social conditions—21st century. 4. Economic forecasting—United States. 5. United States—Economic conditions—21st century. I. Title.
HQ1064.U5E97 2014
305.260973—dc23

2013032061

St. Martin's Press books may be purchased for educational, business, or promotional use. For information on bulk purchases, please contact Macmillan Corporate and Premium Sales Department at 1-800-221-7945, extension 5442, or write specialmarkets@macmillan.com.

First Edition: April 2014

10 9 8 7 6 5 4 3 2 1

TO ISABEL

CONTENTS

ACKNOWLEDGMENTS

Right from the start, this project enjoyed the assistance of so many kind and talented people. My agent, Joseph Spieler of the Spieler Agency, initiated and framed the effort. Laura Honsberger's research assistance was invaluable. Not only did she delve deeper into all sorts of evidence than I am sure I could have, but her questions forced much clearer thinking on me. Shirley Tomkievicz read early drafts, and her objections changed the book's organization into something much cleaner, clearer, and more straightforward than I originally contemplated. Holly Miller's unflagging interest and encouragement carried me through frequent losses of confidence.

Once the manuscript was done, it benefited enormously from the careful editorial work of, first, Angela Pullen Partington, who worked to a severely tight deadline, and then Edward Mansour, who gave freely of his spare time. Michelle Toto and Naya Oktoratos also gave generously of their spare time to prepare and correct the manuscript. Each showed unbelievable patience with a never-ending series of rewrites. Specific points and questions raised by Professor Ian Partington, late of Oxford Brooks University, sharpened the argument, as, in a more general way, did my ongoing conversations and debates with colleagues Zane Brown and Robert Morris.

Once Thomas Dunne Books of St. Martin's Press accepted the manuscript, it benefited further from the team there, from Thomas Dunne's general suggestions and guidance, from Senior Editor Robert Kirkpatrick's fine editorial skills, and from Fred Chase's remarkably thorough copyediting. Margaret Brown and then Nicole Sohl, both also of Thomas Dunne, did yeoman's service shepherding this book, and me, through all the many steps to publication. While I am noting the patience, kindness, and sensitivity of others, I offer a special thanks to my daughter, Isabel Ezrati, who tolerated my many doubts and always showed a soothing confidence in the project.

All these people made this a much better book than it otherwise would have been. Still, for all their efforts, there are undoubtedly errors and other failings. These belong entirely to me.

PREFACE

This book is a forecast. It begins with the rec- ognition that populations in America, Europe, and Japan are aging. It then goes on to explain how this inexorable trend will impose tremendous economic pressure and force huge adjustments, including a massive extension of globalization. All these changes, of course, will in their turn create pressures of their own that will engender still further change.

In assessing these layers of adjustment, especially because the book considers such a long time horizon, I have resisted the temptation to extrapolate. Popular as it is these days to create exciting, extreme conclusions by extending recent trends into a distant future, such "forecasts" are always wrong. Reality seldom works that way. Trends never run uninterrupted. People, firms, and governments refuse to stand passively by while their would changed. They react. In so doing they take matters in new directions, which create new pressures and elicit additional reactions that then move matters in still other directions. These twists inform this and any reasonable long-term forecast.

The analysis offered here takes in more aspects of life than I had expected it would when I began. Though economics and finance dominate, as one would expect, matters of culture, social organization, and politics intrude throughout. Some of this material yields rich veins of interest. Mining them was inviting but also threatened to make the discussion ungainly. Worse, such tangents threatened to obscure the underlying argument. To keep the book on track I have at times only sketched the otherwise rich details behind certain issues, pointed to the conclusions of other research. I reserved most of my attention for how matters fit with the other elements of the larger argument. I have, however, referenced this material for any reader interested in more detailed investigation.

What I offer is, I believe, an accurate picture of the future for this and other economies. There is, of course, plenty of room for error. Though demographic trends change only very slowly, and so offer a solid basis for analysis, responses of individuals, firms, and governments are much less predictable, especially over such a long period. With these I have relied on plausibility and practicality, assuming, I think reasonably, that people, firms, and governments rationally follow their own interests, at least over the longer run. But even when reality deviates from these expectations, and at times it inevitably will, the analysis should, nonetheless, help investors, businesspeople, and governments position themselves for this long future, for I identify not just likelihoods but also the potential pitfalls and alternatives that will emerge as events unfold and pressures build. This background should equip readers not only to assess for themselves the ongoing flow of information but also to weigh the probable effect of unforeseen events.

In pulling together these many and, as I discovered, diverse elements, I was continually reminded of the great pitfalls of any temptingly elegant interpretation of reality. These can account for neither all we know nor, of course, the unforeseen, but they still serve a crucial purpose by giving those involved a notion of the forces at work and offering a means to distinguish between the probable, the plausible, and the merely possible.

It was, I am sure, with similar distinctions in mind that General Dwight Eisenhower told his staff on the eve of the D-Day invasion of Europe that the plan was "useless," but the planning was "indispensable."[1] He knew that the shooting would immediately spin events to veer in unexpected directions. But he had confidence that the effort to pull together all the pieces would, nonetheless, give his officers an understanding of capabilities and constraints, and so also give them the ability to judge how matters were likely to take shape even in the face of inevitable surprises. If this future will likely avoid the carnage of D-Day, this intense economic, financial, political, and social reality nonetheless will, as with that battle, move away from the details of even the most carefully constructed outlook, making the analysis behind the plan infinitely more valuable than its specific conclusions.

In assessing these anticipated actions and reactions, and in making recommendations for future actions, the analysis will, from time to time, seem to argue from contradictory political ideologies. Sometimes the text will support active government—in areas such as training, for instance. At other times it will seem pro-business when, for example, it advocates government-business partnerships for research and development. And sometimes it will take a seemingly strident, free-market tone that would have government step out of the process altogether, as, for instance, when I point out how regulations can stifle innovation and impede needed adjustments. The ideological confusion emerges from my commitment to practical perspectives and a reality that is too complex for ideology.

The end product will, I hope, bring clarity, even if it frustrates simplistic interpretations. I am confident that the analysis will open much room for disagreement. In the belief that men and women of good will can differ, I look forward to an active correspondence with those who find flaws, those who see how subsequent events complicate matters in ways that I have failed to anticipate, and, of course, those who take issue with my conclusions about what needs to be done, by either individuals, governments, or businesses.

In preparing this book, I have used insights gained from my two major professional affiliations. The opinions and conclusions expressed here are, however, strictly my own and in no way reflect those of my employer or the Center for the Study of Human Capital, Technology

Transfer and Economic Growth and Development at the State University of New York at Buffalo.

New York City
April 2013

Thirty Tomorrows

1

Growing Old Gracefully

The West and Japan are aging. Decades of de-clining birth rates have reduced the proportion of young people in these populations, creating increasingly severe shortfalls in the number of new entrants into their labor markets. At the same time, increasing life expectancies have swollen the ranks of their dependent retired populations, redoubling the burdens on these limited labor resources. The change by itself will impose severe growth constraints on these economies and even threaten existing living standards. In stark contrast, the emerging economies—India, Brazil, and China prominent among them—enjoy the benefits of large, youthful, and eager workforces, and will do so for years to come. These differences will set the economic and financial tone for the next 30 years at least.

It would be hard to overestimate the economic and financial ramifications of these demographic trends. The developed economies, to avoid economic setbacks, will come to rely more and more on the product of the emerging economies to support their outsized retired populations. The focus of economic and financial power will shift accordingly. To survive in such an environment—to have something to exchange for these imports—these developed economies will need to increase their emphasis on research, innovation, training, and education. The process will force huge industrial adjustments, change attitudes toward work and retirement, raise levels of immigration, and greatly accelerate the pace of globalization. To sustain such essential adjustments, the leaderships of these countries will need to disarm a dangerous, protectionist backlash that would block their access to emerging economies. China, India, and other emerging economies will have to make their own fundamental adjustments, too. While much can occur naturally without overarching direction, the entire effort, nonetheless, will demand purposeful leadership within each economy and globally.

Changing America's Self-Image

Though America finds itself under less intense demographic pressure than Japan or Europe, it will in many respects have the greatest trouble adjusting. Unlike Europe and Japan, America has always seen itself as a youthful society and has long claimed the virtues of youth: energy, optimism, physical strength, impulsiveness, perhaps even insouciance. It has left to other societies the virtues of age: prudence, patience, sensibility, composure, and care. But as America's reality becomes less and less youthful, certainly compared with China, India, and other emerging economies, it will have to abandon these attitudes. Its prosperity, in fact, will depend on its ability to seize the advantages of age. Though in some ways the work of change has already begun, the adjustment will not proceed easily. Nor will it proceed easily in aging Japan and Europe, even though these countries have relied less on a cult of youth.

Until recently America's identification with youth had a basis in reality. The nation was in fact young. Large families and huge waves of eager immigrants kept the average age of the nation's population low.[1] The physical structure of the economy was also young and ripe with development opportunities. From the eighteenth century to the middle of the twentieth, this young and growing workforce earned huge commercial dividends as it turned this New World's vast tracts of wilderness into farmland and interconnected it with new roads, canals, railroads, and eventually air links. And, as the existence of this infrastructure facilitated industrial development around previously untouched natural resources, the economy significantly increased those returns.

Of course Europe during this time also enjoyed great economic leaps. Strides occurred especially in technology, transportation, communication, construction, and production. But there was a fundamental difference between Europe and America. Europe's economies had already established themselves around older technologies. As they applied the new, they were not so much developing as redeveloping, modifying and refining, improving something that had already existed. Industry focused on efficiency, quality, sometimes variety. America, building new, oriented itself toward things more basic: size, volume, raw power. Its continental-sized national market reinforced the difference from a more economically Balkanized Europe.

Especially in the early stages of industrial development, these differences impelled Europe to lead in knowledge-based products. It invented mechanized spinning and the mechanized loom, the steam engine, the railroad, and the locomotive.[2] America applied itself chiefly to the challenges of vast distances and mass production. The United States had its inventions, of course. It pioneered standardized parts and invented the cotton gin as well as the reaper.[3] Not surprisingly, even America's inventions aimed at volume. It was not until much later in the nineteenth century, when much of America's de novo development was complete, that its inventors began to refocus innovative energies along lines that Europe had followed for years.

Still, these different emphases persisted right up through the Second World War and even into the second half of the twentieth century. Of course America, as it became ever more completely developed, could rely less and less on opening new areas and did begin to feel the Old World's need to find its commercial returns in replacement, rebuilding, and refinement. But in the popular imagination, the old distinctions remain stark. America even laid its victory in the Second World War at the feet of its youthful, overwhelming force. The German Tiger tank, it was said, outclassed America's Sherman tank, but the United States won the war anyway by producing its tank in overwhelming numbers. As one German tank commander noted, just one of his more sophisticated and better armored tanks could take out eight or nine of its American counterparts, but the Americans always sent 10 or more against him.[4] In the air, too, against both Germany and Japan, the message of victory came in America's ability to build more planes and throw more weight. Quality was claimed but was less obvious. Even America's great wartime invention, the atomic bomb, spoke to overwhelming force and certainly not to refinement.

It was not until the Cold War that the relative reality, if not quite the imagery, began to change. America's competition—economic, military, and diplomatic—had by then shifted east, to a still larger and less developed continental power. The Soviet Union was doing more de novo construction than America, certainly of industrial facilities, and tapping resources across a much wider range. The emphasis on mass production fit better there, and when the Soviet leader Nikita Khrushchev, in 1956, assured the world's diplomats that Soviet Russia would "bury" the West, presumably in production, if not literally, it was believable.[5] The difference showed vividly in the great competition of the time: space exploration. The Soviets emphasized force. Their bigger, more powerful rockets could lift more weight out of the atmosphere than the American rockets. The United States could meet the challenge only, it seemed, by taking a page out of old Europe's book. Deploying greater refinement, America concentrated more on sophisticated electronics, more precise and careful guidance, and miniaturization to do more with less weight.[6]

Now demographics will draw America still further from its historically youthful image and all that that means. Ancient as the cultures of China and India are, these countries, not America, hold the great, unexploited continental reaches ripe for development. They can take American, European, and Japanese innovations and apply them to regions that, if not virgin territory, are nonetheless barely touched by modern development. They have youthful, eager populations with which to do it. China's working-age population of 965 million is almost five times that of the United States. Though China's median age of 35 years is only slightly lower than America's 37, the gap will widen. India's median age today is a youthful 26 years, and its working-age population of 744 million is more than three and a half times that of the United States. Brazil, to round out the picture, has a smaller working-age population than America but a much younger population, with a median age of only 29 years.[7]

In such circumstances, the United States can no longer use its old, youthful approach as a guide. Energy and opportunity combined with overwhelming volume and force will lie increasingly with the emerging economies. America must adapt, as it did in the Space Race with the Soviets, by meeting the challenge of China, India, and other emerging economies much as Europe once met America's challenge. It must recognize that its advantages increasingly will come from refinement and innovation rather than through mass production—not in every case but generally. There is an urban myth from the 1920s that wonderfully captures the difference. As the story goes, right after the First World War American industrialists, though bigger, richer, and more powerful than their European rivals, chafed at their reputation for volume over refinement. A Connecticut copper mill challenged its British rival by sending over a length of tubing with the dare to produce something with a diameter as narrow and as consistent. When the response arrived in Connecticut, the Americans at first could find only their original tube. It took a while for them to realize that the British producers had threaded inside it their much finer piece of tubing.[8]

Making the Adjustment

Today, in matters much more sophisticated than copper tubes, American producers must meet the challenge of the emerging economies, much as the British rival met its Connecticut competitor. Old attitudes and approaches will cease to work.

Even if people have a hard time accepting the change, the demographics will force it on them. As the dearth of youth in the developed countries creates a shortage of labor, certainly compared with their outsized retired populations, these economies will adjust, or the strain will cut into their living standards. Business no doubt will try to relieve the pressure by keeping existing workers on the job longer and turning to immigrant labor, but because such remedies can only go so far, producers will increasingly look overseas for relief. Business will find it in the emerging economies' abundance of young, inexpensive, if not especially well-trained workers. By importing simpler products from them, those that require a lot of labor input, the developed economies can relieve much of the strain on their own limited workforces and, consequently, on their living standards. To have something with which to trade for these imports, production at home will need increasingly to leverage the superior training and production facilities in the developed world, emphasizing increasingly sophisticated, complex, and high-value products.

To its credit, American industry and commerce have already made great strides in this adjustment. Without any overall perspective or guidance, market signals and profit pressures have already begun the shift away from crude mass production, leaving those activities to the emerging economies, and toward more sophisticated and complex products. The United States, for instance, no longer produces inexpensive garments, plastic toys, even structural steel girders and concrete reinforcement bars. These mass-produced items come from South Korea, India, China, and elsewhere in the emerging or recently emerged world. In their place, America increasingly has emphasized technology, specialty products, and other, high-value items, as well as services. American producers have begun, as it were, to thread their own, finer tubing into that offered by China, India, et al.

Extending these adjustments, the economies of America, Europe, and Japan will increasingly have to act their age. Given the record of recent decades, there is every reason to believe that they can leave off other more muscular, obvious sorts of processes and make their money increasingly with products that require more concentration, training, and patience. This process, however, will take a change in attitude as well as action. Business will make the move under the tyranny of the bottom line. Matters in national capitals, and with the public generally, will be more problematic. Perhaps the aging baby boomer generation, less able to compete with the energy and raw power of youth, will at last come to value patience, diligence, and the products that rely on such mature virtues. Since baby boomers have always insisted that the larger society accommodate them, they just might shift the orientation of society overall, too. But the change will not come easily.

Of all the actors in this drama, the politicians in Washington and other capitals will surely have the most difficulty with the changes. They live in a world of power. Overwhelming force in output, money, and votes is what they understand and sometimes all they understand. Both Congress and the White House enjoy the idea of the United States as the biggest and most forceful in every way. They may like the idea of more refined products, but they apparently see no need to yield in the manufacture of girders, concrete reinforcement bars, and the like, no matter how compelling the economics. They will resist the change instinctively. Like their counterparts in Japan and Europe, U.S. politicians are also highly vulnerable to voters who complain about the very real pains of these adjustments, especially since those who have successfully adjusted, having no need of political assistance, will remain quiet and so effectively invisible to those in the various congresses, parliaments, and executive mansions.

However much the United States and other developed economies will struggle, the emerging economies should embrace the arrangements. Trade is their primary engine of growth. Without it, these economies would have difficulty employing their increasingly restive populations and would face severe social unrest. Though eventually their domestic consumer sectors will grow big enough to offer a market for their impressive production potentials, this will take decades. In the meantime these economies need access to the rich markets of Japan and the West. They also need trade to procure the complex goods and services essential for development and that, despite the impressive strides they have made to date, they still have trouble producing for themselves, and will for years, maybe decades, to come. They will also want the transnational investment flows on which they rely to secure the development funds that they need to build their industrial base and secure the essential management and financial expertise available only in the developed West and Japan.

Change Begets Change

But such seismic economic shifts will produce new ruptures of their own, not all of them pleasant and some dangerous. Certainly the shifting industrial emphasis, though essential to protect living standards generally, will create considerable pain and dislocation in particular sectors, industries, and geographic regions, in both the emerging and the developed economies. These hardships will generate an ever-growing resistance to globalization. They already have. It would be a mistake to underestimate the strength of such feeling. There are already ample signs of its influence in the highest reaches of government. The United States, for example, has threatened a tariff wall against Chinese products and China has promised retaliation. It would be an even bigger mistake to underestimate the extent of the danger in such trends. Protectionism, if it sometimes helps particular groups within an economy, has always hindered general economic growth and will do so especially when taking into account the future's demographic imperatives. Economies, at least those that want to prosper, will need to disarm this sentiment and meet the needs of the new economic environment by dealing with the pain of transition.

Two areas in particular cry out for such remedial action. One involves employment and wages, the other finance. Whatever benefits increased trade has brought and will continue to bring, nations can no longer ignore the tendency for it to throw people out of long-held jobs and hold back wages at the middle and lower reaches of the income distributions, seemingly killing America's middle-class dream and its equivalents in Japan and Europe. Nations must also wake up to the association between globalization and the horribly destructive boom-bust financial cycles of recent years, most notably the disastrous collapse in 2008–09. Unless the world's economies can address these and other ills the backlash against globalization will deprive them of the welcome relief it can offer from demographic strains.

Given these needs and dangers, it is sad how most nations to date have such a patchy record relieving the strains of globalization and the social tensions created by them. The United States, true to its traditions, has left its financial markets to swing, almost unimpeded, up and down under the influence of global financial flows. It has left most workers displaced by globalization to find their own way back into new economic structures. The more controlled economic systems of Europe and Japan have fared no better. Their financial markets have fallen into a boom-bust pattern as well, while their extensive welfare policies have failed, even more thoroughly than America's neglect, to reintegrate workers into new economic structures. On the contrary, Europe's and Japan's welfare schemes have simply warehoused workers and wasted their talents. These nations have also squandered public funds on subsidies to threatened industries or regions, fighting a losing battle at great expense. Rather than continue in these failed patterns, nations must find new and better ways to deal with the hardships imposed by globalization, in the financial sphere and among workers displaced by the process in one way or another.

On the financial side the direction is clear, if not especially easy. The ill effects of globalization have found definition in a number of painful and destructive cycles since the process gained momentum. The pattern first became clear in the Asian financial collapse of the mid-1990s, moved through the technology bubble that burst with the new century, and most recently contributed to the real estate collapse and attendant financial failures of 2008–09. Doubtless new regulation will play a role in the solution, especially if coordinated internationally. But since regulation alone never answers the need for financial stability, it is apparent that matters also call for a change in monetary management, to control the tendency for international financial flows alternately to glut markets with financial resources and then to starve them. It is fortunate in this regard that most central banks already have the tools necessary to insulate domestic financial markets from these effects. Control, however, will require new, more global policy perspectives and protocols at the Federal Reserve, the U.S. Treasury, and their equivalents abroad.

On the economic side, issues of employment, wages, and the destruction of the middle class are more subtle and obscure. To some extent the economic transformation itself, even as it displaces workers, also offers avenues for relief by creating new industries and new ways of doing things, and in the process creating powerful demands for workers with the necessary skills. Facilitating this adjustment will require a powerful focus on technological advancement and on an innovation-friendly environment to allow these economies to exploit new opportunities. For the sake of workers, the new industries, and social cohesion, success will demand a stronger commitment to training and education to prepare workers for their new work environment. Private-public partnerships will have a place in the effort, as will government tax and other funding incentives, but the adjustment will also require sensitivity on government's part to when it needs to step back from the process.

Emerging economies, too, will have to change. At present they count almost exclusively on exports as an engine of growth, especially China. This economic development model will doubtlessly work for a considerable time to come, but, as with all things economic, it will pay diminishing returns. These economies must, then, develop with an eye to broadening their respective sources of growth beyond today's exports, and anticipate that time when they will need to rely increasingly on their domestic consumer markets. Even at this relatively early stage these economies must allocate resources to foster growth in their domestic markets. Part of that effort must redistribute more of their growing wealth toward a larger portion of their respective populations. These nations must look to integrate all parts of their economies so that incomes can rise beyond those narrow parts of their population directly engaged in international trade.

A failure to make such accommodations will threaten countries' respective expansions and their continued role in the world economic system. It would also threaten well beyond their borders, since the codependent nature of the world's economic system makes it vulnerable to failure anywhere. Of course smaller emerging economies, such as relatively more developed Singapore and underdeveloped Vietnam, probably can proceed without too much concern for this anticipated change. Their longer-term economic niche probably lies in exporting, importing, and transshipping product, as Hong Kong has done for years and Singapore, too. But China, India, Brazil, Indonesia, and other larger emerging economies must keep this ultimate shift in mind as they develop. In this regard India's and Brazil's more organic, if slower, economic growth paths, with their ongoing attention to domestic development, show greater long-term promise than China's heavily export-oriented dash for rapid growth.

The oil-producing economies face a particular peril, not because they can hold back a precious resource, which they sometimes do, but because of their seeming inability, despite their great wealth, to integrate their economies domestically and into the world trading system. Oil has cursed these nations, it seems, by alone generating enough income to tempt them away from such necessary, broad-based development. From Qatar to Russia to Venezuela, they neglect self-development and rely on the sale of a single resource, oil, to buy what others produce. They have, as a consequence, remained entirely dependent on the price of oil and upon other economies as a source of wealth and income. Saudi Arabia and the Gulf emirates may have an excuse. They have few economic options for broad-based development beyond oil. But Russia and Venezuela have no such excuses. They have many avenues for development, most of which, sadly, they have chosen to neglect. Having weakened their own economic prospects, they have weakened the world's ability to adjust—if not fatally, then significantly.

Thirty Futures

The world, then, faces two possible futures. One secures growth by adjusting successfully to globalization and to each nation's comparative economic advantage. The other fails to make the adjustment and stagnates or worse. Each year will bring a raft of such choices, making the project one of a new tomorrow each year of the next three decades. Indeed, such choices will occur across so many dimensions, a more accurate characterization might look for thirty tomorrows a year for the next thirty years. Given the promise of one and the pain of the other, the choice, for those not blinded by narrow interests, seems obvious.

Success, however, will nonetheless require leadership. Many of these needed adjustments will grow naturally out of innumerable individual economic decisions guided by longer-term self-interest, something akin to Adam Smith's "invisible hand." The process, however natural it is, will still demand a source of vision and a constant, influential presence to retain a focus on the longer-term interests of business, individuals, and government. Both political and industrial leaders must head off the demagogic appeals of protectionism and instead foster a flexible and innovative economic environment, reintegrate those workers displaced in the process, and help nations enter into the global economic system as fully as possible.

In this regard the United States again becomes the indispensable nation. Japan is too weak, China and India too underdeveloped and partisan, and the European Union too conflicted internally to play such a role. America has had practice in this, too. If it has not always abided by its own ideals, it can nonetheless draw on the experience of the last 60-plus years during which it has, more than any other nation, encouraged broad-based global economic development, cultivated free trade and free financial flows, and worked, if sometimes sporadically, to persuade others to do likewise. America must keep this long-term focus, facilitate the entry of all nations into the world trading system, and set an example for the developed world by finding ways to adjust and help those of its own citizens displaced by the changing environment.

2

The Demographic Imperative

If demographics is not destiny, it is about as close as one can come where economics and finance are concerned. Japan and the developed West will, increasingly in coming years, feel the economic and financial drag, as past decades of falling birth rates slow the flow of youth into their workforces, even as increased longevity enlarges their dependent retired populations. Since the retired still consume actively, even as they cease active production, a considerable production burden will fall on these relatively diminished workforces. Even if output per worker were to soar, the demographic pressures will constrain growth potentials and put these countries at a still greater competitive disadvantage to emerging economies, which will face no such demographic strains. Japan, Europe, and the United States will, no doubt, try to adjust their domestic economies in order to cope, but in the end their aging demographics will force them to look abroad for relief.

Mysterious Whys, Obvious Strains

An element of mystery will always hang over why fertility rates have fallen so suddenly. Some point to the invention of the birth control pill in the early 1960s and the return of women to the workforce. Others cite tremendous advances in wealth and the opportunities it has brought to populations in the world's established, rich nations. Still others point to a kind of spiritual malaise that makes people in Japan and the developed West less interested in, or confident about, the future. The pattern may change. New York's Manhattan is experiencing a sort of baby boom these days, and the fashion for children may well spread. But even if fertility rates were to rise abruptly tomorrow, it would take at least 20–25 years for the change to increase flows of new workers. The economic reality over the next 20–30 years, the available workforce, will take its shape from the fertility declines of the past 50-plus years, and especially the last 30 years.

The figures in Exhibit 1 nearby tell the tale on fertility. Throughout the developed world, average lifetime births for women in the population have dropped precipitously. The United Kingdom has seen the least change, but even there births over a woman's lifetime have fallen from 2.2 in 1950 to 1.8 at last measure, an 18 percent drop. France has a modestly higher fertility rate than the United Kingdom, at 1.9, but France has experienced a bigger drop, 30 percent, from the 2.7 births averaged in 1950. Germany, Italy, and the United States have seen declines of more than 40 percent, and Japan, with almost 60 percent fertility drop, from 3.0 births in 1950 to 1.3. Of these six developed countries only the United States, with 2.0 births, retains a fertility rate able to sustain the existing domestic population.

It is less of a mystery why life expectancy has increased. Improved public health, a better understanding of healthy lifestyles, vastly increased access to medical services, and startling advances in medical and pharmacological science have extended longevity to previously undreamed-of levels. As Exhibit 2 nearby shows, both the United States and the United Kingdom have added 10 years to life expectancy at birth, from 69 years in 1950 to 79 at last measure, a jump of more than 14 percent.

Other developed nations have extended life expectations even further. Germany has seen an increase of 13 years, France 14 years, and Italy

Exhibit 1. Fertility in Major Developed Nations

	Fertility*					
	U.S.	Japan	U.K.	France	Germany	Italy
1950	3.5	3.0	2.2	2.7	2.2	2.4
1980	1.8	1.8	1.8	1.9	1.5	1.5
1990	2.0	1.5	1.8	1.8	1.4	1.3
2000	2.0	1.3	1.7	1.9	1.4	1.3
2010	2.0	1.3	1.8	1.9	1.3	1.4

Source: United Nations World Population Prospects, Population Database.
**Children per woman during lifetime.*

Exhibit 2. Longevity in Major Developed Nations

	Life Expectancy at Birth*					
	U.S.	Japan	U.K.	France	Germany	Italy
1950	69	64	69	67	67	66
1980	74	77	74	74	73	74
1990	75	79	76	77	76	77
2000	77	81	78	79	79	80
2010	79	82	79	81	80	81

Source: U.S. Bureau of the Census, Japan Statistical Yearbook, Central Intelligence Agency World Factbook, *United Nations Demographic Yearbook, and United Nations World Population Prospects, Population Database.*
**In years.*

15 years. Japan has gone from the lowest of the group, at 64 years life expectancy at birth in 1950, to the highest, 82 years at last measure, a jump of 18 years, amounting to more than a 28 percent expansion in the average lifespan.

For all the specific differences, the confluences of these trends tell the same story for each country. The distributions of these populations, as Exhibit 3 nearby shows, have shifted from youth toward age. Older age cohorts have increased more rapidly than the younger—that is, at the expense of the future workforce. In the United States, for instance, the young have dropped from almost 27 percent of the population in 1950 to barely over 20 percent at last measure, while those of retirement age have risen from 8.1 percent in 1950 to almost 13 percent. Japan has seen the most radical change, as its youth fell from 35.5 percent of the population in 1950 to 13.5 percent at last measure, and its pensioners rose from less than 5.0 percent of the population to over 22 percent. The same pattern has repeated to varying degrees in the nations of Europe.

As the relative size of each economy's workforce shrinks, it will face increasingly constrained production capabilities, certainly relative to the economy's needs. Demographers capture this economic effect with a metric that they call the "dependency ratio," a measure of how many working-age people each country has available to support each dependent retiree. Nearby Exhibit 4 shows that Japan, for instance, once had more than 12 people of working age for each retiree but more recently has seen that figure fall to less than 3, a mere quarter of the relative labor power that it enjoyed in 1950. Germany and Italy have each seen the relative size of their working-age populations drop by more than half during this time, to barely over 3 for each pensioner at least measure, while the United Kingdom and France have each seen their relative available labor power drop by more than 30 percent, from almost 6 workers to support each person of retirement age to just over 4. The United States enjoys the best metric, with just over 5 people of working age for each retiree, but still has almost 36 percent less than the 8-plus it enjoyed in 1950.

By comparison the emerging economies face little such strain. Of course, all populations are aging; improvements in public health and medical science are global, at least to a degree, and have extended life expectancies most everywhere, while even emerging economies have experienced declining birth rates. But these economies face far less acute circumstances than do Japan and the nations of the developed West. As Exhibit 5 nearby makes clear, the median age in China, India, and Brazil remains young, and the proportion of the population of re-

Exhibit 3. Population Distribution in Major Developed Nations

	% < 16 Yrs						% of Working Age						% > 65 Yrs					
	USA	Japan	UK	France	Germany	Italy	USA	Japan	UK	France	Germany	Italy	USA	Japan	UK	France	Germany	Italy
1950	26.9	35.5	22.7	23.3	23.3	24.5	65.0	59.6	66.1	64.6	67.3	65.9	8.1	4.9	11.2	12.1	9.4	9.6
1980	22.5	23.6	20.6	22.3	18.1	22.0	66.2	67.3	64.3	63.6	66.4	64.5	11.3	9.1	15.1	14.1	15.5	13.5
1990	21.5	18.5	19.2	20.1	14.9	16.7	65.9	69.5	65.0	65.1	69.7	68.8	12.6	12.0	15.8	14.8	15.4	14.5
2000	21.5	14.8	18.9	19.4	14.3	15.2	66.1	67.9	65.5	65.6	68.7	67.6	12.4	17.3	15.6	15.0	17.0	17.2
2010	20.2	13.5	17.0	18.6	13.6	13.5	67.0	64.3	67.0	65.0	66.1	66.3	12.8	22.2	16.0	16.0	20.3	20.2

Source: U.S. Bureau of the Census, Japan Statistical Yearbook, Central Intelligence Agency World Factbook, *U.K. Government Actuaries Department, United Nations Demographic Yearbook Historical Supplement.*

Exhibit 4. The Rising Burden of Dependent Retirees

(Number of working-age people per those over 65)

	U.S.	Japan	U.K.	France	Germany	Italy
1950	8.1	12.2	5.9	5.8	7.1	8.0
1980	5.8	7.4	4.2	4.5	4.3	4.8
1990	5.1	5.8	4.1	4.4	4.5	4.7
2000	5.3	3.9	4.2	4.4	4.0	3.9
2010	5.2	2.9	4.1	4.1	3.3	3.2

Source: United Nations World Population Prospects, Population Database.

Exhibit 5. Demographic Benchmarks for Select Emerging Economies

	China	India	Brazil
Median Age	34.1	25.3	28.6
Fertility Rate*	1.8	3.1	1.9
Life Expectancy at Birth	73.0	64.0	72.0
Portion of Population over 65	8.1	4.9	7.0
Portion of Population of Working Age	72.1	64.3	67.3
Number of Potential Workers per Retiree	8.9	13.1	9.6

Source: CIA World Factbook, *United Nations World Population Prospects, Population Database.*
**Average lifetime births for each woman.*

tirement age is low. The same is true throughout the emerging world. Only in China, after decades of the one-child-per-family policy, is the median age above 30, and even there a mere 8 percent of the population is above 65. Dependency ratios in emerging economies all compare favorably with the developed countries. China, for instance, has about 50 percent more working-age people per retiree than the United States, and an even wider margin compared with either Japan or Europe. India has almost three times as many as does the United States and five times as many as Japan.

These differences will only intensify in coming years. Past declines in fertility will further constrain the relative labor power in developed economies, just as the retirement of their respective baby boom generations will bloat the proportion of their dependent elderly. United Nations estimates, shown in Exhibit 6 nearby, indicate that by 2030 the United States will have barely 3 people of working age for each person older than 65. The United Kingdom, France, and Germany will have less than 3, while Japan will have less than 2. Though the emerging economies will also age, their legacy of past high fertility rates will nonetheless provide a relatively abundant flow of new labor for years to come. China in 2030 will still have 30 percent more workers available to support its retired population than the United States and 50 percent more than Japan and much of Europe. India and Brazil will have even more abundant labor resources. These U.N. projections do indicate narrowing disparities in the later period up to 2050, but too much else can change in this exceptionally long interval to make such projections of much practical value. The figures up to 2030 are, however, practical, reflecting as they do birth patterns that have already occurred.

Exhibit 6. Comparison: Number of Working-Age Population to Those over 65, Present and Projected

	U.S.	Japan	U.K.	France	Germany	Italy	China	India	Brazil
2010	5.2	2.9	4.1	4.1	3.3	3.2	8.9	13.1	9.6
2015	4.3	2.3	3.6	3.3	3.1	2.9	7.6	12.5	8.7
2020	3.7	2.1	3.4	3.0	2.8	2.8	5.9	10.6	7.3
2025	3.3	2.0	3.1	2.7	2.5	2.6	5.1	9.3	6.2
2030	3.0	1.8	2.9	2.4	2.1	2.3	4.2	8.3	5.1
2040	2.8	1.5	2.6	2.2	1.8	1.7	2.9	6.5	3.8
2050	2.8	1.3	2.5	2.1	1.7	1.6	2.6	5.0	2.8

Source: United Nations World Population Prospects, Population Database.

A Huge Economic Drag

Such vast demographic disparities cannot help but have profound economic implications. The shortage of raw labor surely will slow the pace of economic growth in America, Europe, and Japan, compared with past trends and certainly compared with emerging economies. For the United States, academic research suggests that the pace of growth will slow by a fifth approaching 2020, with the economy's competitive prowess suffering accordingly. Other estimates for Europe and Japan, where demographic circumstances are more acute, show greater strains and even worse outlooks.[1]

Some, of course, cannot resist hyperbole. Peter Peterson, for instance, former secretary of commerce and a man never accused of optimism, has argued that "aging could trigger a crisis that engulfs the world economies [and] may threaten democracy itself."[2] Journalists, too, have frequently extrapolated the implicit pressures to draw pictures of future dystopias. One article, for instance, forecast a "self-centered generation [of elders] just sucking down all the resources."[3] Even if such exaggerations can be easily dismissed as so much needless drama, the economic significance of the situation remains.

Behind all these assessments, reasonable or not, lies a relative shortage of labor. Fewer workers to produce for each dependent retiree will cause all these economies to struggle just to meet the consumption demands of their outsized retired populations. Even if that retiree has saved an ample nest egg, the present workday economy must produce what he and she consume and must do so with the existing workforce. Consider, then, that by 2030 each worker in the United States will have to produce enough for him or herself, his or her own family, and on average one-third of the entire consumption needs of each retired person. In Japan and parts of Europe, each worker will need to produce for his or her own family and half the consumption needs of each pensioner. The implied strains are obvious. Before even considering other economic and financial ramifications of the demographics, these basic shortfalls in relative labor resources raise significant questions about how much room these economies will have for growth. Of course older people can continue to work and expansions in output per hour and immigration can also provide a measure of relief, but these answers can only mitigate, not offset, the strain implicit in the intensifying shortage of conventional domestic labor.

Today high unemployment in the United States and Europe makes it difficult to envision a labor shortage. Though it will, no doubt, take a while for the demographic trends to assert themselves, ultimately the present high unemployment rate cannot offer an antidote to those basic imperatives. Today's joblessness has its roots in periodic cyclical phenomena, severe to be sure, and stubborn, but, as with all other cycles, something that will reverse in time. The economy's cyclical upswing, modest as it is, will gradually reduce the unemployment. Meanwhile, beneath these cyclical influences, and at times disguised by them, the demographic effects will unfold, bringing labor shortages long after today's unemployment overhang is forgotten, as past cyclical labor gluts and shortages are long forgotten today.[4]

Even if the level of unemployment never gets back to its historical lows, either absolutely or as a percentage of the workforce, it will result less from a fundamental abundance of labor power than because some workers will lack the skills needed by employers. Indeed, if a part of the workforce lacks necessary skills, then the effective working-age population will be that much smaller, making the effective labor shortage even worse than the raw demographic figures imply. The unemployable class will only add to the burdens on the even smaller numbers with the skills that the economy needs. And whatever measures the economy takes to get the most out of its effective labor, labor shortages will nonetheless impose economic limits.

Precise estimates of the economic drag are elusive. As already cited, academic research estimates a reduction by one-fifth in America's historical growth rate, but a glance at the dependency ratios makes that estimate look mild. Because America will, over the next 20 years, see its working-age population fall from 5.2 for each person of retirement age to 3.0, the 48 percent drop in its relative labor resources implies an annual erosion of 2.5 percent a year in its raw productive power, enough to erase some two-thirds of the economy's historical annual trend growth rate of 3.0–3.5 percent.[5] Of course an expansion in productivity, by increasing each worker's output per hour, could mitigate this adverse growth impact. But to make a difference, productivity would have to exceed its past trend growth of about 1.5–2.0 percent a year,[6] and there is some question whether an aging population could even sustain the old rate. Neither do these estimates take account of the prospect of an expansion in an untrained, unemployable class among working-age people. The constraints look much the same, or worse, for other developed countries.[7]

Raw labor power, however, is not the only issue. Shortages of effective workers will have an additional, adverse economic effect by raising wages. Though no doubt a boon to worker spending power, especially to those at the lower end of the wage scale,[8] rising wages would also increase production costs generally, and so prices, too, driving up living costs for the general population. Wage increases also would further erode the ability of developed economies to compete with low-wage emerging economies. Again, precision is elusive. Research into a period when the demographics went in the opposite direction might, however, shed light on the possibilities: back in the 1970s, when the youthful baby boomers were just beginning to enter the workforce, they created something of a labor surplus that, the findings indicate, brought down starting wages some 6.0 percent below trend.[9] It remains an open question whether the coming labor shortage, accompanied as it is by the retirement of those same baby boomers, will simply turn that effect around, but the upward push on living costs, and competitive disadvantages associated with that trend, are clear nonetheless.

The aging trends also raise questions about future innovative abilities. Many scientists and social historians, Albert Einstein and the great mathematician John von Neumann among them, have argued that only youth can produce the great scientific advances on which economies grow.[10] Einstein's own career offers evidence for his assertion. After all, he published his groundbreaking theories when he was only 26.[11] Considerable research shows that most great conceptual artists and thinkers create their masterworks before they turn 30.[12] Still other studies show that most Nobel laureates in economics make their conceptual advances before they reach age 25.[13] Research into more prosaic aspects of life shows that younger workers adjust more readily and completely to new situations than older workers and are more willing to migrate and to make adjustments that enable economies to sidestep disadvantages and take advantage of new opportunities.[14]

Though from this perspective, prospects for innovation look less than promising, not all the advantage lies with youth. After all, Frank Lloyd Wright, Henrik Ibsen, and many other creative individuals made their biggest contributions after the age of 60.[15] Studies of Nobel laureates in chemistry and physics and other natural sciences suggest that innovation in these fields peaks in those aged about 40 and that barely over a third of those who received Nobels in science did their significant work before the age of 35.[16] (Perhaps the implication here is that economics is a less mature field than the natural sciences and, therefore, more readily mastered in youth.) Some research distinguishes between conceptual advances, which seem to favor the young, and analytical advances, which seem to favor the more mature.[17] In the workforce, however, age seems to have the edge, since available evidence concludes that younger workers can take a while to match skills to jobs, creating inefficiencies avoided an older workforce,[18] which has learned over time to adapt its skills and can bring the advantages of its greater experience and discipline to bear upon challenges.

But if points on innovation and flexibility are ambiguous, the ill effects on crucial business decisions are clear enough. Business spending on new equipment has always propelled growth by expanding and modernizing productive facilities and improving worker efficiencies. To some extent, rising wages will inspire such spending as business seeks to economize on expensive labor. But higher pay scales associated with a labor shortage will also prompt business to move facilities abroad to hire cheaper labor. By squeezing profitability in domestic enterprises—by as much as 10 percent, according to several studies[19]—rising wages will further dampen business's willingness to expand, as well as its ability to finance any such expansion. A shortfall in savings will compound the problem. Because people cease saving as they retire,[20] and also start tapping their nest eggs, business will lose an important pool of assets on which it draws to finance its capital spending, either by borrowing from banks, issuing bonds, or floating new stock offerings. Though, sadly, no study as yet offers an authoritative estimate of these debilitating effects, there can be little doubt of the direction of influence.

Compounding financing problems, aging economies will also siphon funds from capital investments by demanding them for growing public pension and health care needs. The trustees of the Social Security and Medicare systems in the United States have long warned how they will need additional funds to sustain benefits as the retired population grows.[21] The most authoritative estimates suggest that these needs will increase their draw on the nation's financial resources by as much as one-third.[22] In Japan, where aging trends are even more extreme, authorities estimate that the pension and medical draw on otherwise investable funds will rise from today's 28 percent of the country's gross domestic product (GDP) to about 50 percent by 2040.[23] A similar picture emerges in Europe. These demands, however necessary and humane, will inevitably interfere with the ability of the business sector to finance expansion and modernization, with clear adverse implications for growth. It is noteworthy, too, that the increased payroll taxes that these systems would use to procure their additional funds would also nullify the advantages of the wage hikes workers might otherwise have enjoyed as a result of the relative labor scarcity, and hold back their spending and living standards accordingly.

Illustrations from Elsewhere

Perhaps the general effect is best illustrated in the record of the very different demographic experiences of Asia's Pacific Rim and Ireland. In both cases the effects on growth were remarkable. Each had been backward for decades. Then Asia in the 1960s, and Ireland more recently, suddenly (and for a while, seemingly inexplicably) took off. Taiwan's economy, for instance, grew at more than triple the pace of the United States between 1960 and 1980, expanding in real terms almost 10 percent a year and more than 8.0 percent a year into the 1990s. As similar patterns emerged throughout the region—in South Korea, Singapore, Malaysia, Hong Kong, and Indonesia most prominently[24]—these once easygoing communities suddenly became fierce trade competitors. Ireland saw its economy take off in the early 1990s, growing 8 percent a year in real terms for more than 10 years.[25] Diplomats and investors, having already dubbed the rapidly growing nations in Asia's Pacific Rim the "Asian Tigers,"[26] named Ireland the "Green" or "Celtic Tiger."

Since then, Ireland has fallen on hard times, largely because of an excessive reliance on debt between 2006 and 2008. But this collapse, though painful, says nothing about the fundamental growth that preceded it, except that financial ineptitude for a time has spoiled the effect of otherwise firm fundamentals. Those underlying influences, both in Asia and in Ireland, reflected a confluence of developments. There were, of course, historical particulars. Asia rode the coattails of Japan's extraordinary growth during much of that time. Ireland benefited handsomely from investments made by the European Union once it had joined, and from the cheap financing available on joining Europe's common currency, the euro, a development that subsequently led to the country's debt problem. But for all the historical particulars, these growth surges in their fundamentals clearly link to similar demographic trends in these countries.

The effects unfolded in several steps. A gradual increase in wealth and improved public health reduced child mortality. Relieved of the need for large broods to ensure that some children survive to later care for their parents, fertility rates fell, freeing the working populations of these countries from a huge burden of dependent young, allowing the existing workforce at last to produce surpluses significantly beyond their nation's daily consumption needs. At the same time the legacy of high fertility rates kept the working-age population growing relative to both old and young dependents. Their new, surplus production allowed people to save for their old-age retirements instead of counting on their surviving children to support them. As savings rates increased, in Taiwan, for example, from 5 percent of overall income in the 1950s to 20 percent in the 1980s, increased pools of funds emerged that businesses could and did invest in production-enhancing capital improvements.

Governments used the newly abundant financial resources to invest in new roads and port facilities and otherwise modernize their economic infrastructures. These "demographic dividends"[27] enhanced growth potentials even as they also improved the global competitive advantages of these economies.[28]

Some Natural Sources of Relief

With demographics in the world's developed economies now the reverse of these experiences, these economies would seem to face constraints as powerful as the advantages that Asia and Ireland once enjoyed. Even so, it would be a mistake to succumb to hyperbole, as some already have. Circumstances do possess natural mitigating influences to counteract some of the growth constraints otherwise imposed by the aging trend.

There is reason, for instance, to believe that the aging may cause less financial strain than might seem to be the case from simple extrapolation of past trends. Longer life expectancies, by extending retirements, may well motivate people to save more and draw down on their savings more slowly in retirement than former patterns suggest. Such behavior would relieve at least a portion of the otherwise anticipated shortfall in funds available to finance investments in productive facilities. Though as yet only little evidence of such change has emerged,[29] there is nonetheless good reason to expect such shifts in savings behavior as people become more aware of the practical financial implications of longer life expectancies.

Economies might find further, otherwise unexpected, relief in the improving health of older people. Demographers have already noted that people remain healthy and more vital for a much larger proportion of their lives than in the past, a phenomenon for which they use the unfortunate phrase "compression of morbidity."[30] No doubt the natural advance of medical knowledge has played a role here, and will continue to do so, but also the prospect of longer life has no doubt induced people, at all stages of life, to pay more attention to their health than they once did. After all, heroic efforts at health preservation hardly made sense decades ago when people lived surrounded by untreatable disease and industrial accidents, and anyway anticipated death shortly after their youthful vitality faded. Smoking and drinking to excess surely seemed like minor issues to the members of a generation that expected to die from other causes by the time they were 60. But if a person expects to reach 85–90 years, as many do today, decisions about tobacco, alcohol, and other health issues change habits of self-maintenance and should lead to an even greater compression of morbidity in coming years.

As such trends ameliorate the otherwise growing health cost burden posed by an aging society, improved health, by allowing people to work productively for longer, could further lift the burden on relative labor shortages.[31] Indeed, recognizing the general economic benefits of better health, especially for nations with aging populations, the United Nations has identified the prevention of chronic health care problems as a major economic growth consideration.[32] Several academic studies have documented a cross section of the productivity advantages from improving health.[33] Further, such health improvements free resources; it could also relieve labor shortages, marginally at least, by freeing for general production those whom the economy might otherwise need in the health care professions.

Relief might also emerge as rising life expectancies justify longer careers. Such a development not only would relieve the relative labor shortage but also would reduce pension-funding needs, leaving more financial resources for business to increase productive facilities. The United States has already responded in just this way by raising the age for full Social Security benefits from 65 to 67.[34] Public and private pension plans in other developed countries have made similar moves.[35] A further extension of the retirement age could relieve more strain. The then-titled U.S. General Accounting Office calculated that Social Security could forgo any extraordinary funding needs by raising the eligibility age for full benefits to 70 or 72,[36] though such a move can create hardship and raise questions of equity and quality of life. Even short of such stark changes, pension plans could relieve their financing needs and encourage work by structuring benefits, as Social Security does, to give a larger payout to those who postpone retirement.[37]

A number of other avenues lie open for these economies to mitigate the demographic impact on their growth prospects and living standards. Increases in worker productivity stand as an option, as does a wider participation of the population in the workforce. Immigration could also help. Some of these palliatives could develop naturally. Changes in public and corporate policy could reinforce their development. But as the next chapters will show, even the best efforts face limitations. They can only mitigate, not overcome, demographic effects. Accomplishing the latter will, ultimately, hinge on matters of trade and globalization.

3

More Work, More Efficiently

The developed economies will not accept the setback passively. They will do what they can to cope with their increasingly severe relative labor shortages. Companies, naturally, without any overreaching guidance, will adjust to find trained employees and get the most out of them. Government policies will doubtless reinforce such private efforts, especially if, in the words of one group of prominent researchers, policy can help channel financial and economic resources "into productive investments, labor market institutions and policies that best facilitate a supply response to labor shortages and [the] high wages [that will result from them]."[1] Still, even with the best policies and most flexible responses, there is only so much that these economies can do within themselves to counter the intensifying economic and financial pressure.

Working Harder for Longer

The most obvious and least risky place to look for relief is through a rise in the existing population's participation in the workforce. Within the working-age population, the greatest leverage lies with women.

Working-age men already have such high participation rates that there is limited room for further expansion. In the United States, for instance, 81 percent of working-age men already have or seek gainful employment, and in the prime working years of 25–54 that figure is 90 percent. But with women, even after the dramatic participation increases of past decades, only some 69 percent of the working-aged have or seek gainful employment, and fewer than 76 percent of those in their prime working years.[2] Outside the United States, the difference is greater still. For all developed countries, as measured by the membership of the Organisation for Economic Co-operation and Development (OECD), only some 51 percent of working-age women participate in the workforce, well up from 41 percent in 1950 but still far below the men's rate of about 80 percent.[3]

Even more potential lies with a jump in the participation of older workers. This would help in two ways: first, obviously, by adding to the working population, and second by reducing the dependent retired population. This process may already have begun. In the United States workforce participation by men and women over the age of 65 has already risen from 15 percent, in the 1980s, to 21.5 percent more recently.[4] If workers in general were to expand their working life from age 65 to 70, America's relative workforce would jump from the expected three workers per retiree, in 2030, to almost four.[5] Still more relief could emerge in Europe and Japan, where labor force participation by elders is, if anything, lower than in the United States

Combined increased participation rates by women and older workers both could markedly ameliorate aging's effects. If the participation of working-age women in the entire OECD were to rise just to the American and Scandinavian rates of 70 percent, the available labor in these economies would rise some 12 percent.[6] If in the United States working-age women were to increase their participation only halfway to the male rate, eight million additional workers would become available, an increase of more than 5 percent. If on top of that older people were regularly to work until they were 70 instead of 65, the number of workers available to support each dependent retiree in America would rise toward 4.5 by 2030, an almost 40 percent improvement on what would otherwise happen to dependency burdens.[7] Such help, of course, would fail to erase all the ill effects of aging demographics, but it would offer major relief nonetheless.

Some of this change will occur organically, as increasingly intense labor shortages raise wages, making paid work more attractive. Individually, people will also naturally opt for longer careers, simply because they live longer and especially because they remain healthier and more vital for more of their lives. The need to accumulate for a longer retirement will reinforce the trend by driving women back to gainful employment and by keeping both men and women at work longer. In time, the stay-at-home spouses will become even rarer than they are today, while the usual retirement at 65 will become a thing of the past. Beyond such natural responses government and business could enhance the participation change by making the workplace more accommodating to the particular needs of women and older workers.

Where women are concerned, surely the most effective policy would find ways to accommodate family obligations, particularly children. Though modern societies have mostly ceased to view child care as the sole preserve of mothers, the reality is that women still shoulder the bulk of these obligations and, consequently, feel the greatest clash between those demands and the time required by full-time or even part-time employment. In most cases this issue explains why women's participation rates, even now, remain so much lower than men's.[8] In the need to offset labor shortages, ultimately it matters less whether policy accommodates the family obligations of men or of women than that it facilitates the return of the main caregiver to the workplace. Affordable, quality child care is one clear solution, and one on which government and business can collaborate.

Business alone will have plenty of inducements to accommodate the child care needs of its workers. Such a desire to help, of course, will emerge less from sudden enlightenment or a new openness to feminist arguments than a pragmatic need to lure whichever workers are available in a labor-short future. Offering child care will in fact allow business to gather needed new workers more cheaply than simply by raising wages. Several firms have already made such accommodations. Food maker Sara Lee, for example, has instituted what it calls its "returnship policy," which eases the transition back to work for employees who have taken "career breaks," mostly for childbirth. Firms such as LiveOps have accommodated family needs by developing an entire industry around customer service people working from home.[9] These and comparable policies by other firms have already resulted in the employment of many who otherwise could not have participated in the paid workforce.

Beyond such responses, it is reasonable to expect, as labor constraints become more acute, that employers will meet the challenge with more formal child care help, whether offered directly or through independent providers. In factories and other large work facilities where thousands of workers congregate, on-site child care would confer special advantages by combining the commute to work with the commute to child care and at the same time by giving parents the peace of mind offered by ready access to their children. Even short of such arrangements, business could lure those who might otherwise stay at home by offering parents the flexibility to take their children to school and bring them to a separate on- or off-site afterschool facility.

Government could help with these initiatives. Since flexibility around each job requires sensitivity to its particulars, government could accommodate the solutions of those involved by loosening federal labor laws on how workers' weeks and hours must be scheduled and paid. Washington, actually, has already acknowledged such a need, though to date has done nothing about it.[10] Tax incentives for companies that provide child care could also help. Direct grants either to child care providers or to the buyers of such services, be they employers or individuals, offer another avenue that government might follow. Universal licensing of child care could encourage the process by relieving many natural parental anxieties. Still more radical changes might alter law to allow parents to enroll children in schools near their workplace instead of near their home. Such a shift would, of course, require modifications in the way public schools are financed. Government might even find in such a change a new source of funding by encouraging business to improve nearby schools in order to lure employees more cheaply than with still higher wages.

Persuading older workers to stay on the job longer would require different accommodations. They, too, will need more flexible work arrangements, but in different ways that allow fewer hours or shorter workweeks. Though older people are much healthier than they once were, they still cannot do physically demanding jobs for as long as younger workers, and even where physical stamina is not an issue, the older worker, at the end of a long career, will balk at maintaining the levels of intensity that younger workers tolerate for the sake of advancement. So far business has made only minor adjustments along these lines, but as the need for workers becomes more intense, management will doubtless become more flexible.

Probably the hardest part of this adjustment will involve new attitudes toward pay scales. Forever, it seems, the seniority-based approach to pay has prevailed in both business and government. The highest wage often goes to those employees with the longest tenure and, presumably, the greatest experience. But with increasing numbers of older workers seeking a modified schedule, the system will have to learn to adjust pay downward as careers enter their later stages.

Some firms have already begun, tentatively, to experiment with ways to overcome both institutional and worker resistance to such transitions. One approach reclassifies older workers from regular employees into temporary status, or establishes in-house consulting arrangements to tap into the greater experience of older workers on a part-time basis. The International Business Machines Corporation in Belgium has set a remarkable example with its consulting company, SkillTeam. This special firm draws experienced, older workers, largely out of IBM Belgium, and allows them shorter and more flexible hours at reduced pay levels. Typically they work about 60 percent of their former hours and receive some 88 percent of their former, full-time salary. IBM makes up the difference with downward adjustments in their bonuses and in the pension contributions made on their behalf.[11] Not all businesses will find it as easy to create such "bridge jobs," but the aging trend and the consequent labor shortages should compel more such solutions.

A shift in pension structure could also keep older workers employed longer. Obviously any increase in the eligible age for receiving benefits will keep people at work longer (as well as relieve financial burdens on pension plans). An increase in the present retirement age, in most of the developed countries, from 65–67 to 70–72 years would fairly quickly achieve the desired increased participation of elders in the workforce. It is with just this effect in mind that the United Nations has noted, some might say cruelly, that circumstances ultimately will require nations to abandon public pension entitlements and, as an incentive to continue working, replace them with minimum welfarelike payouts designed simply to keep the nonworking elderly out of poverty.[12] Of course there are political and legal limits to how far either business or government can go in this regard, but if these limits constrain how much change in pension structures can take place, there are other ways business and government can induce older workers to stay on the job.

Pension plans can, for instance, cease penalizing work. Social Security once reduced benefits to working pensioners by 50 cents for each dollar they earned. With other taxes this penalty left older people with as little as 20 percent of their pay, hardly much incentive to work. Although Social Security has long since abandoned such policies,[13] some company pension plans retain such disincentives, as do many public and private pension plans outside the United States. In Belgium, Germany, France, Italy, and the Netherlands, for instance, the combination of lost benefits and tax on older workers amounts to 60 percent of any pay they might earn on the job.[14] Of course pension managers will resist reforms that allow pensioners to keep their benefits even after returning to work (in the hope, presumably, that the denied benefits would relieve the pension plan of a portion of its obligations), but the need to draw more labor out of the existing population will surely overcome such resistance. The European Union has already recognized the need to follow the example of Social Security and make such changes.[15]

In addition to encouraging older workers to stay actively employed, changes in health care policy can also reduce the need for health care workers and so presumably free scarce labor for other work. Here, too, the United Nations has made what some might regard as harsh recommendation: that nations replace conventional health care benefits with minimum payouts. The U.N. has argued that such a policy would reduce the number of needed health care workers by promoting family care over hospitals and nursing facilities.[16] Though such a plan might save on health care funding, it is not apparent that it would do much to alleviate labor shortages, since an increase in family care would surely hold back the workforce participation of those who stay home to care for elderly relatives.

If U.N. recommendations would both help and hurt, Japan has developed technological solutions of greater promise, both in holding down health care costs and in reducing the need to draw health care workers from a limited labor force. Japanese health services, for instance, have installed integrated television and local area networks into the homes of elderly citizens to allow them to take their own basic health care measurements, such as blood pressure, temperature, even blood sugar, and transmit them automatically to health centers. Also, by using sensors in refrigerators and other appliances, such as tea- or coffee-makers, to monitor the daily rhythms of life, Japanese services can monitor the elderly at home without an excessive invasion of privacy, sending assistance only if something seems amiss. Japan has also experimented with robots to perform household chores for the elderly and the infirm and to provide them with company.[17] Such innovations not only reduce the costs of health care but also, importantly, relieve the strain on limited labor resources by reducing health care staffing needs.

Getting the Most out of Each Worker

Besides all such avenues for relief, economies can further mitigate the effects of labor shortages by finding ways to increase the hourly output of each worker. Clearly if the economy can produce more per worker, then the impending labor shortage will have less impact on output, growth prospects, and living standards. Those at work will produce more of what they need to support themselves, their families, and those many in the economy who will have retired from active production. The potential for relief here is actually larger than it seems at first, since every advance in worker productivity multiplies across all workers. Though some productivity advances will occur naturally under the strain of labor shortages, government assistance and policy accommodations can reinforce such helpful trends.

Output per worker certainly should benefit, as increased proportions of older workers remain on the job and bring their experience to bear for longer. It will get an additional boost as extended careers invite more workers to invest in education and training. Business has long recognized that the longer a worker's employment horizon, the greater his or her interest in education and training.[18] With workers increasingly contemplating longer careers and striving for skills that will enable them to stay employed after their youthful vitality fades, the incentives for education and training will become that much greater, with increased product quality and productivity an inevitable by-product.[19] In recognition of these kinds of productivity dividends the Harvard Initiative for Global Health encourages official support for policies to promote "life-long education programs as a way to ameliorate the general economic ill effects of population aging."[20]

The economy could produce more gains along these lines from increased investment in new business equipment, research, and innovation. There are few clearer statistical links than between productivity growth and such business spending.[21] The picture is certainly evident in the great post–Second World War productivity surge. Because of the enormous effort to build up the economy's productive capacity during that war, and also after it, to convert the war production to civilian applications, the productive power of each employee leaped during the 12 years between 1943 and 1955. Real or inflation-adjusted business spending on plant and equipment increased more than six-fold, or at an astronomical average annual rate of 16.5 percent[22] and after a brief lag, while the now enhanced facilities came online, output per hour surged accordingly, growing almost 3.0 percent a year between 1949 and 1962, a multiple of the pace averaged during the previous 30 years.[23]

The evidence from Europe and Japan during these early years is, if anything, even more compelling. With their business's productive capacities destroyed by the war, the European and Japanese economies after 1945 began an immense capital-spending drive. By 1962 continental Europe dedicated between 25 and 30 percent of its GDP to this effort and Japan dedicated as much as 35 percent,[24] high figures compared with the prewar practice and with the United States, too, where even the capital spending surge amounted to only about 9.1 percent of the economy.[25] Accordingly, European and Japanese output per hour soared. Tokyo recorded an average annual rise of 8.6 percent between 1950 and 1960, France 3.6 percent, and Germany 7.6 percent. Because the United Kingdom had much less need for industrial recovery, it spent relatively less on new equipment and structures, and, accordingly, the productivity of British workers expanded only 2.0 percent a year on average.[26]

Figures have become less dramatic in more recent years, but the evidence is, if anything, even more convincing. In the 1980s and 1990s, for instance, the United States enjoyed a leap in technological applications, and business stepped up spending on equipment and software to gain from the advances. Rising at an average rate of 7.1 percent a year, spending on equipment, systems, and software advanced from 7.8 percent of the overall economy in 1985 to almost 10 percent of it in 1999.[27] Output per hour surged accordingly. The consequences of this development were felt chiefly after this capital spending had had time to permeate the production process. Between 1990 and 2005, manufacturing productivity rose by a startling 5.1 percent a year, more than half again faster than it had during the previous 20 years.[28] Because Europe and Japan were slower to buy and apply the new technology, their worker output per hour grew more slowly than in the United States, at an annual average of 3.7 percent in Japan between 1990 and 2005, 3.9 percent in France, 3.2 percent in Germany, and 3.4 percent in the United Kingdom during the same period.[29]

As with training and education, much of this productivity support should occur without overall direction in response to demographic imperatives. Rising wages in a labor-short future certainly will induce business, if it can procure the financial resources for such spending, to seek laborsaving techniques, substitute equipment for labor in the production process, and search for innovations that improve efficiency. Government can assist this process with tax incentives for firms that spend on equipment, systems, software, and research, as many governments have done in the past and many still do. Direct research grants could help, too. Those actively applied during the Cold War, for instance, though aimed purely at defense or the Space Race, nonetheless yielded tremendous unintended economic benefits. It was, after all, in a defense-related government project that Bell Labs invented the transistor in December 1947,[30] a breakthrough that then led to tremendous innovations now so famous as not to require elaboration here. Government could amplify this effect with a return to the partnerships that it once promoted with universities and by encouraging university-business partnerships in research and innovation, again with grants and tax incentives.

Government support may actually be more important than in the past. Because the aging demographics, as described earlier, will create a savings shortage and otherwise siphon off funds from business purposes into pensions and health care, firms will have less of their own resources for such spending. Apart from direct government grants and tax relief, policy could also promote free flows of what private financial resources are available. Certainly any measures that can offer business a ready flow of financial capital promote increased output per hour by encouraging investments in newer, more effective equipment, systems, software, and research. More open and active financial markets will help identify the projects and activities most likely to offer the greatest returns, thus allowing the economy to use most effectively what financial resources it has, and consequently realize the greatest productivity advances possible, given the constraints in the situation.

Though government policy can do little directly to promote free flows of financial capital, it can at least avoid impeding the process. In this regard, it needs to review all regulations to test if they interfere with free flows of funds and the information on market preferences that they carry. Even otherwise necessary regulations should interfere as little as possible. Inevitably, the painful experience of 2008–09 has created an environment where most people think of free financial flows as dangerous and see regulation as effective only by constraining them. Understandable as this reaction is, it would, if followed, misguide policy and hold back needed productivity improvements. Regulations can provide necessary safeguards and still avoid unnecessary impediments.

Take, for example, the Sarbanes-Oxley legislation that followed the devastating bankruptcies of Enron (2001) and other once popular investments in the early years of this century. In its effort to stop misleading corporate reporting, "Sybox," as the legislation is called, stipulated that chief executive officers sign all reports to shareholders and subject themselves to punishment for any inaccuracies, even the risk of imprisonment.[31] It captured the spirit of retribution that prevailed at the time, but the draconian nature of the rule, and its inability to distinguish between honest error on the one hand and willful fraud on the other, simply convinced executives to offer the minimum information in reports. Whatever the legislation's good intentions, it stymied the flow of critical bits of business intelligence and consequently made financial markets less efficient.

Such constraints multiply throughout the financial regulatory regimes in the United States, the United Kingdom, on the European continent, and in Japan. A list would fill several volumes. But, apart from the almost infinite detail, they generally offer opportunity to improve matters by recasting rules, not simply to free executives and their firms from penalty but rather to promote freer flows of funds and information. Indeed, by focusing rules effectively on issues of fraud and abuse and by insisting on transparency, regulation, though typically set in opposition to free financial flows, can actually enhance them. Confidence that regulation ensures accurate information and honest dealing frees investors from time-consuming checks and investigations. It fosters trust, reasonable risk taking, and efficient exchanges that actually enhance the dynamism and effectiveness of financial markets.

For all the promise of productivity enhancement this effort, too, would fall short of offering a complete remedy for these demographic disadvantages. All these efforts will mitigate the economic ill effects of demographically created labor shortages, as will increased labor force participation rates, improved education, and better training. But for these aging economies to sustain growth and maintain their standards of living, they will have to look beyond the clear limits of such purely domestic remedies. As the next two chapters will show, immigration has significant limits, too, but increased trade offers the promise of almost complete relief, though not without complications.

4

Immigration Cuts Two Ways

Immigration would seem to offer a powerful solution to the developed world's relative labor shortages. It has already reached high levels and will no doubt increase of its own accord as the need for trained labor becomes more acute. Even where policy tries to block the flow, the powerful lures of better pay and better jobs will prompt illegal immigration, as they already do. The United Nations expects that during the next 45 years some 22 million people will migrate from poorer nations into the established economies of Japan and the developed West.[1] But there are limits. Not only would any migration sufficient to fill the labor gap impose unacceptable immediate demands on already burdened public services, and exacerbate the already severe financial strains imposed by aging demographics, but also a huge flow of immigration would further exacerbate existing, severe social strains.

Social Strain

The social drawbacks of such flows are clear in the tremendous numbers of immigrants required to offset demographic disadvantages. According to calculations by the prestigious RAND Corporation, continental Europe would need a 30-fold increase in immigration over the next 25 years to offset the effects of aging on its workforce.[2] Few societies could remain stable in the face of such a volume. Japan estimates that even a doubling of immigration would have hardly any effect on its overall workforce needs.[3] South Korean figures suggest that immigration would have to rise to a socially explosive six million—more than 12 percent of the population—to counteract the effects of aging on that nation's native workforce.[4] Other research on the financial aspects of the aging trend in Germany indicates that even a doubling of current rates of immigration would fail to compensate for the demographically induced savings shortfall and at most would add only 1.0 percentage point to the national savings flow—hardly enough to make a significant difference in even that single aspect of the matter.[5]

Making things still more problematic and potentially disruptive are the already large sizes of existing immigrant populations. Germany, for instance, already has a foreign-born population of almost seven million, or about 8.5 percent of the population, and this figure fails to account for the children of past generations of immigrants, Turks who came in the 1960s and 1970s, and who still live unassimilated in ethnic enclaves. France's foreign-born population already amounts to more than 8 percent of its workforce.[6] By some accounts, immigrants total nearly 12 percent of Belgium's current workforce and 24 percent of Switzerland's.[7] In Spain just those immigrants who have gained Spanish citizenship have risen to 12 percent of the population, a sudden socially disruptive jump from a mere 3 percent just 10 years or so ago.[8] Japan, in recognition of its aging problems, quadrupled its immigration flows between 1990 and 2010 and consequently already has an immigrant population equal to some 1.2 percent of its population,[9] a huge figure for a country renowned for its xenophobia and with no immigrant tradition whatsoever. Estimates for the United States put the immigrant population, legal and illegal, at 35 million, or more than 11 percent of the population.[10]

Discord has already risen, even before any additional flows. The United States, despite its strong immigration tradition, is showing enough strain to create an intense, awkward, and self-contradictory national debate. The government has decided to build a wall along the border between the United States and Mexico but is proceeding only hesitantly.[11] Private, so-called Minuteman militias patrol the border to stop what they refer to as a "human flood of illegal immigrants,"[12] while the state of Arizona has found itself in conflict with the federal government over its zealous enforcement of immigration laws.[13]

Sentiments cut across the usual political divides. Pro-immigrant, free market ideologues and business groups stand in an unusual alliance with civil rights organizations and ethnic advocacy groups, while an odd collection of cultural conservatives, labor unions, and environmentalists stand against immigration.[14] These crosscurrents have stymied policy reform efforts, including one not long ago by an equally unlikely alliance of Republican president George W. Bush and late, liberal Democratic senator Edward Kennedy.[15] More recently President Barack Obama, for all his rhetoric about laying out a "path to citizenship," has fallen back on the same mélange of enforcement policies that circumstances imposed on Bush.[16] That is true of recent legislative proposals.[17]

The emotional level of this debate has brought out some strange arguments on all sides. Typical is a piece from the usually progressive Cultural Change Institute at the Fletcher School of Tufts University. The author, Lawrence Harrison, after establishing his nonnativist bona fides, his immigrant heritage, and his minority roots, goes on to sound remarkably nativist, demanding: 1) an immigration law that considers only the country's economic needs and that weighs each immigrant group's record of "acculturation," 2) that the United States declare English as the "national language," and 3) that the United States "discourage the proliferation of Spanish-language media."[18] From another point on the political spectrum, Peggy Noonan, conservative journalist and former speechwriter for presidents Ronald Reagan and George H. W. Bush, succumbs to a similar sentiment. Referencing her Irish forebears, she speaks of how they had to "wait in line," pass "the tests," and "get permission" to exit Ellis Island.[19] In fact, the United States did not even require passports before 1918, making the term "illegal immigrant" meaningless until that date. But rational, accurate, or neither, such emotionalism points up why even now, long before numbers have grown large enough to begin to address future labor shortages, the immigration answer cuts two ways for the United States.

Matters in Europe are still more intense and chaotic. There hostility to immigrants runs much deeper than in the United States.[20] Unlike America, which, for all the hostility of select groups, has never entirely closed itself to all but natives, Europe has. In the 1970s, for instance, Europe, after a rather open policy in the 1960s, just about shut its borders. Many governments at that time even tried to persuade resident immigrants to return to their country of origin.[21] One German official captured the tone of the time, and perhaps also today, when he dismissed immigrants out of hand, describing Germany bluntly as "not an immigrant nation."[22] Though Europe's immigration laws were liberalized again in the 1990s, that former wariness has returned more recently, in both official and unofficial circles.[23] Capturing this renewed hostility, Éamon Ó Cuív, Ireland's minister for community, rural, and Gaeltacht affairs, not too long ago told *The Irish Times* that much more immigration for whatever reason would simply cause "one million and one" problems.[24]

If anything, Minister Ó Cuív understated the depth of bad feeling at all levels in Europe. Large majorities in the United Kingdom and on the continent not only object to new immigrants but, as in the past, want to send existing foreign residents home. In one U.K. survey some three-quarters of the respondents thought that officials should force unemployed foreigners out of the country. A general European survey showed that a decided majority of the continental population had similar attitudes.[25] In Italy the anti-immigrant sentiments ran even stronger than in Britain. Even in Spain, which has a reputation for being the most welcoming European country toward immigrants, less than half those responding to a nationwide survey saw migrant flows as positive.[26] Celestino Corbacho, Spain's labor and immigration minister, recently linked immigration to unemployment and threatened to stop the flow altogether. Though he later withdrew his remarks, Spain joined the rest of the EU in a crackdown on illegal immigrants and actually offered to pay even legal immigrants their unemployment benefits up front if only they would go home immediately.[27]

Voting has followed such attitudes. Already one-fifth of Belgium's Flemish voters back the far-right, anti-immigrant Vlaams Belang Party, while in Denmark the voters recently gave the anti-immigration Danish People's Party still more seats in their parliament. In Switzerland, the xenophobic Swiss People's Party received almost one-third of the nation's vote.[28] Hostility to immigrants was certainly evident when the French rejected the European constitution in May 2005. Voters feared the proverbial "Polish plumber," who, they said, would steal jobs and undermine the existing French social contract.[29] Not too long after the vote, then presidential candidate Nicolas Sarkozy, sensitive to the mood, trimmed his political sails accordingly and won the presidency after adopting much of the anti-immigrant rhetoric of the right-wing National Front Party. He spoke loudly of "inculcating French values."[30]

Law naturally has followed sentiment and politics. The Netherlands and Germany have joined France in imposing more severe restrictions on the Muslim headscarf. The Vatican has effectively endorsed these moves, characterizing such garments as exhibiting "disrespect for local cultures and sensibilities." Jack Straw, British Parliament member and former foreign secretary, effectively endorsed the Vatican when he criticized traditional Muslim dress on the grounds that it "separates people."[31] Germany has reversed its once liberal immigration policy and has just about closed its labor market to foreigners, even to other EU workers. When, in 2007, Central and Eastern European governments protested against the German position, the best Berlin could offer was a promise merely to reconsider at a later date.[32] Germany still insists on a language test before an immigrant can enter the country.[33] Entry requirements have become so strict that, it has been claimed, the only way even educated foreigners can get into the country is to show the promise of a salary higher than that of a typical German managing director.[34] Italy has new laws that make it easier to expel even other EU citizens, while France's new Ministry of National Identity and Immigration has proposed quotas on migration and has restricted immigration for family unification, sometimes insisting on DNA testing.[35]

The hostile tone and stronger legislation has brought out more zealous enforcement. In 2008 alone Italian officials summarily expelled some 12,000 illegal immigrants.[36] In the same year France increased its expulsions—by half—sending home some 24,000 illegal immigrants,[37] and recently even turned on its Gypsy population.[38] Spain has gone from authorizing more legal immigration, in 2005, to recently endorsing the EU's "Return Directive," which allows member nations to hold undocumented aliens, including minors, for up to 18 months.[39] When the free travel and migration rules within the European Union went into effect in 2007—the so-called Schengen Agreement—some 40,000 German police protested, warning about a "wave of migration and crime."[40]

Vigilantism has increased as well. Reports have emerged from Italy of frequent action by neo-Nazi, anti-immigrant groups in Rome, Milan, and Naples. A recent Rome attack saw swastika-wearing gangs run through the trendy Pigneto district, beating up Chinese and Indian shopkeepers and shouting "get out bastard foreigners."[41] Then–prime minister Silvio Berlusconi saw his popularity rating jump 17 percentage points when he adopted anti-immigrant rhetoric.[42] For all these headlines Morten Kjaerum, director of the EU's Fundamental Rights Agency (FRA), concluded in a recent study conducted by his agency that "crimes with racist motives and discrimination in the EU are [already] more widespread than individual member states admit."[43]

And all of this only hints at the extent of bad feeling in the general population. The most virulent is anti-Muslim. It has become commonplace in Britain and on the continent, for instance, to refer to anyone who sympathizes with Muslim immigrants as *dhimmi.* Since this Arabic word is used in Muslim countries to refer to the second-class status of non-Muslims, the use in Europe suggests that any conciliatory gesture toward Muslims invites a diminished status for the native, non-Muslim population. A leading German feminist, Alice Schwarzer, recently speculated ominously in *Emma* (a popular feminist journal) that Islamists "probably and unfortunately can no longer be stopped with only democratic means." Anti-Muslim Web sites have sprung up across the continent. One, Pax Europa Against Eurabia, has called for provocative demonstrations in Muslim neighborhoods, to applause from similar sites, such as Deus Vult Caritatum (in the Latin, "God wills kindness"), a name that draws on the rallying cry of the First Crusade, Deus Vult ("God wills it"). Still another site, Gates of Vienna, offers a cap with the motto (in several languages) "Islamaphobe and Proud of It."[44]

No Help Without Integration

Not surprisingly the milieu makes it difficult for existing immigrants to join the larger economy, a necessary step if immigration is to help with labor shortages. Emblematic of the situation, surely, are the Paris riots of fall 2005. Official France and the international media initially tried to connect the violence to radical Islam. National deputy Jacques Myard described the disturbances as "an anti-French, ethno-cultural bias from a foreign society [that] has taken root on French soil."[45] But it soon became clear that the trouble came more from frustration over a sense of isolation and a lack of economic opportunity.[46] Nor are such problems confined to France. In Germany, more than half the resident Turks say discrimination against foreigners is widespread, blocking their ability to enjoy employment opportunities and thereby make much of an economic contribution.[47] When Chancellor Angela Merkel tried to explain immigration regulations, Turks in Germany gave vent to their frustrations, translating her remarks as "Merkel defends discrimination against Turks."[48] Four major Turkish associations refused to participate in Chancellor Merkel's second National Integration Summit.[49] She has responded by concluding that multiculturalism in Germany has "utterly failed."[50]

Against such a backdrop, increased immigration for any reason would seem problematic at best, especially in the massive numbers required to answer future labor needs. Even a small increase in immigration, it would seem, threatens to rend Europe's social fabric, with much worse implications for growth and wealth than the aging trend. There is even the possibility that deteriorating circumstances could exacerbate Europe's demographic problem by prompting emigration, either because a more heavily immigrant society would make natives feel alienated or because a growing immigrant presence, particularly a Muslim one, could create a violent backlash that would prompt better-positioned Europeans to flee.

Indeed, there are already signs of such effects. In 2006 those leaving Germany outnumbered those entering by 155,000. Some 52 percent of German university students say they would like to leave Germany, complaining about "social decline" and the sense that they "no longer feel at home in a country whose cultural appearance is changing dramatically." The Netherlands, also in 2006, the latest year for which data are available, saw 130,000 more leave the country than enter it. Dutch emigrants and their sympathizers explained their decisions in terms of the assassinations of Pim Fortuyn, an anti-immigrant politician, and of the filmmaker Theo van Gogh, both killed by Muslim extremists. Some Dutch referred to the "Trojan horse of Islamism." In Belgium annual rates of emigration have picked up by 15 percent in recent years, and in Sweden the rate has grown by 18 percent. In 2007, more Swedes left their country than at any time since the nineteenth century. Some 200,000 people left Britain in 2006.[51]

In the event of a general flight, the United States, Canada, and Australia would no doubt loosen their existing immigration laws. These are already the primary destinations of these emigrants and South Africa for the Dutch. Those fleeing Europeans would also look attractive as an answer to the demographically induced labor shortages in these destination countries, while at the same time promising easier integration than most other groups. The relative benefits and losses would exceed mere numbers, too, since the most likely emigrants would include those with ability and means. University of Bremen sociologist Gunnar Heinsohn noted: "The really qualified are leaving. The only truly loyal to France and Germany are those who are living off the welfare system."[52] Should such patterns gain momentum, they could in some ways resemble the flight of Europe's educated from Nazism and Fascism before and during the Second World War, to the benefit of destination economies and cultures and to the detriment of Europe's. In such a modern reprise of the movement, however, the aging demographics would exaggerate the economic and financial benefits to the destination countries and exacerbate the disadvantages to Europe.

Such events would, of course, create a social, economic, and financial calamity for Europe. And, if such speculation on mass middle-class European immigration gets ahead of events and even future probabilities, it nonetheless grows naturally out of an already difficult environment that clearly blocks much more immigration as an answer for Europe's looming labor shortages. Even so, there are steps that Europe and other developed regions could take to alleviate this situation, not only allowing greater immigration but also offering more effective relief from demographic burdens by allowing existing immigrants to make more thorough economic contributions.

Some Sources of Relief

In this respect areas of relative success in the United States, Canada, and other immigrant nations may serve as guides. Though neither the United States nor Canada nor Australia is tension-free, these countries nonetheless have avoided the permanent immigrant underclasses so common in Europe and made so obvious by Turkish complaints in Germany, in the riots in the *banlieues* of Paris, and in the attitudes of the native European public. It also speaks to the relative success of these nations that immigrant incomes in the United States and Canada rise more rapidly toward comparable native wages than they do in Europe. A recent study by the Pew Center notes that children of immigrants in America actually achieve higher median incomes, more university degrees, and lower poverty rates than people in the country generally.[53] Perhaps even more telling, immigrants to the United States and Canada also tend to marry outside their ethnic group more readily than they do in Europe.[54] As much as 25 percent of the children of immigrants marry outside of their race or ethnicity. And the evidence suggests that rates of assimilation in North America are actually accelerating.[55]

Historically, the United States has had a much easier task with its immigrants than has Europe. Its long immigrant tradition makes it harder for native-born Americans than for Europeans to associate nationality with ethnicity. Even when Americans worry about the impact of immigration on traditional culture, their concern is less pronounced than in Europe or Asia, where some surveys show 90 percent of the population concerned about cultural adulteration.[56] Also the cultural divide between America's so-called Anglo population and the Hispanic culture of the vast majority of its immigrants is much narrower than between Europe's traditional culture and its predominately Muslim immigrants from Turkey and North and East Africa. After all, in America both groups share Judeo-Christian ethical and religious roots, whereas Europe's native population and its Muslim immigrants can only look back over centuries of intense mutual hostility. Hispanics and Anglos in America know each other's cultures much better, even before contact is made, than do Muslims and the native populations of Europe.

For all the cultural and historical hurdles, Europe could still gain from a look at American practice. Education stands as one important avenue. Though America's system affords much scope for criticism, in general and compared with Europe, it is much more accommodating of immigrants. It offers, for instance, high school equivalency certification that gives adult immigrants a useful, career-enhancing credential that barely exists on the other side of the Atlantic and that makes them more useful to the economy. America's greater flexibility toward late-blooming students also helps immigrants. Because European countries often divide university-bound students from others early in their education—Germany, for instance, at age 10 (12 in Berlin)[57]—youthful immigrants have their fate sealed, so to speak, before they have had time to overcome their obvious but ultimately temporary language and cultural disadvantages. The tendency in American schools to resist such early tracking, and to make exceptions if it is done, relieves immigrants of the worst of these impediments to their economic advancement and, by implication, to their economic contribution.

Accommodations concerning language have helped keep tension levels lower in America and Canada than in Europe. The practice of allowing immigrant schoolchildren to attend class in their native language is common in the United States. Schools sometimes also provide language programs for immigrant parents. Even with all the reasonable questions about the long-run efficacy of such bilingual programs, the practice nonetheless highlights an effort on behalf of immigrants that hardly exists in Europe. If such programs accomplish nothing else, they remove one source of immigrant resentment. In recognition of this American success, Germany has actually made its own tentative steps on language, except that the German authorities have emphasized special instruction in German in order, according to then interior minister Wolfgang Schäuble, to avoid the creation of a "parallel society."[58] If this German plan is less welcoming than the American approach, it may have greater practical value and, importantly, it does at least show more effort on behalf of immigrants than existed previously.

Progress might also come from a greater tolerance of outward signs of cultural difference—the willingness of schools, for instance, to accept cultural attire, such as turbans and headscarves, and the willingness by the police and military to accept modifications to their uniforms, as Canada has done with Sikh turbans. French schools could, after all, make some accommodation on the issue of wearing the Muslim headscarf. The issue, of course, carries great complexity, touching on women's rights and other questions of gender-based religious practice. But such an accommodation need not address such matters. Neither need it threaten what the French claim is 200-plus years of commitment to secularism, though strict secularist rules in France really date back only to 1905.[59] Still, it might disarm some of the tension if the French establishment were, for instance, to allow the scarf where students socialize, if not in the classrooms. An Irish compromise allows Muslims to wear headscarves if they are the same color as the school uniform.[60] Such accommodations, by their nature, satisfy neither side completely, much less some of the more subtle issues, but they can nonetheless relieve some bad feeling, relax tensions, and help to generate the desired economic dividends.

Europe might also benefit from some form of the American- or Canadian-style programs of official outreach to immigrant communities, including forms of affirmative action. Indeed recent French policy, referencing the American example, has begun to take just such steps. Immediately after the Paris riots the government established special priority education zones—ZEP using the French initials—in order to recruit immigrant students into elite universities. The government also appointed its first minister of equal opportunity, Azouz Begag, to head investigations of employment discrimination against immigrants.[61] It is doubtful that France or other European nations, much less Japan, could go as far as the United States and effectively reserve places at premier schools or in workplaces for otherwise disadvantaged minorities. But an active effort to guide otherwise ill-informed immigrant communities in the steps needed for educational and career success could go a long way to relieve the immigrant feelings of isolation and oppression that have so interfered with economic integration, and consequently blocked immigrants making an increasingly necessary economic contribution.

Other North American practices might also serve a more general need. Both the United States and Canada have invested in immigrant literacy programs, use bilingual signage on roads and in public buildings, have established family health programs for immigrants, as well as other underprivileged groups, and in some districts have promoted integration through breakfast and lunch programs for mothers to join their school-age children. The United States, like some places in Europe but unlike Japan, routinely offers immigrants the right to have language interpreters in courts and facilities to take a driver's exam or read a ballot in their native language.[62] Canada might provide a still more effective model. Its Immigrant Settlement and Adaptation Program offers newcomers a raft of assistance, including connections to volunteer programs to help them find work.[63] If France and Germany have so far ignored such examples, they have considered the adoption of the American and British practice of allowing dual passports in the hope that immigrants will more willingly accept their new society if they do not have to reject their homeland to do so.[64]

Many argue, no doubt correctly, that the immigrants should do more on their own behalf. Certainly they have huge economic incentives to do so. And many immigrants do make tremendous efforts, though culture and the dubious comforts of victim status can often trump even powerful economic incentives. But though such arguments for immigrant effort make sense, they are also almost pointless from a policy perspective. Even were it entirely justified, neither America nor Japan nor Europe could create policies to goad immigrants into trying harder. Officials can only make policies for the larger society, and must consequently address the issues largely from the side of the still majority native population. Neither does pushing immigrants to help themselves, however justified, do anything to advance the objectives of easing social tension or getting the full benefit from immigrant labor and talent that economic integration might provide. It certainly does nothing to relieve tensions sufficiently to allow still more immigration to help with future labor shortages.

There are, however, helpful policies besides accommodation. Developed countries could restrict inflows only to those with needed education, skills, and integration promise. Canada, even as it has shown a most welcoming face to immigrants, has taken the lead in this regard. Its point system for admission discriminates according to the immigrant's professional and language skills, as well as to his or her openness to Canadian society and culture.[65] The United Nations indirectly has recommended similar immigration policies, stressing the need to favor the young, the better educated, and the better trained.[66] So far Europe has rejected these approaches. But with an eye to similarly desirable effects, the European Commission has considered something equivalent to America's legal residence arrangements, commonly called a green card, as a way to attract and retain skilled foreign workers.[67] Though either approach would deprive the emerging economies of their most talented and well-trained workers, and would hardly serve overall humanity's broad aspirations, each would offer a genuine economic and social benefit to developed economies.

Surely imaginative policymakers can improve on these suggestions and devise still more effective ways of defusing tensions in either Europe or Japan or America. To the extent that they succeed, immigration flows can rise to levels where they do more to mitigate labor shortages, if not entirely erase them. The intention here is not to create a complete catalogue of what can be done but rather to give a general idea of what is needed, what has been tried, what has worked, and where the limitations lie. The composite effects of immigration, raising the levels of productivity, and increasing rates of participation in the workforce will certainly ease the labor strains imposed by aging demographics. But even the best efforts in these areas can only lessen, not dispel, the economic and financial disadvantages of the demographics. Increases in international trade, financial flows, and a general intensification of globalization do, however, promise to do more and consequently safeguard living standards.

5

A Global Means to Relief

Globalization can, however, offer complete relief. By importing goods and services from emerging economies, the United States and other developed economies can sidestep the otherwise severe limits of their pinched demographic situations and meet the material needs of their outsized retired populations. And they can do all this even as the labor used to produce those needs stays in their home country. It is an easy answer in some regards, too, because the emerging economies will welcome the arrangement. Trade is, after all, their best means of employing their huge, comparatively unskilled workforces and, with international investment, offers support for growth and development. If this codependence between the developed and the emerging economies has already largely evolved, demographic imperatives promise to intensify it to a point at which the change will seem less one of degree than of kind.

Advantages to All

History certainly testifies to the perennial role of trade as the way for economies to alleviate their weaknesses and capitalize on their strengths, whatever the underlying causes.[1] Holland's merchant empire of the seventeenth century amounted to nothing more than international links. Though Britain's agricultural and industrial revolutions of the eighteenth century stemmed from domestic innovation, they had their full effect only because Britain could export the product of its sudden manufacturing might, import raw materials to feed its productive machine, and, in time, import food so that it could still more thoroughly shift the focus of its domestic workforce from agriculture to industry.[2] Some hundred years later, Germany followed very much the same pattern.[3] The United States for much of this time depended on trade to procure needed manufactures, even as it capitalized on its position as a supplier of agricultural products and raw materials to Britain. Then, later in the nineteenth century, as America developed its own industrial infrastructure, it depended on trade as a sales outlet.[4] Clearly such cursory descriptions cannot do justice to this complex economic history, but the issue here is less that of historical detail than how economies always, and naturally, turn to trade to deal with their weaknesses and strengths.

This next wave of trade will answer the increasingly desperate needs of the developed economies to use imports from the labor-rich emerging economies to supplement the product of their relative lack of working hands. By outsourcing services and bringing in goods, especially those that require a lot of labor input, the developed economies will find a way to service the demands of their outsized retired populations even as they ease the productive burden on their limited workforces. By reorienting their existing productive effort toward more sophisticated, high-value, capital-intensive production, they will use their advantages in training and education, and their access to sophisticated equipment, to best advantage and have something with which to trade for the labor-intensive imports. As in the past, the process will allow both groups to sustain their growth trajectories and protect their living standards. How far trade will need to grow to accomplish these goals will, of course, depend on how successful the developed economies are with other means to mitigate the ill effects of labor shortages. But given the limitations of increased immigration, greater labor force participation, and enhanced productivity, some significant increase in trade and globalization is inevitable.

If the alternative mitigators were to fail, and international trade had to bridge the entire workforce gap, then a truly astounding acceleration in the pace of globalization would be in prospect. In America, for instance, the long-term expected 40 percent drop in relative labor strength (from 5.2 of the working-aged for each retiree presently to 3.0 in 2030) would force imports and outsourcing to rise from 18 percent of today's economy[5] to 30 percent. Comparable calculations for other developed economies[6] indicate a rise in imports to 25 percent of the Japanese economy by 2030 and to 35 percent of the British economy. France, Italy, and other continental European countries, where trade already dominates, would see imports climb to more than half their respective economies by 2030. By adding to an already impressive import-growth momentum, the demographics could easily drive imports to much higher proportions.[7]

Obviously these calculations hardly cover all the possibilities.[8] On the one hand, success in ameliorating the ill effects of demographics by other means would relieve some of the need for increased globalization. On the other, there are separate, powerful trends toward increased trade. These have already increased imports in the United States from 10.5 percent of the economy in 1980 to 18 percent more recently.[9] Superimposing the demographic need on top of this considerable momentum could more than triple the pace of globalization in the American economy.[10] Similar comparisons would apply in Japan and Europe. Such prospects explain why some researchers conclude that world trade will rise from slightly more than 30 percent of global gross domestic product today to well over 50 percent by 2030, and likely quite a bit higher.[11]

The evident need for increased trade in the developed world can only come as a boon to the emerging economies. The trends promise them increased growth, employment, and development. After all, the bulk of their progress so far has rested on exporting to Japan, Europe, and especially to America. China's desire for exports is crystal clear. That economy's astounding overall average real growth of 10.8 percent a year during the last 10 years was only possible because its exports grew at a still more remarkable 25 percent a year. Throughout, their importance has intensified. Exports have risen from 18 percent of China's economy

10 years ago to 40 percent more recently.[12] India's figures are slightly smaller, but otherwise they tell the same story. That country's powerful 7.1 percent average annual overall growth during the last 10 years was clearly driven by an 18.6 percent annual surge in exports that took their significance to the economy from 7.8 percent of the total 10 years ago to 14.4 percent more recently.[13] Similar, if sometimes less impressive, patterns are evident in all other emerging economies.[14]

More than just an engine of growth, production for export is, for the time being, the only way these economies can employ their people. China is archetypical. Some 50 percent of the nation's population still live on the farm in dire poverty. One million or more of these people *a month* migrate into the coastal cities in search of work and a better life.[15] Especially because these new workers are neither particularly skilled nor even literate, "labor-intensive production and exports" are, in the words of Qu Hongbin, an economist at HSBC Bank, the "only means for China to absorb its surplus labor and improve rural living standards and buy social peace."[16] The government in Beijing explicitly concurs[17] and notes the monumental scale involved, estimating that already the country has 225 million former farmworkers whom it must keep employed, "140 million of which are migrant."[18] (Just this migrant group alone rivals the size of America's entire labor force.[19]) The export dependence actually goes beyond such mind-boggling figures, since a large portion of that economy's retailers and other domestic producers depend for their sales on exporters and those whom they employ.[20]

Critical as such immediate growth and employment benefits are, exports also support a longer-term, more fundamental development agenda. At the very least, the incomes from selling toys and textiles, and by running call centers, allow the emerging economies to buy the complex, sophisticated products that they cannot produce for themselves—the high-level electronics, the heavy earth-moving equipment, generators, locomotives, computers, and such—but that they need to modernize their economies and prepare for future growth and development. Still more, the trade connections themselves bring these economies essential information. There decision makers learn of global product preferences that can guide factories in what to produce and to which specifications.

The links to Japanese and Western trading partners, and to the sophisticated products and systems that they buy with their export earnings, also, critically, expose the emerging economics to modern production techniques that can improve the efficiency of their production processes and the quality of their products. Zhang Yansheng, director of China's Foreign Economic Research Institute, captured these essential but mostly nonquantifiable benefits in remarkably poetic language by describing international trade as a means to "open the eyes of 1.3 billion people."[21]

Research to quantify the precise degree of this export dependence has failed to reach a consensus, but it universally concludes that overseas sales are critical for these emerging economies.[22] The smallest estimates for China ascribe to exports fully one-quarter of that economy's remarkable growth.[23] Some research concludes that as much as 30 percent of all China's new jobs stem from exports alone,[24] while other research, which takes into account the domestic jobs indirectly dependent on exporters and export workers, concludes that sales abroad are responsible for some 330 million jobs, or about one-third of all Chinese employment.[25] Much of this work underlines China's increasing dependence on exports, and shows how that economy would stagnate without them.[26] But if this careful research were not compelling enough evidence of the crucial nature of exports, the message has come home brutally whenever trade flows have suffered the least interruption.

The global recession of 2008–09 are a case in point. The loss of markets in Japan and the developed West during that time quickly put these emerging economies into a desperate situation. America's recession engendered a 26 percent decline in its purchases from China in only six months. Even China's chronically optimistic official forecasts could not ignore the matter and called for an overall economic growth slowdown, from a 12 percent yearly rate to just 7–8 percent. Though robust by the standards of other economies, that pace was slow by Chinese standards and, critically, barely enough to absorb China's seemingly endless flow of new job seekers. And matters threatened to deteriorate further.[27] India's situation was almost as dire. As its exports fell at almost a 50 percent yearly rate during that same period, the growth pace of India's overall economy slowed by almost half, to 4 percent yearly. Indian manufacturing output even declined for a time.[28] Elsewhere among emerging economies Brazilian exports fell at an overwhelming 80 percent annual rate, stalling that economy's growth.[29] After years of rapid expansion most of Asia's Pacific Rim—South Korea, Malaysia, Taiwan, Thailand prominent among them—faced outright economic declines.[30]

Layoffs soared almost immediately. China sent some 20 million migrant workers back to their inland rural villages[31]. Matters looked grim both to officials and for the workers. Though there is always considerable migration in China, officials noted in 2008–09 that migrants carried televisions and even refrigerators with them, implying that they expected to stay away from the coastal factories.[32] As India's critically important garment exports plunged almost 30 percent, some 1.5 million lost work right away,[33] and just as quickly the Indian government announced that some 10 million more jobs were at risk.[34] Similar stories of severe layoffs came out of the emerging economies elsewhere in Asia and in Latin America.[35]

Concurrently, the threat of violence rose. India's middle class, even before the recession, worried over "waves of violence."[36] Brazil, by spring 2009, saw job riots in Rio de Janeiro and São Paulo, and the pattern repeated elsewhere in Latin America.[37] Even more developed South Korea, Malaysia, and Thailand fret over the threat of labor unrest.[38] China was so concerned that police in Guangzhou met returning migrants standing in close phalanxes along the walls and fences of the railroad station.[39] And yet violence still erupted. When, for example, Kader, a Chinese toy manufacturer based in Dongguan, canceled 400 worker contracts late in 2008, those who were displaced immediately ransacked the factory offices.[40] Riots in China's northwest provincial capital of Urumqi resulted in the deaths of 184 people.[41] Beijing had to send troops to keep order, and an embarrassed President Hu Jintao had to return from his appearance at the July meetings of the Group of 8 most developed economies (G8) in Italy.[42] Though the killings took on the color of ethnic conflict, Beijing had no difficulty tracing their origins to a brawl miles away among workers displaced from an export facility in southern Guangdong province.[43]

Chinese premier Wen Jiabao's response seemed to speak for all the emerging economies. Even before the worst of the rioting began, he made clear his belief that only by "sustaining economic growth" could China maintain stability,[44] and he then went on to confirm the export link by vowing to answer the growth and jobs needs by opening "new [export] markets."[45] Chinese commerce minister Chan Deming underscored the critical role of exports by emphasizing China's determination to grab more of a suddenly limited global export market.[46] So determined was China to sustain its export edge that it quickly adjusted its currency policy. Between 2005 and the troubles of 2008, China had allowed its yuan to rise on foreign exchange markets, even though the currency action raised the global price of Chinese goods and so created a modest headwind to export growth. But with the recession of 2008–09, Beijing abruptly stopped all yuan appreciation.[47] So desperate was China for exports that it could not yield even the slightest competitive advantage with even the smallest rise in the price of its currency. China, in its perceived desperation, leaned on the All-China Federation of Trade Unions (ACFTU) to cease unionizing, striking, and collective bargaining.[48]

As it turned out, the worst of the recession in the developed world dissipated faster than many had anticipated. Buying resumed, and some of the worst fears for the emerging economies never materialized. Still, the sudden setbacks, the almost immediate violence, and the desperate responses of business and political leaders showed more dramatically, if not more precisely, than any statistical analysis how thoroughly these economies depend on exports. Silence overcame those who had previously argued that China and many other emerging economies had grown beyond such dependence—had "decoupled," as it were, from the developed world. The export dependence was clear, leaving China, India, and other emerging economies inclined to treasure the opportunity implicit in the impending labor shortages in Japan, Europe, and the United States.

Last a Long Time

In time, of course, these circumstances will change. Domestic markets in the emerging economies will gain sufficiently to replace exports as an engine of fundamental growth and employment. Ultimately, too, training and production prowess in these economies will improve so that they will gain the ability to manufacture sophisticated products for themselves. When that day arrives, they will cease to need the rich economies of Japan, Europe, and America quite as much, either as markets for their products or as sources of high-level equipment and business expertise. But that time is a long way off. The differences now between the developed and the emerging economies are so vast that it is reasonable to view the horizon for such change more in terms of decades than years.

Certainly income gaps indicate that it will take a long time before workers in emerging economies have sufficient income and wealth to substitute for the rich markets in Japan and the West. Even after the impressive wage gains of recent years, China still counts good pay for a production worker at the equivalent of just $2,500 a month[49] and average pay at closer to $300 a month[50]—both a far cry from counterparts in Japan, Europe, or the United States. General development levels tell an even more dramatic story. It is easy, of course, to miss the development gap in the showcase city centers of Beijing, Shanghai, Mumbai, Hyderabad, São Paulo, and Rio de Janeiro. But the shortest trip outside those centers shows how very long it will take these economies to bring their transport, communication, and production facilities up to the standards of the developed world. The average Chinese worker, for instance, has barely 5 percent of the productive equipment at his or her disposal that American, European, or Japanese equivalents have at theirs.[51] Most of China's local country roads still remain unpaved.[52] In India, almost half the country's rural households still lack electricity.[53] The same can be said in varying degrees of otherwise impressive economies elsewhere in Asia and Latin America.

Neither do the education levels compare with those of the West and Japan. While literacy in China stands at 91 percent of the population, it falls well below the better than 99 percent functional literacy rate in the developed economies, and China is the best in the emerging world. Only 89 percent of Brazil's workforce can read and only 90 percent of Indonesia's and Vietnam's. India has only a 61 percent literacy rate.[54] The gap is as vast with general education levels. The average worker in China has 6.4 years of formal education, in India 5.1 years, and Brazil 4.9 years. In the United States the average worker has more than 13 years of formal education, in Europe eight to 10 years, and in Japan some 9.5 years.[55] Even those workers in emerging economies with well-developed cognitive skills are less familiar with the systems, equipment, and practices of modern production than are even the most backward workers in Japan and the developed West, where everyone literally grows up amid such systems and equipment. In the words of one prominent observer: "Most developing regions have abundant labor, but rarely abundant skilled labor."[56]

None of this is to say that India, China, or other emerging economies lack for talented people. Quite the opposite is true. These nations produce a remarkable number of impressive scientists, engineers, businesspeople, entrepreneurs, artists, and political leaders. But these special people stand less as representative of than in contrast to the general mass of workers. Whatever the talents of the elite, it is the general run of workers that determine what an economy can effectively produce. It is hard, for instance, to mount a sophisticated production effort when one worker in 10 or more cannot even read his or her own language. And while no one can deny the impressive skill and training involved in the traditional handicraft industries that so dominate in these emerging economies, such highly specific training helps little with modern production processes and may actually impede a person's ability to function in such an environment. What is more, the steady flow of even less well-educated new entrants from traditional rural communities,[57] which typifies these economies, will extend the time needed to reach the general skill levels typical of workers in the developed economies.

So it seems that a codependent trade relationship between the developed and the emerging economies will remain viable for some time to come. Emerging economies will eagerly produce and sell to the developed world the abundance of simple, labor-intensive goods and services that will help relieve demographic strains. Japan and the developed West will continue to finance these purchases by selling the emerging economies the kinds of products that require the sophisticated workforce and industrial structure that the developed economies possess and the emerging economies will lack for decades to come.

Finance and Investment, Too

Under this intensifying globalization, the developed and emerging worlds will also find remarkable complementarities in finance and investment. The aging populations of Japan, Europe, and America increasingly will look to the fast-growing emerging economies for the high-returning investments to sustain them in their long retirements, investments that will become harder to find in their own, growth-constrained economies. And, as with trade, the emerging economies will welcome the heightened investment flows as a support for their own ambitious development objectives.

Viewed from the relatively slow-growing economies of Japan, Europe, and the United States, the investment allures of the fast-growing emerging economies are unmistakable and will become irresistible. Of course growth is only ever a piece of the investment puzzle. Asset prices can run counter to economic fundamentals, sometimes for years. But over longer time horizons, fewer links are stronger than those between rapid economic growth and superior investment returns. Such links go back, in fact, as far as data exist. This common trend was certainly evident when the Dutch merchant empires arose in the seventeenth century, during Britain's industrial revolution in the eighteenth century and in America's remarkably rapid development during the nineteenth and early twentieth centuries.[58] And the picture will continue to repeat itself in today's emerging economies.

Certainly the record of the last 30 years confirms the investment attractions of rapid development. Whatever may have happened in response to recent burdens, equity returns in the fast-growth emerging economies, when measured over sufficiently long time horizons, have outpaced those in the slower-growing, established economies. Contrast, for example, the about 8 percent average yearly advance of America's main stock measure, the S&P 500 Index, over the past 35 years with the

16 percent advance of India's Bombay Stock Exchange Index, or SENSEX, and the 20 percent of Brazil's Bolsa de Valores de São Paulo, or BOVESPA, stock index. Even the slower 9 percent average annual advance of the Taiwan Stock Exchange Capitalization Weighted Stock Index, or TAIEX, and the 9.3 percent of South Korea's Index Korea Composite Stock Price, or KOSPI, offer considerable return over the American index when compounded over these longer time spans. China's stock markets have existed only since about 1990, but during that time the Shanghai Stock Exchange Composite Index has risen at a superior 13.3 percent average yearly rate, far above America's 6.9 percent during the same period. Most other emerging markets show varying degrees of superior gains.[59]

Especially as demographic imperatives further constrain growth potentials in developed economies, their investors will find a greater allure in the rapid growth rates of the emerging economies and the superior performances of their asset markets. Funds will flow accordingly, as is already evident. The American data are indicative of the unfolding trend. Investment flows from American citizens, firms, foundations, and other institutions into emerging markets during the last 10-plus years have grown far faster than flows into almost every other major investment category. Naturally, given the conservative nature of most investors, the bulk of American money has stayed at home, but flows of new money overseas, from whatever source, have raised the proportion of American investments in the fast-growing emerging economies from negligible amounts in the 1990s to more than $1.5 trillion recently. Such exposure in American investment portfolios has risen from nothing to as much as 7 percent of all investments. The amounts and the proportions are still rising fast.[60]

Perhaps more significantly, companies will continue to pursue investment opportunities in emerging economies. Recognizing the huge potential of rapid growth and development, especially in contrast to the demographically constrained developed economies, businesses have already made significant moves into the emerging economies, actively placing their own subsidiaries there and establishing a broad array of joint ventures. American ownership of enterprises in emerging economies generally has leaped more than 11 percent a year during the past 10 years. In China those interests have grown 14 percent a year, and in India they have risen a stupendous 28 percent a year.[61] If anything, European companies have shown even greater enthusiasm. Western European businesses have expanded their ownership of Chinese enterprises 12.3 percent a year during this recent 10-year stretch, and in India European interests have grown 21 percent.[62] Japan has joined in, too. Concentrating mostly on China, Japanese businesses during the past 10 years have established almost 40,000 new ventures and committed the equivalent of more than $60 billion in capital.[63] In 2009 all direct foreign investment flows into emerging economies actually surpassed those crossing borders among the developed economies.[64] Trends have accelerated since.

No doubt, as this momentum picks up, some officials in the emerging economies will hesitate over foreign ownership, foreign control, and even use words like "imperialism." But apart from such obvious political impulses, economics and finance will offer a number of reasons for these countries to welcome the investment dollars, euros, yen, or whatever, as eagerly as individuals and firms in the developed economies want to make the investments. At the very least, the investment flows will provide a rich source of financing for machinery and the construction of housing, roads, rail links, ports, airports, warehouses, factories—all of which these economies lack and in some cases desperately need to enhance their productive potentials and living standards.[65] But more than this, and in a manner entirely analogous to trade, direct investments also bring access to advanced technologies, management skills, financial acumen, and production practices that these economies also lack and need, perhaps even more than the financing itself, to enhance their productive efficiency and effectiveness.

Though easy to overlook, it is hard to overstate the value of these skills transfers. Not only will the investment flows, like trade, help focus production on global trends and preferences, but they also will accelerate development by bringing to bear the composite expertise of a worldwide pool of business and financial talent.[66] Though no manager will explicitly consult this talent pool, it will nonetheless pass judgment by determining which projects win financing from global capital markets. To be sure, such expertise often fails in a world of great complexity and uncertainty, a reality to which the recent, painful financial crisis speaks loudly. But it is nonetheless a more effective basis for economic decision making than the alternatives, which in emerging economies are often otherwise based on political connections, family ties, regional loyalties, and, all too frequently, graft.[67] Even in the United States, where business plays a greater independent role than in most emerging economies, political, as opposed to economic, decision making often builds "bridges to nowhere."[68] With the insight and expertise delivered through such foreign financial flows, emerging economies can look forward to fewer false starts and less waste. By so making the best use of both economic and financial resources, the emerging economies can also anticipate greater economic stability and enhanced growth prospects both.[69]

Direct investment flows will add further to development efforts by bringing access to the technologies, management practices, and systems rare in emerging economies but widely used in more established economies.[70] Trade, of course, also gives such access, but the actual investments bring a much more thorough integration. When, for instance, a firm from the developed world sets up even a simple operation in an emerging economy, it not only brings otherwise scarce, sophisticated systems and machinery into the economy, but it also trains local workers on their use in modern production, including how to apply global communications and transportation links. Such matters might seem obvious to those already working in established economies, but this kind of training is precious in emerging economies. Its effects multiply as these trained workers take their new skills with them to new jobs. Some foreign investors, especially the Japanese, serve development efforts still more broadly by actually establishing schools to improve the literacy and cognitive skills of their workers, and even their workers' children, to lure the best talent and to ready the next generation of workers.[71]

If, as always, the complexity of all these influences defies precise measurement, scholarly research agrees that emerging economies should welcome investment from abroad as a means to accelerate development. In the words of one recent broad-based study, if "it is difficult to establish a robust causal relationship" between any one of these influences and growth, the overall pattern is "nonetheless clear."[72] It is certainly clear that, among emerging economies, those most open to foreign investment tend to grow much faster than those closed to it. One authoritative listing, without the usual blizzard of metrics and coefficients, clearly identifies economies more open to foreign investment, such as China, South Korea, Singapore, Thailand, Malaysia, India, Chile, and Indonesia, as having universally faster growth rates than those more closed to such investment, such as Paraguay, Haiti, Niger, Nicaragua, Ecuador, Peru, Côte d'Ivoire, and Togo.[73]

Helpful as this openness to trade and finance is, to both the emerging and the developed economies, it will force significant and sometimes painful adjustments. Some of these changes will build on already well-established patterns. Some will seem wholly new. As these transformations proceed, and indeed accelerate, these economies and societies will inevitably face hardships alongside the clear benefits. Together, the adjustments and the sometimes adverse political responses to them will force further change on all in coming years and decades.

6

Forcing Change in Industrial Structures

As these codependent patterns intensify in coming years, the trade, as ever, will prompt economies to specialize. The developed economies will increasingly yield the more labor-intensive activities to the emerging economies and focus themselves on more sophisticated, high-priced products. The specializations will, of course, reflect what each economy wants and needs of the other. But, more than this, those specializations will reflect each economy's competitive advantages. The abundance of less well trained and low-wage labor in emerging economies is suited to the manufacture of simpler, cheaper products that require considerable labor input, whereas the better education, training, and industrial infrastructures of America, Japan, and Europe are suited to the production of sophisticated, high-priced products. In the inelegant jargon of economics, the emerging economies will specialize in the labor-intensive and low-value-added, while the developed economies will concentrate on the capital-intensive and high-value-added. The pattern is already well established.

Who Does What and How

These future leanings will dominate not only what each economy produces but also how it produces. The patterns are already evident. Emerging economies use labor lavishly because it is abundant and because each worker brings relatively little training and productivity to the game. The emerging economies can pull this off profitably because labor is also relatively cheap. The average Chinese worker, for instance, earns little more than 1/100th–1/50th of his or her American, European, or Japanese counterpart, and the average worker in India or elsewhere in the emerging economies earns only slightly more.[1] In contrast to their approach to labor, emerging economies conserve equipment, which is far less abundant and relatively much more expensive than it is in the developed economies. The picture in America, Europe, and Japan is just the reverse. There producers do whatever they can to conserve their expensive labor inputs and will do still more in the future as labor becomes even more scarce and expensive. But with their relative abundance of machinery and productive infrastructure, much cheaper and more accessible than in the emerging economies, the developed economies make lavish use of equipment, not the least because their workers are well trained and can use it.

Such production orientations are especially evident in the popular practice called "de-engineering." Typically managers in emerging economies disable the cutting-edge capabilities of equipment when it is delivered from Japan or the West. A grader, for instance, may quickly "lose" a computer-based system to reset its blades automatically, leaving only manual means. These managers, far from being Luddites, have two very practical reasons for their actions. First, by ridding the equipment of much of its labor-saving capacity, they can employ more people, usually to meet government-mandated aims. They have little trouble bowing to such demands, since generally low wage scales allow additional employment with little impact on profitability. Second, their changes make the equipment simpler to use and maintain. Though the de-engineering renders that equipment less flexible, efficient, or precise, the workers, who almost always lack training and experience, would not know how to use the more advanced features anyway or effectively service them.[2] Needless to say, in developed economies where wages are higher, the absence of labor-saving features and flexibility could destroy a whole project's profitability.

These huge differences are especially evident in a comparison of construction activity. In China, India, and other emerging economies, construction crews consist of hundreds of men with shovels, lined up to dig a ditch or grade a road. In American, European, or Japanese construction, shovels hardly make an appearance. Instead, a wide array of trucks, earth-moving equipment, and grading machines replaces the men and the shovels of the Chinese and Indian picture and does the work in less time.[3] In these emerging economies the ranks of men are cheaper than a backhoe or a bulldozer, which in any case would be as hard to find as it would be to locate a worker who could operate it. In the developed economies the backhoe is cheaper, and many of the men and women involved know how to operate and maintain it.

An American businessman on a visit to China observed still other evidence of such distinctions. En route to a meeting in a suburban location, he passed a small gang of workers at the side of the road. They were using hand tools to cut stone blocks from a huge boulder—for construction materials, he was told. Returning from his meeting at the end of the day, he noticed these same workers at the same task, having made only slight progress. When he asked his Chinese hosts if there was not some cutting equipment to break the boulder into blocks more quickly and efficiently, they assured him that such equipment was very expensive, not readily available, and, in any case, the workers would not know how to use it.[4] At their low wages, however, what in America would count as a wasted day nonetheless paid a return.

Comparisons of these sorts multiply across every aspect of economic activity. Factories in emerging economies employ hundreds, sometimes thousands, of laborers toiling with every aspect of the work at hand, manhandling materials, loading, unloading, forging, and assembling items. In Japanese or Western factories the shop floor has few employees and even fewer doing heavy work. That is done almost entirely by machines.

The men and women on the shop floor work less on direct production than on managing and maintaining the machinery. It does the actual production, loading, and so forth. The picture differs in other significant ways as well. In the emerging economies the workers repeat hundreds of simple manual tasks in parallel, each focused solely on his or her immediate task. In contrast, the machine tenders in the developed economies often perform complex, varied tasks that clearly need considerable training and, critically, an ability to coordinate with others, which in turn requires an understanding of the overall effort and the purpose of the others' functions.

China's problems during the 2008–09 global recession testify in another way to these defining differences. The lack of social infrastructure in China's cities drove many workers to leave as soon as they were laid off from their export jobs. They had no choice but to return to their hometowns in the hinterland. But once they were home, the country's transportation infrastructure made it difficult for them to return quickly when export orders began to pick up again. Poor communications compounded the problem, as did the inability of these workers to estimate the likely duration of the layoff period. The lack of information and transportation and their ignorance of what was fundamentally happening made them insecure about what they would find if they returned to the cities, or less secure than they otherwise might have been. Such circumstances left China's factories short of needed staff for some time after export orders resumed, so that they missed deadlines.[5] Without such disadvantages the developed economies are much more flexible. And since a more sophisticated and complex product mix requires much greater coordination among workers and facilities, the differences become even starker when producing these sorts of products.

Generalizing from such specific examples shows how production orientations of the different economies deal effectively with their comparative advantages and disadvantages. The relative abundance of workers in emerging economies naturally pushes them toward the labor-intensive side of the production spectrum, while their low-wage structure gives a comparative profit edge in the production of low-value-added items. These include textiles, handicrafts, toys, plastic parts, the straightforward assembly of retail electronics and automobiles, generic chemicals, structural steel, other raw or semi-finished goods, and in some services, retail call centers, for instance. These sorts of activities have further appeal because they require less sophisticated equipment and systems. Because they lend themselves to rote repetition, with little need for worker communication or coordination, they further sidestep problems implicit in limited training, even literacy. Furthermore, because repetitive assemblies absorb masses of identical inputs, they can accommodate huge, sporadic deliveries and thereby minimize problems presented by unreliable transportation networks.

The developed economies with their high wage scales and limited labor resources have difficulty competing in the production of these simpler, low-priced, mass-market goods. But superior industrial infrastructures, an abundance of sophisticated equipment, more highly skilled workforces, better communications, and superior transportation networks give them a decided advantage in the more specialized, complex, and demanding products, especially because they frequently must tailor them to specific customer needs. Not surprisingly, these include research, technology, software, design, consulting, specialized chemicals, pharmaceuticals, finance, law, engineering, management, and the production of advanced machinery, such as fine machine tools, electronics, telecommunications equipment, aircraft, railroad locomotives, earth-moving equipment, heavy vehicles, and generators. And because these sophisticated, often customized products also demand a constant coordination throughout the production process, they further underline the advantages of superior transportation and communication networks, as well as a superior knowledge base. Because these products also command higher prices for each hour of labor input involved in their production, they can support the higher wage structures of these economies.

Reality's Complications

Obviously reality is never so consistent, neatly divided, or balanced as generalities imply. Parts of the emerging world will pursue sophisticated tasks that require the coordination of highly trained workers and a considerable investment in research, equipment, and systems. China and India's space programs stand out as prime examples.[6] Simple, labor-intensive activities will continue in parts of Japan, Europe, and the United States, too, a fact to which any stroll down the main street of a tourist town will attest, though increasingly even there, the inane T-shirts and "gift" items are made in Asia and Latin America. But if easy research can turn up long lists of exceptions, these general tendencies and the remarkable complementarity that they create between developed and emerging economies will prevail, while demographic pressure naturally will extend and exaggerate them.

The evidence certainly suggests that the world is moving toward just these divisions of activity. In the emerging economies, the growing momentum of globalization has intensified the preference for the simple, the cheap, and the labor-intensive. China's own government describes its entire industrial effort as oriented toward the production and export of simple "traditional, labor-intensive sectors such as spectacles, ornaments, shoes, and [retail] electronic goods."[7] For all the noteworthy progress that India has made in upgrading its production effort, its integration into the global economy has actually increased its bias toward these low-value-added, labor-intensive products. During the last 35 years, during which India has increasingly become involved in global trade, this sort of production has risen from 34 percent of the economy's export mix to 45 percent.[8] Brazil, in addition to the agricultural and mineral exports typical of less developed economies, has a manufacturing effort that centers on footwear and transportation equipment, mostly automobile assembly, the most labor-intensive, least-sophisticated part of automobile manufacturing, though Brazil has also developed a niche in aircraft manufacturing.[9]

Textiles, garment manufacturing, and handicrafts—the quintessential simple, low-value, labor-intensive products—dominate all emerging economies. Over half of India's exports lie in these areas,[10] with garments alone constituting almost one-third. Textiles employ almost 80 percent of India's industrial workforce,[11] though because of the product's low unit value, they earn barely 20 percent of profits from exports,[12] account for only 14 percent of the value of all industrial production, and constitute only 4 percent of India's GDP.[13] The story is the same for other emerging economies.[14] Some 53 percent of Sri Lankan exports are in garments and other textiles, as are 95 percent of Bangladesh's exports, 93 percent of Laos's,[15] and 90 percent of Vietnam's.[16] China employs a massive 20 million people directly in textiles production, with official figures identifying as many as 100 million indirectly dependent on that industry—a significant 12.5 percent of China's entire workforce.[17]

The evidence also shows conclusively that China, India, and the other emerging economies have grown increasingly dependent on the developed economies for their more sophisticated, capital-intensive products. China's major imports, apart from raw materials, focus exclusively on such high-value items, prominently refined petroleum, nuclear fuel, chemicals, metals and metal products, instruments, specialty electrical, telecommunications, and transportation equipment.[18] China has to import almost all the high-value technological parts and components used in its assembly efforts, especially semiconductors and microprocessors. Indeed, it depends so heavily on imported parts that technology imports rise and fall in lockstep with China's technology exports.[19] India's economy, though it produces fully 92 percent of all labor-intensive, low-value-added products for itself,[20] has to import more than 44 percent of its machinery and technology. Brazil, too, imports most of its more sophisticated, higher-value, capital-intensive products, such as fine machinery, electrical equipment, electronics, chemicals, and parts for its automobile assembly effort, including engines and transmissions.[21]

Even where emerging economies have a presence in industries generally considered more sophisticated, they lean toward the simpler, labor-intensive sides of the spectrum. China's "high technology" production, for example, consists mostly of the assembly, in the words of one prominent researcher, of "high volume, commodity-like product[s] sold primarily by mass merchandisers," such as notebook computers, mobile phones, and DVD players.[22] Among commercial services, an area that includes the famous Indian call centers, China and India focus on services for transportation, travel, and retail technology support, all aspects known in the industry as less demanding. More than half of China's services exports lie in these simpler areas. India is only slightly more sophisticated. Meanwhile, these economies have to import the more sophisticated commercial services of the sort used in marketing support and technological consulting at business or government levels.[23]

India, for all the headlines about its technical prowess, has only a tiny 15 percent of its exports in programming, medical support, research, and other knowledge-intensive products.[24] And even there the concentration lies in what India's own government describes as an "employment-oriented export strategy for those unskilled and semi-skilled."[25] If software equals some 60 percent of all Indian technology exports,[26] its focus is much more on execution and implementation than on the more demanding design aspects. One industry observer characterized Indian software projects as "small and undemanding (and responses to a survey of Indian software firms indicated that its 'most important project . . . had a small median size of only 150 man months')."[27] too limited for anything sophisticated. India's pharmaceutical industry runs true to this form as well. Its exports focus almost entirely on generics and straightforward, active ingredients for use overseas, what the trade calls "bulk drugs."[28] The same is true of Brazil's otherwise impressive pharmaceutical industry.[29]

As one would expect, the developed economies show the other side of this exchange coin. They have begun to relinquish to the emerging economies the production of textiles, handicrafts, and the bulk of inexpensive mass merchandise. Increasingly, they have pursued their relative advantages in more sophisticated high-value goods and services. Even when they remain in textiles and the like, they lean increasingly either toward highly mechanized production techniques, such as commercial carpeting in the United States, or specialized, high-end products, such as designer footwear in Italy.[30] Though not every one of their products is sophisticated or high-value, the tendency is clear. Capturing the difference in a single metric, the U.S. National Association of Manufacturers recently noted that China manufactures about as much as the United

States in unit terms but only half as much after taking into account the value of the output.[31]

These same divides appear in software development. Though much has indeed gone to India, which since 1980 has seen its software industry explode by 30–40 percent a year to employ more than 450,000 people at present, activity and sophistication levels still pale alongside the United States, which employs eight times the number in information technology[32] in an overall workforce less than one-third the size of India's.[33] And in stark contrast to India, America emphasizes the more demanding, high-value design aspect of the business. The same researcher who noted the relative simplicity of Indian software projects also noted that "requirement analyses and design, not to mention the creation of new products and 'solutions,' is still mostly the province of the U.S."[34] A similar picture emerges in Brazilian aircraft production. Though the United States, Europe, and Brazil each produce airframes, Brazil's otherwise impressive small-jet manufacturing remains far less sophisticated than either America's Boeing or Europe's Airbus.[35]

Similar distinctions are evident on the services side of the production equation. Though India has grown remarkably as a service outsourcer—now ranking sixth globally—it has, as in so much else, focused on the simpler, lower-value areas. The developed economies, particularly the United States and the United Kingdom, remain the top global outsourcing destinations, largely because of their huge financial services and legal industries. To be sure, India and China have more people involved than the United States or the United Kingdom, but the higher value commanded by American and British services gives them much higher revenue per employee and far greater revenue overall. In fact, the United States and the United Kingdom bring in so much more from outsourcing that even netting out what they outsource elsewhere, their respective surpluses stand at three times that of India and more than 12 times that of China. When it comes to more complex computer and infrastructure services, no emerging economy even registers as a significant outsourcing destination. China and Brazil actually outsource far more of this sort of activity to America and other developed economies than others outsource to them.[36]

Durable Divisions

The emerging economies will in time close the development and training gap with Japan, Europe, and the United States. As is already clear, it will surely take them decades to do so, but ultimately the catch-up will occur, and these relationships will make yet another adjustment. Still, even if the development gap were to close tomorrow and the established, developed economies were to lose all the tremendous advantages that they now enjoy—in training, systems, infrastructure, productive capital, and the like—they would still retain a similar orientation in the international exchange of goods and services. Even then the emerging economies would continue to concentrate on simpler, cheaper, more labor-intensive products, and the older, established economies on more expensive, sophisticated, knowledge-intensive products.

Why the pattern will persist, even after all today's absolute advantages disappear, harkens back to the remarkable insight of the early nineteenth-century British economist David Ricardo (1772–1823)[37] and the thought and research that has built on his work.[38] The focus of an economy's productive effort, Ricardo pointed out, has little to do with any absolute advantages it has over other countries. The important comparison is not between economies but rather within each economy's own capabilities. If the United Kingdom, for example, can produce more value in manufacturing than in agriculture, it will focus its efforts there, where, to quote Ricardo, it has a "comparative advantage" within itself. It will do so no matter how great or feeble those abilities may be relative to other economies. Even if Britain were superior to other economies in every way, it would still get more by concentrating on the areas in which it has its greatest advantage. There it can get the very best out of its labor, capital, and other economic resources and thereby maximize its output and its returns. It can then use excess production from that area where it is strongest within itself to buy from other economies more of the other products than it could produce for itself. This insight explains why weaker economies produce where their disadvantages are least pronounced.

Even Ricardo, notoriously known for his impatience with and intolerance of those who questioned his reasoning, admitted that the concept is highly abstract and slippery. His illustrations are too outdated to offer much illumination, but his point may be clearer in a simple example drawn from daily office life. If under time pressure an executive and his or her assistant need to produce several copies of a glossy client report and coordinate its distribution, they might best divide their last-minute effort with the executive doing the copying and binding and the assistant doing the word processing and the creation of exhibits. Though the assistant, no doubt, is more effective at both these activities than is the executive, his or her greatest advantage no doubt lies in word processing and PowerPoint. Though the executive is certainly less effective than the assistant at copying and binding, he or she does these things less badly than the other activities. By apportioning their efforts in this way, the pair maximize their combined skills, such as they are, and produce the most in the least time, even though the assistant could otherwise perform both functions better than the executive.

In much the same way, economies will maximize overall global output if they divide activities according to what each does best or least poorly. Suppose for the purpose of argument (and without any pretense of a forecast) that 30 years from now India were to surpass America's productive ability in every sort of activity—labor- and capital-intensive, simple and complex, high- and low-value. India nonetheless would still enjoy a more generous supply of labor, and so exceed America by a wider margin in the straightforward, low-value, labor-intensive side of the production spectrum. Indian producers would continue to identify the greatest profitability and get the most out of their economy, by emphasizing those areas where they can outdistance America by the greatest margin. America, though disadvantaged in all activities, would still see its smallest shortfall in the production of more sophisticated goods and services, causing its businesses to focus there, where they also can get the most out of their economy. Though India in this example could cut America out altogether, it could only do so by diverting resources to tasks where its economy is less thoroughly advantaged. India would, as a consequence, produce less overall while it and the world would lose out on America's production altogether. Both India and America would benefit if they concentrate on their respective comparative advantages and trade to satisfy needs not met by their own production.[39]

Such illustrations doubtless explain why economists have such a widespread reputation for implausible abstractions. Reality is never so cut-and-dried. Economies are never the same size, nor are they consistent throughout. They also always have many more than only two choices. But the exercise, abstract and unrealistic as it is, nonetheless demonstrates three critical considerations. First, even if at some distant date India or another emerging economy were to overtake the production advantages of the United States, and by implication the rest of the developed world, natural economic choices would still give America and the other developed economies a role in the international exchange of goods and services, in this case with the production of sophisticated, capital-intensive, high-value products. Second, even in this extreme case, both the emerging and the developed economies would benefit from the trade. Third, any economy, even one that outpaces all others in every way, gives up a lot of potential wealth and income by cutting off trade and producing all its needs for itself, even if in the process other economies suffer more.[40]

Over any reasonable time frame such speculation obviously is purely academic. As the previous chapter made clear, the developed West and Japan will for a long time retain not only comparative but absolute advantages over emerging economies in the production of pricier, more sophisticated products. Speculation on the state of affairs decades from now might instruct, but any projection at such a distance is dubious at best. Over a more manageable 20- or 30-year time horizon, however, economic fundamentals point conclusively to these expected divisions of economic endeavor—with such an increased intensity, in fact, that the process will overhaul respective industrial organizations as well as worker-management relationships, especially in the developed economies.

7

Still More Exaggerated Change

The intensification of globalization will exag- gerate these economic differences. Old, labor-intensive industries will disappear entirely from the developed economies. Reorganizing around sophisticated products and processes, firms will demand ever-more-skilled and better-trained workers, a circumstance that will change industrial-labor relations, the role of management, and even the way people live. For many, the change will offer an improved life, but the adjustments will undoubtedly also produce great strains, enough to stiffen the already ample resistance to globalization. Since any effort to stop the process would ultimately create much more pain than globalization itself, these economies have powerful reason to manage the transition, embracing the alterations even as they relieve the strains that they cause.

Business Well into the Process

A glimpse of this future, or at least part of it, flashed across the financial pages in 2004. IBM had decided to abandon the production of personal computers and sell its entire operation to the Chinese producer Lenovo.[1] Though many people still see PC production as cutting-edge technol-

ogy, IBM clearly thought otherwise. The nature of the deal revealed IBM's judgment that PC production had become too standardized to command its former high-value status and so no longer suited America's high-wage structure. Perhaps IBM could see that the technology of Apple's iPod, also launched that year and initially aimed at music, would eventually replace the PC's dominance in text and data manipulation. Since then the rise of smartphones and the iPad have confirmed IBM's judgment. Perhaps IBM determined for other reasons that the PC no longer offered much growth potential. Whatever the specifics behind the decision, IBM got a jump on this future by jettisoning what it clearly saw as a less demanding, lower-value endeavor, reserving its American operations for more sophisticated and profitable activities. Consulting services were mentioned in the press release accompanying the sale.[2]

Similar harbingers of change have appeared elsewhere. Japan's Kutch Chemical Corporation not too long ago entirely abandoned to China and other emerging economies the production of polyvinyl chloride (PVC), an inexpensive plastic used in everything from deck chairs to drainpipes. It reserved for its domestic Japanese operation the production of more sophisticated and pricier products, such as polyphenylene sulfide, a complex, heat-resistant plastic used to house electric motors and similar items.[3] In much the same way, the Nagoya-based machinery manufacturer Yamazaki sent all the production of its less sophisticated equipment to its Chinese plants, holding for its domestic Japanese operation complex machine tools, such as its trademark multitasking lathes. Another Nagoya-based firm, Brother, relocated its straightforward fax machine production to China and Malaysia, but retained all the design and management at home, along with the production of its high-end, precision industrial sewing machines.[4]

Repetitions of the pattern have become widespread. General Electric has divided its massive power equipment division, sending the routine, lower-value assembly and parts manufacture to various emerging economies but retaining for its more expensive, better-trained American workforce the pricier and more complex areas of management and maintenance, and the customized aspects of power plant design and construction, including installation.[5] Similarly, the German firm Siemens has divided its medical equipment division, sending its more routine, less knowledge-intensive parts manufacturing to emerging economies but keeping at its Forchheim plant near Nuremberg the more demanding, high-priced, knowledge-intensive design, service, and customer relations functions.[6] Apple assembles its eminently successful iPhone and iPad products in China, but retains the more complex, high-value design, marketing, packaging, and retail efforts for its American workforce.[7] South Korea's Korean Investment and Securities, also recognizing comparable advantages, has outsourced all its complex information technology design to IBM, which, after framing the project, made its own global distribution, keeping the more complex aspects in America while subcontracting the simpler activities to operations in emerging economies.[8]

In some cases whole industries have shifted. Japan's petrochemical industry moved the production of straightforward, commodity-like products, such as ethylene, to its overseas operations, retaining for its Japanese effort the more sophisticated production of the chemical compounds used in flat panel display screens.[9] These and similar decisions in other Japanese industries have allowed business in that economy to so sidestep areas where China holds advantages that today almost 80 percent of Japanese exports to the United States face no Chinese competition.[10] American companies in the chemical industry have done much the same as their Japanese counterparts, yielding the production of simpler products to operations overseas while emphasizing at home what it calls specialized engineering firms (SEFs) that focus on the newest process technologies and services, all of which command high value through licensing and consulting.[11] Textile firms, in much of the developed world, have long since left conventional woolens and cottons to producers in emerging economies. They have moved either toward highly mechanized operations for the production of synthetic, industrial fabrics or toward higher-priced specialty products.

All these shifts, as they continue to unfold in the future, will fit the general patterns dictated by the comparative advantages of these different economies and described in the previous chapter. The mass production of simpler, lower-value items—those that need cheap, mass employment—slide off to the emerging economies, while the more complex, specialized, higher-value efforts—those more oriented around complex customer specifications—remain with the more highly trained and expensive workers in the developed economies. The small island of Guernsey in the English Channel made this all explicit in the press release that accompanied its own adjustments. Guernsey, it said, would outsource "labor-intensive, low-margin activities" such as simple "software development and call centers," but it would keep the "high-margin activities" for its own highly trained workforce.[12] And whether it is Guernsey or some industry elsewhere in the developed world, all recognize that intensifying circumstances will force accelerated efforts to keep their domestic endeavors at the cutting edge of newer technologies and capabilities, especially those that are more sophisticated and more complex.

Yielding once staple industries to emerging economies can obviously cause considerable pain and dislocation, but the process can create significant gains for firms and workers as well. At the very least, each shift abroad requires larger operations at domestic headquarters, especially in communications, management, and technical support. Any new overseas operation also demands additional output of capital equipment, typically produced only in the developed economies. Subsequent upgrades of overseas operations create similar demands. None of these activities would exist had all production remained domestic. Furthermore, the transfer of routine tasks overseas frees more highly trained domestic workers from drudgery and allows them and their domestic divisions to pursue new, more profitable, higher-paying endeavors and innovations. Meanwhile, by expanding the general scope of the firm, overseas operations offer returns from a broader application of original designs and patents. They also allow an expansion in the often lucrative ancillary activities involved in getting the products to market, including marketing, advertising, packaging, and the like, something that would not occur so broadly had all the effort remained only in the domestic realm.

The British firm Globeleq offers a vivid, if extreme, illustration of the process. Launched in 2002, this company acquires electricity-generating capacity across fast-growing, emerging economies wherever it anticipates rapid increases in the usage of electricity. Globeleq does not manufacture anything. It merely facilitates. Yet its efforts to find the most effective sources of production generate gains to both developed and emerging economies. The returns to the emerging economies come pretty obviously from the expanded generating capacity. Returns to workers and firms in developed economies are no less significant. Aside from the incomes of its relatively small British staff, which only accrue because of its ventures overseas, Globeleq's efforts bring back to the United Kingdom and other developed economies all the returns surrounding the design and construction of the generating equipment it places, from shipping to installing to servicing and training. These returns all accrue to various manufacturing and consulting firms largely in the United Kingdom and other developed economies.[13] None of the associated business or jobs would exist were it not for Globeleq's effort, or at least not to the same extent.

The Hong Kong–based cosmetics company Beauty China operates on a less august scale but accomplishes much the same thing. Capitalizing on its physical proximity to China and its cultural knowledge, the firm generates ideas for women's makeup, its packaging, design, and marketing campaigns. Once it has set its design, it outsources the rather simple, labor-intensive manufacturing and packaging activity to independent operations in China. It also outsources the equally low-value, labor-intensive distribution activity to agents in China, which in their turn contract with hundreds of small outlets to sell Beauty China's latest product.[14] For all the business activity it generates in China proper, not to mention the boon of affordable glamour to Chinese women, Beauty China gains for itself, its employees, and more developed Hong Kong ample returns from the high-value design and marketing aspects of the cosmetics business—employment and income that would not exist were it not for the China venture.

In these adjustments, the future of cross-border investing has also made its appearance and shown its potential for huge returns as well. Apart from fees for investment management and consulting, investment professionals in developed economies have demonstrated an ability to use their connections and expertise to earn considerably more on the investments that they control than emerging economies earn on their investments in developed markets. They often earn these additional monies simply from redeploying official Chinese reserves placed in U.S. Treasury securities, earning on average a remarkable premium return of 5 additional percentage points a year.[15] Such additional earnings, just on the foreign holdings of U.S. Treasury securities, bring the American economy a net flow exceeding $150 billion a year.[16] That figure amounts to more than one-third of the nation's deficit between imports and exports of goods and services, though for some reason government statisticians exclude such financial earnings from their calculations.[17] The actual returns are surely much greater, since flows into Treasury securities are only a small part of all foreign financial investments in American markets.

A Changing Work Culture, Too

These are just a few current manifestations of this future. There are others, and they will multiply, creating advantages even as they disrupt past patterns. But the trend will go much further than an industrial reorientation and the placement of business operations. In time the changes impelled by these circumstances will alter the entire nature of the workplace, the way people live, and even relations between employer and employee. Tentative signs of these coming changes have also begun to emerge, even before the responses to demographic imperatives have made themselves felt. The picture, remarkably, has emerged in two otherwise very dissimilar places, Texas and New England.

Texas still has its oil roughnecks and its cowboys, but under the pressure of globalization it has increasingly emphasized knowledge-intensive business. Firms and individuals naturally have followed their profit opportunities and moved toward pricier products, leveraging the state's well-developed, modern industrial infrastructure, its easy access to sophisticated technologies, complex equipment, and an increasingly well-trained workforce. The Federal Reserve Bank of Dallas has documented this increase in the "skill intensity" of the state's production processes and its product offerings. Today as much as 26 percent of the state's export jobs lie in computers and electronics, and 16 percent in sophisticated machinery—well up from the past, and well ahead of the country as a whole, where only 16 percent of export jobs are in electronics and only 12 percent in complex machinery. Texas also has reoriented its target markets ahead of the rest of the country, doing much more business with emerging economies—Mexico, obviously, for geographical reasons, but also Asia's fast-growing economies. The entire shift, according to the Federal Reserve Bank's extensive research, has given the Lone Star State a 75 percent advantage over the rest of the United States in trade with all emerging economies.[18]

New England, too, has transformed itself along broadly similar lines and for much the same reasons. Having lost most of its once great textile wealth—first to cheaper labor in the American South and then overseas—the region has responded to the global challenge, also without any central direction but rather from each firm's and individual's recognition of its relative advantages. It has built on its strong standing in higher education, emphasizing it as a major product in itself but also extending it to related high-value efforts in finance, health care, and professional services, especially law, computer-related support, scientific research, development, industrial design, and consulting. Employment in textiles has all but disappeared, while Boston and environs now proportionally employ about twice as many in these high-value endeavors as is typical in the United States, and many multiples of what the sparse statistics show is the case in emerging economies. In offering this peek at the future, New England has raised the region's relative income, wealth, and land values from mediocre to the top rank in the United States.[19]

The European Union has sought its own, similar transformation, striving to close what it calls the "research, education, and development gap" with the United States.[20] The British have claimed to be in the vanguard, taking comfort that they have moved away from low-value manufacturing faster than has continental Europe, and boasting that Britain now employs more than 40 percent of its workers in "knowledge-intensive services" compared with only 33 percent in Germany, 36 percent in France, and 30 percent in Italy.[21] Even barely emergent Portugal has made a transition. Faced with competition from still less developed Eastern Europe, it has cut its dependence on exports of textiles, clothing, and footwear from 40 percent of the total economy early in the 1990s to only 23 percent while raising the proportion of more capital-intensive exports, such as chemicals, paper, machinery, vehicles, and precision instruments, from 16 percent in the early 1990s to 46 percent.[22]

Such shifts will, of course, also force a change in the nature of the workplace. Hints are already evident in how business has chosen to spend its money and in the kinds of jobs it increasingly has emphasized. Foremost is the ever greater emphasis on research and development, not just new ideas for new products but also an ever more widespread application of technology throughout the production process. R&D has long held a special place in American industry.[23] It already absorbs a huge proportion of the economy's business spending, more absolutely than any other combination of countries, but proportionally more as well. At last measure, R&D spending by American business as a proportion of GDP stood well above that of Europe and Japan and at more than twice the proportion of such spending in China, Brazil, India, or any other emerging economy.[24] That difference should persist, even redouble, under pressure from demographics and more intense globalization.

The growing research emphasis should change R&D's nature as well. The laboratory work, often done remotely from the production site, will accelerate and bring its advantages to the workplace. It will target the productive effort around superior products, while the fruits of this research—embodied in more sophisticated equipment, infrastructure, and systems—will themselves bring efficiencies and greater effectiveness to the production process. But in addition to this well-known, more or less top-down benefit, firms increasingly will add a bottom-up element. Because they will have more highly skilled workers who understand much or all of the productive process, they will effectively have a huge source of innovative talent on site, a kind of in-house consulting group on every aspect of the firm's products and how they are produced. This source of innovation will itself become increasingly important, especially as firms move toward a higher-value and concomitantly a more customized product mix that will require a more flexible productive process, one that orients itself ever more responsive to customer specifications and evolving technologies. Indeed, since much of the high-value-added output will revolve around products made to customer specifications, more and more, customers, too, will become a source of innovation, and suppliers, too.

This whole process will urgently demand more worker training and education. Responding to existing pressures and seemingly anticipating this future, workers already have dramatically upgraded their skills. As mentioned earlier, American workers today have on average 13.1 years of formal education, up by almost one-third from the 10.1 years averaged 35 years ago, when globalization was only just gaining momentum. Indeed, educational demands have already become so severe that those without such upgraded skills suffer much less job security. Though the average job tenure of experienced, trained American manufacturing workers has remained pretty much unchanged over the last 40 years,[25] less well-trained workers have universally suffered shorter and shorter tenures as the weight of globalization has impelled ever greater demands for better skills.[26] As these pressures intensify, they will impel the less well trained increasingly to rectify their shortcomings in this regard. Meanwhile, those with skills adequate for the present will have to upgrade continually—run faster, so to speak, just to keep what they have.

All these changes will in their turn erode the old hierarchical approach to industrial organization and industrial-labor relations. The need for old-fashioned supervision cannot help but fade as mechanization does the more routine functions and better-trained workers become increasingly involved in innovation while, necessarily, also becoming increasingly aware of the overall production process. So, too, the distinctions between managers, technicians, and workers will fade. The staff increasingly will supervise itself. Those in the executive offices will shift from supervisory functions toward a more outward focus, maintaining the right R&D focus, for instance, networking to procure a steady supply of needed inputs from a greater variety of sources. And because an increasingly sophisticated product mix will become more specialized and tailored to buyer specifications, they will need to work increasingly with customers. Because so much innovation will need to emerge from staff, suppliers, and customers, the executive suite will, if it wants to be successful, need to listen more and command less, at least until after management has digested the various inputs.

Cutting-edge firms have already signaled this future. In the American chemicals industry, for instance, the proportion of the whole workforce involved in supervision has dropped by almost 5.5 percent in just the past few years, while the proportion of those in business planning, design, and related areas has risen 22 percent. In the paper industry, the proportion of headquarters staff dedicated to managing production workers has fallen 22 percent, while the proportion in planning and design has risen nearly 19 percent.[27] Even within the strict production areas of manufacturing firms, proportionally fewer workers than before focus on straightforward production. The dominance of more complex products, those with more demanding specifications, has naturally forced a relative increase in inspectors, testers, and quality-control people. In just the last few years the fabricated metals industry, for instance, has seen the proportion of those involved in such functions rise 10 percent. Transportation equipment manufacturers, including autos, aircraft, and railroad equipment, have seen the proportion of their staff in these same groups rise by more than 12 percent.[28]

Decentralization will exaggerate these organizational changes. In the old model, the one that still largely prevails today, the production process was linear. Each step depended entirely for its input on the output of another division of the single, overarching firm. Everything was located in close proximity. But as specialized, high-value production replaces the mass production of relatively simple items, this structure will no longer serve. In a globalized environment, where production gets placed according to relative advantages, each operation will seek its inputs and customers in many places. Firms increasingly will source and sell across a web of suppliers and buyers, not necessarily divisions of the parent firm. An operation that assembles, say, electric motors might buy its coils outside its parent firm—wherever, in fact, it can find better quality at a lower price. It might choose a different supplier for its casings and a third still for its platforms. It might then sell its assembly to any number of firms, sometimes foreign, sometimes divisions of the parent company. Economists have tracked the development of this growing interdependence with gauges that they call "multipliers." All show that a significant shift toward such networking is already in place.[29]

Changes in steel production—an otherwise archetypical old industry—provide an illustration. Because steel felt the pressure from foreign competition early, it has, despite its backward image, anticipated this future. Along with straightforward efforts to increase efficiency and productivity, the industry closed its older, larger, integrated mills and turned to more specialized "mini-mills." These often locate away from the old centers of production and closer to customers, not just for shipping convenience but also because they often tailor their small runs strictly to customer specifications. No longer does a single overarching organization oversee every step in the production process from the mining of iron ore and coking of coal to the final huge runs of standard structural girders or standard sheets. Now the much smaller mini-mills find their inputs—iron ore, or sometimes scrap steel—not necessarily from other divisions of their parent firm but from other firms, either within the United States or abroad, and then sell their high-value, specialized output, perhaps as input to another producer, also either in the United States or abroad.[30]

The general effect of all these shifts on industrial-labor relations has increasingly had a refection in the changing structure of organized labor. In heavy industry, for example, where the labor movement got its start, unions have long since lost ground, even before these changes gained momentum. The old, integrated manufacturing industries were ideally suited to union activities. There, workers "gathered in large groups under a single factory roof, sharing similar working conditions and interests."[31] But as this structure has broken down—and manufacturing has become more sophisticated, decentralized, and mechanized, often located far away from the original locales of the earlier operations—unions have found it difficult to organize. Compounding that problem, the growing proportion of better-educated, more highly trained workers, concentrating less on raw output and more on inspecting, testing, and quality control, has eroded the old-time sense of common worker interests and even the sense of opposition to management.

As though anticipating the future, union membership in industry has declined, both absolutely and particularly as a proportion of the working population. From a 1940 peak, in which almost 36 percent of workers affiliated themselves with a union, the figure dropped to 22 percent by 1975, to 18 percent by 1985, and recently stood at less than 12 percent. In terms of outright numbers, total union membership peaked in 1979 at some 21.2 million. Even as America's overall workforce has grown, that figure has fallen by almost a third to 14.3 million at last count.[32] The only significant union successes during this time have occurred among teachers and civil servants, two groups that have remained unaffected by the trends imposed on the industrial community and in which the old, integrated model of organization still prevails.[33]

Globalization has introduced other reasons for workers to question the value of a union affiliation. Traditionally unions organized to protect workers from management abuse, but as the main threat to workers' well-being has shifted from management to foreign competition, unions have had trouble adjusting. Indeed, the growing significance of foreign competition has driven management and workers into an alliance of sorts to meet the common foreign threat, leaving unions with a less significant role. Organized labor has tried, even so, to rise to the demands of the times and frequently has lobbied Washington on trade issues, but seldom has it done so in a particular industry as effectively as management or a joint management-worker effort can.[34] Even the United Auto Workers, which showed great political power managing Washington's response to the failures of Chrysler and General Motors, has failed in its antitrade lobbying efforts. Union loyalty has weakened accordingly.

Not surprisingly, the same forces weakening union strength and altering industrial organization will add to their powerful effects on society in general. Certainly the greater geographic dispersion of industry will extend already powerful suburbanization trends, while the telecommunications revolution will push that movement into exurbia as well. At the same time demands for more sophisticated, better-educated workers will continue to give societies throughout the developed world a still more middle-class character. Older communities will dissolve, as will old identities and old political alliances—trends that political scientists and sociologists have long noted, though for different reasons.[35] The nature of suburbia and exurbia also will continue to change. Whereas once suburbs served almost exclusively as bedroom communities for major urban centers or centers of integrated industrial activity, the more networked nature of industry has seen a growth in the suburbs as settings for work as well.[36] To be sure, there is much more than economics behind such trends, but there can also be little doubt that networked business structures have fostered them as well and will continue to do so.

A little imagination could draw these threads out to paint a picture of a future that looks very different from the present. Some of this picture may appeal; some may not. Judgment will depend on each observer's biases and tastes. The object here, however, is not to paint futuristic pictures, tempting as that might be, but to signal the extent of the adjustments required and indicate what their nature will be—whether they are good, bad, or indifferent. The changes, however welcomed by some, even a majority, inevitably will generate grievances among those hurt in the process, as they already have. These grievances will feed the resistance to globalization, however helpful and necessary it otherwise is. Nations and economies will need to address these complaints, if they hope to rely on trade and globalization to relieve their demographic pressures and protect their living standards.

8

A Tide of Resistance

Already, even in their beginnings, these changes have elicited great resistance. People, with considerable justification, associate globalization's imports, outsourcing, and offshoring with lost jobs. They link globalization to a widening income gap between rich and poor and the destruction of middle-class dreams in America, Europe, and Japan. They complain, understandably, about destructive financial swings, and they fear the rising political, financial, and military strength of emerging economies. If their concerns are frequently overblown, they surely carry enough truth to gather political support. In fact, there is an increasing danger that a protectionist political response could stop globalization, creating still greater economic havoc. Better, then, that these nations disarm antiglobalization resistance by addressing popular concerns, channeling trends to alleviate the adjustment pains, and turning those adjustments to each economy's advantage.

Enthusiasm Turns Sour

People were not always so wary. On the contrary, not too long ago most welcomed free trade and free financial flows as agents of prosperity, peace, and a more liberal political culture around the world. The greatest enthusiasm, not surprisingly, emerged in the early 1990s, as the Berlin Wall fell and the Soviet Union imploded. On both sides of the old Cold War divide people hailed the triumph of liberal democracy, freedom, and market economies. The end of the great communist tyranny had, it seemed, lifted the threat of nuclear annihilation, loosened constraints on all international interactions, and brought hope for more open, more rewarding, and more profitable global interchanges.[1] Those nations that had shouldered the onerous costs of the Cold War looked forward to a "peace dividend" that would enable governments to direct monies formerly aimed at defense toward more productive initiatives, or at the very least to tax relief.[2] Businesspeople across the globe looked ecstatically to the opening of new markets.

Back then, the positive power of globalization took on an almost religious character. Conservative, centrist, and left-leaning editorialists caught the positive mood, as did columnists, academics, and policymakers. These people rhapsodized about the "civilizing influence" of commerce or how "more trade and more growth would lead to more democracy and freer elections."[3] Others predicted that growth would surge as the developing world "throws off its socialist shackles and moves toward capitalism."[4] They emphasized "the intimate relationship between political and economic freedoms."[5] Even in Japan, never a paragon of economic openness or a firm supporter of free trade, establishment opinion commended international economic interdependence as the "strongest guarantee of peace."[6]

Not all interests embraced the globalizing trends. Organized labor resisted, as did some populist thinkers on both the left and the right. In the early 1990s, for example, Texas industrialist H. Ross Perot based his 1992 presidential bid in large part on opposition to NAFTA, the North American Free Trade Agreement that allows free trade among the United States, Canada, and Mexico.[7] But these were minority positions. As newspaper columnist Thomas Oliphant said at the time, it was a great myth "that the NAFTA opposition was ever on the verge of victory."[8] Surveys from 1990 through the 1993 NAFTA vote and beyond showed approval ratings for free trade and open markets of more than 70 percent in the United States, Canada, and most European and Asian countries.[9] Magazines urged small and medium-sized businesses to "go global," as the new political-economic milieu seemed to demand.[10]

Politicians mirrored the positive public mood even as they reinforced it. In 1989, right after the Berlin Wall fell, President George H. W. Bush immediately endorsed globalization as the natural next step for the United States and the world. Both sides of the aisle in Congress applauded when in his 1990 State of the Union address he referred to changes of "almost Biblical proportions" and to "a new era in world affairs." He got enthusiastic bipartisan support for his vision of a "widening circle of free governments and free markets" and a "growing commonwealth of free nations."[11] Bill Clinton followed with an even more enthusiastic tone, describing a new "global economy" as a means to create "a higher rate of economic growth, improved productivity, more high-quality jobs, and an improved economic competitive position in the world." He went so far as to insist that the country's "economic growth depends as never before on opening up new markets overseas and expanding the value of world trade." During his 1997 State of the Union address, Clinton spoke glowingly, also to bipartisan applause, of the "new promise of the global economy" and the need to "tear down trade barriers" in order to further "the cause of freedom and democracy around the world."[12]

There were indeed sound reasons for optimism, or at least there seemed to be. Budget relief was one of the most obvious. In 1989, the United States spent $362.2 billion on defense, an astronomical amount for the time, approaching 7.0 percent of the nation's GDP. During the Cold War years, 1945–90, defense spending had often risen above 10 percent of GDP and averaged close to 1989's 7.0 percent. These relative rates dwarf even the 3-plus percent of GDP spent on defense during the height of the Iraq War.[13] It was easy and pleasant in 1989 to envision how these hundreds of billions of dollars would turn toward research, education, roads, other needed public works, environmental relief, a reduced tax burden, or any number of other productive endeavors. Some saw an opportunity for more effective foreign aid unfettered by Cold War imperatives. All promised better lives for Americans and for people overseas. Presidents Bush and Clinton provided long lists of such hopeful uses for those monies.[14]

Most promising were the potentials implicit in the destruction of Cold War barriers and suspicions. People previously trapped in the Soviet and Chinese communist spheres looked forward to better lives from greater access to superior Western products, Western investment, and Western ideas. In America, Europe, and Japan people and businesses enthusiastically anticipated outsized gains from growing markets in Russia, China, other former "enemy" nations, and previously nonaligned states, such as India, which during the Cold War had only limited dealings with the West. Africa and Latin America also seemed poised to gain as the great powers ceased to use them as proxy battlefields, and they could instead enjoy more productive interactions with both Western governments and businesses.

The sheer size of the populations involved seemed to give substance to the dreams. In 1990 the Soviet Union, the People's Republic of China, India, and other nonaligned nations, as well as Africa, had more than half of the world's population but produced less than 10 percent of its GDP.[15] If free trade could lift these economies only partway up to Western and Japanese living standards, people reasoned, global growth would enjoy a huge boost for years to come. In the more open political environment, people could also imagine a productive exchange of ideas, including technological advances and innovation, which would further heighten growth and prosperity.

Such astronomical potential swept away reservations even among confirmed skeptics. Linking advances in trade and economic development with political stability, popular opinion looked forward to a virtuous cycle in which economic growth would lead to freedom, which would then foster more growth and opportunity. American political scientist Francis Fukuyama made himself famous by laying an intellectual foundation for these hopes. Taking a remarkably progressive, almost Whiggish view of history, he argued persuasively at the time that the end of communism was the last of a series of steps to bring the world to a more ideal system. First in a 1991 article and then a year later in his book *The End of History and the Last Man*, Fukuyama stated that "the triumph of liberal democracy had freed governments around the world from the internal contradictions present in other systems."[16] The ensuing "liberal revolution in economic thinking"[17] was a natural outgrowth of "the logic of modern natural science"[18] and would end "history as a simple, coherent, evolutionary process."[19] Though in retrospect these arguments sound quaint, they dominated intellectual discussion at the time.

In that enthusiastic milieu officials used the machinery of the General Agreement on Tariffs and Trade (GATT) to create the more broad-based, dynamic, and powerful World Trade Organization (WTO). Like GATT, the WTO had a clear mandate to promote trade liberalization, but unlike GATT, it had policing powers to ensure adherence to those agreements.[20] Initially the WTO got a warm welcome. An opinion article in London's prestigious *Financial Times* hailed the chance to breathe a "hearty sigh of relief."[21] Japan's *The Daily Yomiuri* accused any who stood in the way of the new trade organization as being an "impediment to peace and progress."[22] *The Boston Globe* said that the WTO "is good for the United States and good for the world."[23] *The Straits Times*, of Singapore, put the WTO and other progress toward free trade on a par with the end of apartheid in South Africa.[24] *The Washington Times* enthused that the WTO had been endorsed by "presidents from Ronald Reagan to Bill Clinton, by organizations from the Consumers Union to the Heritage Foundation and by leadership associations from the National Governors Association to the National Association of Attorneys General."[25]

Yet feelings quickly changed. By the late 1990s surveys throughout the developed world revealed a clear decline in the once almost universal support for globalization.[26] Dramatic signs of the change shocked received opinion late in 1999, when street riots greeted the WTO's Seattle meetings.[27] Tens of thousands of protesters from around the world accused the organization of a massive betrayal of public trust and of every crime, from raping the poor to stealing jobs, from destroying the environment to undermining democracy and national sovereignty, from ignoring women's rights to trampling on indigenous cultures and weakening the family farm. In the years that followed, the intensity of negative feeling grew and showed again and again in protests at WTO and International Monetary Fund (IMF) gatherings in Prague, Gothenburg,

Quebec City, Genoa, and Washington, D.C.[28] The turn in opinion gained especially dramatic and sad expression at the WTO meeting in Cancun, Mexico, when a South Korean protester, Lee Kyan Hae, overcome with emotion, stabbed himself to death in front of the building where the delegates met.[29]

The media reversed itself and turned hostile. By 2004 *The Boston Globe* had given up its previous enthusiasm and began to worry about "job security in a changing globalized economy."[30] Even the always pro-business *Wall Street Journal* said that the "net effect of transferring work abroad remains unclear."[31] In 2005, to much press attention, masses of Norwegian farmers marched in protest to WTO headquarters in Geneva.[32] By that time even the pro-free-trade *Economist* wondered if there was "More Pain than Gain" in the process of globalization.[33] The IMF itself suggested that globalization was hurting working men and women throughout developed economies.[34] *The New York Times* noted that "Americans Are Losing Their faith in Globalization,"[35] and the *Financial Times* ran several articles arguing against global financial flows.[36]

A 2006 study of Associated Press reports described the shift comprehensively. Of all articles on globalization, the study noted, those that linked the trend with heightened growth had fallen from 40–50 percent in the late 1980s to barely over 15 percent by 2003–04. Over that same period articles linking globalization with poverty rose from 5 percent of the total to 25 percent, articles linking globalization to unemployment rose from 12 percent to 22 percent, and those linking globalization to environmental degradation from 7 percent to 18 percent.[37] Media attitudes, not surprisingly, correlated to public attitudes. By 2008 a Pew Research survey noted an almost 20 percentage point drop in American support for free trade over the previous four years and a similar, if slightly less dramatic, decline in Europe.[38]

The Pain Is Real

No doubt fashion had something to do with the change. Everyone likes to take new perspectives, intellectuals perhaps more than most. But the shift also had a genuine basis in unfolding realities. Though open market trends had, as expected, benefited many in the intervening years and continued to do so, globalization was also creating much more pain than most had expected, a pain that promised only to intensify. This less happy result gave substance to the widespread feeling that reality had betrayed the great hopes of the late 1980s and early 1990s.

Worse was to come. By the turn of the century Al Qaeda and other terrorist groups had shattered the feeling of security that followed the collapse of the Soviet threat. That was all too real for most. The development of the Chinese military undermined the sense of security as well, especially for Americans and Japanese. Neither did liberal democracy grow as luxuriantly as Francis Fukuyama had predicted. Most significantly, the benefits of trade and free flows of financial capital spread less consistently than people had expected. The protesters and their placards may, as one economist said, have made "the output from a monkey's romp on a keyboard look more coherent,"[39] but many observers sensed that the folks in the streets were nonetheless on to something real. If people overlooked the protesters' silly sloganeering, they could agree that globalization had done much more harm than expected, even if few could detail all the causes and effects.

What really happened is now evident. Instead of finding millions of consumers in the once communist and developing world, businesses, individuals, and governments faced a huge influx of cheap labor. By some estimates the entry of these emerging economies into the unfolding globalized environment doubled the labor available in the world's marketplace.[40] The competition from this huge supply of inexpensive workers began to impose itself quickly on the established, developed economies in America, Japan, and Western Europe. People suffered losses where they had expected gains. Instead of greater security they faced more uncertainty and a widespread uneasiness about the basis of past prosperity. Workers in the developed economies suffered the bulk of the pain in lost jobs, lost industries, and widening income differentials between rich and poor. Globalization now seemed to promise financial instability as well and generally worrisome shifts in relative economic power. As people sensed these burdens, implicitly if not explicitly, it is hardly surprising that enthusiasm about globalization ebbed.

Low wages in the emerging economies were the main impetus behind the shock. Chinese workers earned a minuscule amount compared with their counterparts in the developed economies, for a long time only one-hundredth of what could be earned in North America, Europe, or Japan. Though their relative position has improved, Chinese workers still earn at best one-eighth of their American equivalent.[41] Relative wages in India were only slightly higher than those in China, and though compensation in Russia and the formerly communist states of Eastern Europe ranged closer to the developed West, they still averaged only one-third of wages in the rich countries.[42] Even considering the better training, education, and productivity of workers in America, Japan, and Western Europe, the competitive pressure from this influx of low-wage workers was, and remains, overwhelming in industries that need a lot of labor in the production process.

Though the globalization enthusiasts of the early 1990s had been largely blind to this effect, it became starkly apparent as the decade wore on, and still more so in the new century. Cheap imports from emerging economies flooded into the United States, Japan, and Europe, displacing many domestic suppliers. Since 1989 the United States has seen more than a 300 percent jump in its dependence on imports, which rose from a total of $591 billion, or 10.8 percent of the economy, to about $2.5 trillion, or more than 18.0 percent of the economy. American imports from China alone have jumped by almost 1,800 percent during the 20 years after the global opening got its start in 1989, rising from a minuscule 0.1 percent of the American economy to almost 2.5 percent—a 23-fold increase in a remarkably compressed period. At the same time, India's share of the American market rose four-fold.[43] Trade figures for Europe and Japan are not as significant but tell much the same story.[44] Meanwhile, the sense of uneasiness has intensified as exports to China and other emerging economies have lagged in comparison.[45]

As imports made their inroads into developed economies, jobs began to disappear. Not only have imports replaced domestic production, but firms in the United States, Western Europe, and Japan also have begun to shift production overseas, to take advantage of low wages in the emerging economies. This process of outsourcing work offshore (or simply, offshoring), has received a fillip from the telecommunications revolution, which has extended the international competition from manufactured goods to services that were once thought immune to the effects of foreign competition. Customer help desks have moved from small-town America to India, the Philippines, and other emerging economies. American hospitals increasingly have shipped X rays to South Asia for doctors there to read. Computer programming has found its way from Houston and Palo Alto to Eastern Europe and India. Wall Street has outsourced some of its research to Hyderabad and other Indian cities. Even if, as should be clear, the more complex functions have stayed home, the trend has affected jobs and people's sense of security.

Matters look most grim in manufacturing. Though the American economy has created some 30 million new jobs in the 20-plus years since globalization got its recent start in 1989, manufacturing has lost 4.0 million positions, a decline of 22.8 percent.[46] Other rich, developed economies have suffered similar strains. Though complete data for Europe and Japan are less current than for the United States, what is available shows a marked drop in manufacturing employment by approximately 11 percent in the Netherlands, 12 percent in France, 23 percent in Great Britain, 26 percent in Japan, and 27 percent in Germany.[47] But perhaps more distressing to public feeling has been the clear sense that firms in the developed economies have simply shifted a greater proportion of new employment overseas. American multinationals are indicative. Whereas in the late 1980s they employed 79 percent of their total global workforce domestically, they, by 2000, had cut that proportion to 75 percent.[48] And although data are incomplete, they indicate that this shift has accelerated so that the portion of domestic employment may well have dropped below 70 percent.

Complex Whys, Easy Blame

Clearly the changes have more complex roots than just relative wages and competitive costs. Certainly faster growth in emerging economies has prompted multinational firms to increase employment there more rapidly than they have at home, all quite aside from any competition with domestic operations. Those jobs—for sales, for client services, for administrative functions—would never have existed had not sales opportunities burgeoned in the new economies,[49] and since this work could not have been done in the multinational firm's home country, it has stolen nothing from domestic workers. Technology, too, can account for many of these lost jobs, quite aside from issues of foreign competition. Modern robotics, computers, systems, and other sophisticated equipment typically substitute for labor. And because business in recent decades has seen sharp drops in the cost of computers and other equipment relative to the cost of labor, the trend has accelerated business's outlays on such labor-substituting equipment[50] coincidentally with, but otherwise quite apart from, the increased momentum of globalization.

Though it is impossible to disentangle all these effects on jobs, some studies have concluded that technological applications have hurt American jobs at least as much as has cheap foreign labor.[51] Some lay only 5 percent of the blame for lost jobs on foreign competition. Most studies, however, settle on foreign competition as responsible for only about 30 percent of job losses.[52] Scholarly conclusions, however, have meant far less to public attitudes than bolder, perhaps more analytically suspect, applied analyses. Forrester Research made headlines, for instance, when it warned of the loss of 3.4 million additional service jobs over 10 years. Princeton economist Alan Blinder also achieved notoriety, not for his scholarly research but for his casual estimate that globalization since 2000 has already taken 6 percent of existing jobs in accounting, radiology, and computer programming and has put 30 percent more of them at risk.[53] Souring public opinion still further has no doubt been the daily flow of media and personal anecdotes about layoffs, closed factories, and sudden poverty, all linked by reporters and commentators to globalization.

Particularly upsetting were the jobs sent overseas by domestically based firms. Jobs lost to cheap imports from foreign-based firms are nothing new, but outsourcing and offshoring have left feelings of betrayal. It surely is significant to public attitudes that most everyone has suddenly realized that the individual handling a credit card complaint, who once spoke with a Southern or Iowan accent, now seems to reside in India. Stoking the resentment, stories of the betrayal of offshoring are irresistible to journalists—and, whatever the analytical ambiguities, these have captured the public's imagination.

Typical is the item about the St. Louis man who suffered what *The Boston Globe* described as a "one-two punch." Managing to keep his job after the breakup of AT&T in 1984, he finally lost it 21 years later to "outsourcing overseas." As it turned out, AT&T actually outsourced very few jobs. But the story still resonated with the journalist, and no doubt with the public, by channeling common fears and insecurities and by giving voice to the popular concern that work arrangements were changing forever. The gentleman who was the subject of the profile surely touched a public nerve when he voiced regrets less about his job than that in America today a person could no longer get "a toe" into a company and have "a job for life."[54]

Other moving news items documented more substantive losses to imports and offshoring, especially among low-skilled and already exploited textile workers. One report told how Laurens County, South Carolina, lost every single textile job to foreign competition. That same report calculated 7,000 additional layoffs at just one Pillowtex mill in North Carolina. One particularly poignant note described how the last task management assigned to its laid-off workers was to disassemble their looms for shipment to Pakistan, where the new mill and their jobs were going.[55] Textile mills closed all over North Carolina, Virginia, Georgia, and Florida—all unmistakably linked by the reporters to outsourcing and other forms of foreign competition.[56] North Carolina's Employment Security Commission had no hesitation stating that foreign competition had cost the state 40,000 jobs. Burlington Industries, a major textile employer, responded with estimates that before matters run their course 80 percent of the state's textile mills will close.[57]

Similar stories emanated from other industries elsewhere in the country. The people in Lancaster County, Pennsylvania, publicly blamed foreign competition for the loss of more than 10,000 jobs between 2000 and 2004. Seven companies—Thomson 60 Case, C&D Technologies,

Heil Trailer, Hanover Foods, Kerr Group, Wyeth Pharmaceutical, and Armstrong World Industries—closed down plants, citing import competition and outsourcing abroad as reasons.[58] Other stories from Pennsylvania, Ohio, and the upper Midwest further depressed the public mood by conflating news of more recent losses to foreign competition with older setbacks from over 30 years ago, when huge industrial firms, such as Bethlehem Steel, closed their operations. The array of articles and the attitudes that they have engendered easily explain why during the Pennsylvania and Ohio Democratic primaries in 2008 candidates Hillary Clinton and Barack Obama competed actively to criticize free trade agreements in particular and free trade in general.[59]

Europe, too, has generated plenty of similar stories. Popular fear was strong enough to compel the European Commission of the European Union to earmark €500 million to retrain workers displaced by "outsourcing and shifting world trade patterns."[60] The pressure in Europe has even affected the great luxury brands. Gucci, Givenchy, Ferragamo, and others have outsourced craft functions to Egypt and other emerging economies. Marketing people in these firms have tried to protect their brand image by tearing out the Egyptian and other non-European labels from the products, at least wherever the law allows. But at the same time, production executives at these brands have admitted to the media that within 15 years they will have outsourced all their work offshore.[61] Though relatively few jobs are involved, the news has had a powerful psychological effect. These brands stand for the craftsmanship that has long served as a basis for national pride and national identity, and something that European workers have long viewed as their trump card against global competition.

Beyond Jobs

Concern over globalization has gone beyond bread-and-butter issues. People have begun to fret about how the process will diminish their nation's relative position in the world. Comparative growth rates alone can frighten. During the last 20 years or so since globalization has gained momentum, the established developed economies seem hardly to have grown at all. The United States, for instance, has expanded at less than 2.5 percent a year in real terms, Europe even less, and Japan just 1.3 percent. Meanwhile China has recorded a growth of well over 10.0 percent a year in real terms and India 6.0 percent, while other emerging economies have recorded similarly impressive rates of expansion. Though many hour slowed more recently, all continue to outpace Japan, Europe, and the United States.[62] At their relatively slow pace of growth, the developed economies will take 30 years or more to double in size, compared with merely seven years for China, at its historic growth rate, 12 for India, and similarly short periods for other emerging economies.

The accompanying sense that China, India, and other emerging economies will soon exceed the economic might of the United States or the European Union seems plausible. Since 1989, for instance, China's economy has grown from just over one-sixth the size of Japan's, and barely one-twelfth of America's, to surpass that of Japan and dwarf those of most of Europe.[63] Already China alone produces almost one-fifth of the entire world's manufactured goods.[64] The IMF expects that the emerging economies will continue to overtake the developed economies, projecting long-term real growth of only 2.2 percent a year on average in the developed West and Japan but nearly 10 percent in China, almost 8.0 percent in India, about 9.0 percent in East Asia as a whole, and almost 8.0 percent in South Asia.[65] Quite aside from value and quality considerations, the picture disconcerts many and instills vague fears of what might transpire when these emerging economies surpass Japan, Europe, and the United States.

China's voracious appetite for natural resources, and to a lesser extent India's, has caused alarm in still other ways. By taking so much of the world's precious resources, their prosperity—and the globalization that has fostered it—seems to have found another route to threaten the comfortable lifestyles of people in the developed economies. Only a decade ago neither China nor India even factored in global calculations on the consumption of oil and other commodities. Yet by 2004, China passed Japan as the world's second-largest consumer of petroleum and other industrial commodities after only the United States.[66] Since 2005 commentators have regularly pointed to the rise and fall of Chinese and Indian demands for oil, metals, and other minerals as a reason for rising and falling commodity prices.[67]

Compounding anxieties is the manner with which China especially has set out to secure these resources. When, for example, Europe and America first sought sanctions to control Iran's nuclear ambitions, Beijing, pursuing its need for oil, worked at the United Nations to block those efforts, while at the same time China, very publicly, secured exclusive oil deals with Iran.[68] Beijing extended its influence in resource-rich Africa, enlarging its trade there seven-fold between 1999 and 2007 and its direct investments 53-fold.[69] As part of its Africa strategy, China refused to disengage from Sudan despite world opinion and pleading by many nations to help pressure the Sudanese government to cease its support for the slaughter in Darfur.[70] China's rising profile in Latin America, though less in conflict with the world than its African and Middle Eastern positions, has proceeded so rapidly that the Inter-American Development Bank recently felt compelled to publish a report tellingly entitled "Should Latin America Fear China?" More recently, Brazil has shown a certain wariness of China's presence.[71]

China has added to Western and especially Japanese concerns by seeking a clearly dominant position in Asia. According to a recent U.S. Federal Reserve study, China has already overtaken the United States and Japan as an influence in the region, especially within East Asia's most prominent diplomatic organization, the Association of Southeast Asian Nations (ASEAN).[72] It does not help that China also plays a high-handed diplomatic game, offering lucrative trade links to those nations that acquiesce to its dominance, referring to them as China's Asian "partners," but leveling pointed threats, or worse, at those that resist.[73] Beijing has used naval maneuvers to intimidate and has used its navy several times to challenge Japan and the Philippines over disputed islands in the East and South China Seas. Beijing has also made aggressive territorial claims in order to drill for oil in international waters.[74] China's nuclear status has, of course, added mightily to the security threat and the ominous nature of Chinese force. Recently confirming the popular perception that China is a threat, the U.S. Central Intelligence Agency and the Department of Defense separately identified China as the primary military rival of the United States.[75]

India also has leveraged its new, greater economic status to enlarge its diplomatic and military profile, though not as aggressively as has China. India's nuclear status clearly counts in this equation and has factored heavily in global fears. When India almost went to war with Pakistan (also a nuclear power) in 2001–02, those capabilities received a lot of attention in the media and in official circles.[76] China, India, and other emerging economies have recently put a seal, so to speak, on their new economic and political stature and called stark attention to the global power shift when they sought a position among the long-established association of the world's leading economies, the so-called Group of 8 (G8) comprised of the United States, the United Kingdom, France, Germany, Italy, Canada, Japan, and Russia.[77]

If all this newfound economic and diplomatic power were not disconcerting enough for citizens in the developed nations, the emerging economies also have quickly gained frightening financial power as well. China is now the biggest foreign holder of U.S. government debt. Great concern has swirled around the harm that China could do to the American economy and its financial markets should it refuse to buy any more Treasury bonds, much less the damage China could do if it decided to sell off its existing holdings.[78] The concern has grown so far beyond financial circles that even the TV show *Saturday Night Live* presented a comedy skit on this disconcerting state of affairs.[79] Matters are more complex than they appear in most media stories (not to mention television comedy) and China's options for mischief are far fewer than they might seem,[80] but financial complexities matter less to public anxiety than the sudden realization of China's tremendous importance in such financial considerations and the globalization that clearly has raised it to such importance.

Only slightly less ominous is the financial influence implicit in what are called sovereign wealth funds (SWFs). These pools of assets—amounting at a recent count to the equivalent of more than $3.0 trillion—are owned and operated by foreign governments, mostly in emerging economies. They invest in Western and Japanese firms. Though so far these funds have kept a low profile—buying only minority stakes in companies and avoiding any effort to influence their management—an ominous potential for control nonetheless remains. Abu Dhabi's fund recently sounded alarms when it declared its intention to become one of the top 10 institutional shareholders in American giants such as General Electric.[81] Both former Securities and Exchange Commission chairman Christopher Cox and former treasury secretary Larry Summers have warned about this sort of unwanted influence.[82] German chancellor Angela Merkel not too long ago urged the European Union to protect itself from the possibility that such funds might use their stakes in private companies for political rather than financial goals.

Though still only a small part of overall global financial wealth, which registers $50-plus trillion[83] in global dollar-dominated assets alone, these funds already have the power to swing markets up or down. And given their stupendous growth rate of 660 percent during the last 20 years, their relative power seems set only to increase. If past trends merely hold, SWFs could control more than $5.0 trillion in global financial assets by 2015. Some analysts put that future figure at $12 trillion.[84] According to one knowledgeable observer, "The scale of the issues around such investments is different than anything the world has ever seen. . . . Neither . . . [governments] nor markets know exactly what to do with the assets."[85] Such fears and uncertainties clearly contributed to Congress's rejection of the 2005 bid by Chinese oil giant CNOOC Ltd. to buy Unocal, and its insistence, in 2006, that a British port manager divest itself of its American interests before selling out to Dubai's government-owned Dubai Ports World, though SWFs were not involved in either transaction.[86]

While all sorts of historical and analytical perspectives might argue against strong public resistance, people need neither analytical nor historical arguments to act on their fears. Two concerns in particular lead them to believe that globalization today weighs too heavily to countenance: a widening income gap between rich and poor and the increasingly destructive boom-bust pattern in financial markets.

9

More Intense Pressures

Of all the concerns connected with globaliza-tion, it is these two strains—the widening income gap between rich and poor and the marked increase in financial volatility—that seem to offer the greatest cause for anxiety. The one threatens the middle-class dream on which the populations of the developed economies have long built their economic expectations for themselves and their children. The other, though less well understood by the general public (or even financial professionals for that matter), threatens the sense of security throughout these economies, raises questions about the ability to plan and save for the future, and even increases people's doubts about their jobs, however much they may have amassed necessary skills. These threats, more than others, feed resistance to globalization, whatever other benefits it brings.

The Death of the Middle Class

A widening gap between rich and poor threatens permanent societal damage. If overall household incomes in the United States generally have grown 3.1 percent a year, in real terms, during the last 20-odd years,[1] the benefits have fallen unevenly. In fact, it looks as though only the upper end of the income distribution has gained much at all. Broad data show that the earnings of the richest 10 percent of the economy have grown five times faster than those in the bottom fifth.[2] Finer distinctions show an even more disturbing gap. The nominal earnings of the top 5 percent of the income distribution have grown 9 percent a year during this time, while the earnings of those in the bottom 5 percent have actually suffered a yearly decline of 2.5 percent.[3] The differences have allowed the richest 25 percent of the country to increase its share of total earnings from 10 times that of the bottom 25 percent in 1973 to over 15 times more recently.[4] Meanwhile the Internal Revenue Service notes that the wealthiest 1.0 percent of the population earned 22 percent of national income recently, exceeding the previous high of 20.8 percent set in 2000, while the bottom 50 percent of the nation's income distribution earned a mere 12.8 percent of the total, lower than the previous low of 13 percent, set also in 2000.[5]

Nor has the United States suffered these trends alone. Europe and Japan have seen real wages for the average worker stagnate even as those at the top of their respective income distributions have continued to expand. Within all developed economies, workers' share of overall income has declined from 61.3 percent in 1992 to 58.9 percent more recently.[6] Even in Japan, which is famous for its relatively flat, equitable income distribution, the gap between rich and poor has widened. In just the last 10 years, even as Japan's overall population has held steady, the number below the poverty line has almost doubled, from five to 10 million people.[7] The United Nations, with its usual flair for drama, has offered an analytically dubious statistic that nonetheless captures the sense of inequality involved. In 2005, its Development Program reported that the richest 50 people on the planet earned more than the poorest 416 million combined, though the program failed to indicate whether that disparity had widened or narrowed.[8]

There are, of course, ambiguities in all these measures. Because they rely heavily on tax return data, the American statistics obscure certain realities at opposite ends of the income spectrum. On the lower end, the real incomes include substantial government flows from Social Security, Medicaid, food stamps, and earned income tax credits, but because these are not taxed, the income gap calculations ignore them. Especially as Social Security, Medicaid, and particularly earned income tax credits have become increasingly important to poorer Americans over time, this oversight has severely understated the growth of their incomes. At the high end of the income distribution such oversights mean less, since either these people seldom receive such benefits, or, when they do, they pay taxes on them, leading the IRS to include them in its calculations and further overstate the size of the income gap. These IRS data may mislead further because of the movement of business income. The decline in personal marginal tax rates over these 20-odd years has induced many business owners to put their business's income into their personal taxes, showing rapid personal gains when only a reclassification has occurred.[9]

Even accepting the statistics at face value, the fluid nature of the American economy raises doubts about a widening wage gap, at least to the extent indicated. Except for a relatively small, permanent underclass, most American workers seldom stay in a particular income group for long. The classic example is the young. Even many who have otherwise promising careers can begin at relatively low income levels before they rise, sometimes very quickly, through the income distribution. Many of those at the low end of the distribution 10 years ago are not there today. The growing income gap between the two ends of the income distribution could reflect changing relationships between starting pay scales and later ones as much as widening differences between the pay scales of more permanent classes of workers.

To overcome this particular complication, statisticians and econometricians at the U.S. Treasury conducted an immense study that actually followed the incomes of specific households over time. The picture painted by this work looks very different indeed from the more popular, aggregate statistics. Between 1996 and 2006 the Treasury researchers discovered that those who started at the bottom quarter of the income distribution saw far greater average income gains in subsequent years than those who began the period higher in the income distribution. They calculated that those in the bottom quartile of this group saw their earnings rise by 6.7 percent a year, while those who started in the top quartile experienced the slowest earnings growth, an expansion of only 1.5 percent a year.[10]

Nor can globalization take all the blame for the growing income gap. Technology clearly has played a role, as it has with jobs. Because computers, software, administrative advances, and improving equipment all tend to replace human effort, their application to the production process has restricted the need for workers, especially those at the low end of the income distribution who perform the more routine tasks that are particularly susceptible to automation. At the same time the increased use of more sophisticated machinery, electronics, and systems in the production process has increased the demand for better educated and better trained workers already higher in the income distribution. The net effect, quite apart from the pressure of globalization, has held back wage gains among the former, already poorly paid group, and heightened those of the latter, already better paid group. Furthermore, technological applications have boosted incomes at the highest end of the wage distribution by giving already well-paid executives the ability to apply their skills across a larger, more efficient business than previously was the case.

Advances in telecommunications offer a good illustration of this effect. Because all forms of instant or near-instant communication—first the telephone, then radio, then television, and more recently the Internet—make it easier for managers to marshal more people and resources from a single location, those operating at that point of power can extend their influence in ways undreamed of until recently and see their incomes expand accordingly. The effect is analogus to that of sports stars and entertainers who can now reach audiences of millions when once they could command those only in a single stadium. Meanwhile, the working man or woman on the factory floor and in the back office has enjoyed none of these benefits. Because technology has reduced the demand for the services of such people, their incomes have suffered accordingly.

But for all the impact of technology and all the statistical ambiguities, there is nonetheless little doubt that globalization has had its independent effect and will do so even more as it intensifies in the future. Just as with technology, globalized connections have increased the breadth and scope of any business, allowing its executives—such as managers, designers, planners, advertisers, marketing directors—earn a greater surplus by directing the output of many more workers worldwide across a greater array of production facilities and still more products and markets than previously. And because overseas workers in emerging economies earn much less than domestic workers, American executives associate themselves with even higher levels of profitability than they had in the past. Their incomes, already at the high end of the distribution, have expanded accordingly and disproportionately.

Globalization has held back relative wages at the lower end of the income distribution in other ways as well. Experienced workers, especially when displaced from their jobs by outsourcing or import competition, have on average suffered a 15–40 percent compensation drop in alternative employments.[11] The anecdotal evidence is striking. Typical is the story of a materials handler who lost his job at the steel mill, where he had earned $16.75 an hour, and settled, after a bout of unemployment, for a position with a large retailer at just $9.35 an hour, or the story of another production worker, who had earned $17.17 an hour in industry but had to settle for a position at an auction facility that paid only $9.50 an hour.[12] These and similar, innumerable anecdotes in the daily press may not count as evidence to scholars, but they do illustrate the way in which globalization has depressed wages at the lower end of the scale, and how the public perceives the effect. And some people never find new jobs. They, too, have brought down the average income at the lower end of the wage scale—or would have, had the statistics in those comparisons included them in the calculation, which has not always been the case.

Just the threat of outsourcing and offshoring has surely depressed wages. In heavily unionized Germany, for instance, companies have extracted wage concessions from their workers simply by floating the possibility of a move to Poland.[13] But there is seldom even a need for such explicit pressure. Workers, and the unions that represent them, know well that wages are lower in China, in India, and elsewhere in the world's emerging economies. They hardly need precise statistics to calculate that aggressive wage demands will only spur management to consider the move abroad, and accordingly they have moderated their pay demands. It is impossible to measure such effects, but the logic can stand even in the absence of statistical precision.

Globalization has widened the income gap in emerging economies as well. Because of the huge influx of technology and sophisticated production techniques, those few with better skills have employment opportunities that previously had not existed, creating a powerful contrast to those left, often undisturbed, in traditional activities such as subsistence agriculture, with their understandably low levels of earnings.[14] Responsibility for such growing wage differences could as easily be laid at the door of technology, for it is superior equipment and techniques that ultimately facilitate the outsized income gains of those higher up the wage scale. But, were it not for globalization, these new techniques would never have made it to these countries.

Academic and government researchers have attempted to dispel the ambiguities in the evidence and measure globalization's particular effect on relative wages. It has failed, not surprisingly, to arrive at a consensus. But in their various ways all the careful studies of these phenomena nonetheless confirm an independent wage impact from globalization, beyond those of technology and all the measurement ambiguities. One impressive effort by the prestigious and notably nonpartisan National Bureau of Economic Research (NBER) found, after adjusting for all the statistical failings, that globalization alone explained between 31 and 51 percent of the widening income gap between the higher and lower ends of America's income distribution. This research generally shows that wage gaps in other developed economies and in emerging economies, though less thoroughly measured than in America, also give reason to suppose a similar impact.[15]

Certainly, the public senses the link between globalization and the widening income differential between rich and poor, and counts it as a major ill. Some 78 percent of Americans, and of Germans, too, worry about the growing income gap and link it to globalization. The same is true of 64 percent of Japanese, 87 percent of Spaniards, and 80 percent of the Asian population.[16] The IMF, responding to such strong reactions, has explained all antiglobalization agitation solely in terms of the widening income gap between rich and poor.[17]

Financial Destruction

Less widely linked to globalization, but perhaps ultimately even more disconcerting than the growing income gap, is the marked increase in financial volatility. It is easy to see how the international financial flows associated with globalization have grown large enough to swamp domestic financial or regulatory power. Global trade alone pushes more than $20 trillion a year unevenly around the globe, while cross-border investment creates additional flows that are at least as large.[18] This financial flood, verging on $50 trillion a year, carries mind-boggling power. It exceeds the size of the entire U.S. economy by a factor of three,[19] and equals the entire annual trading volume in U.S. government securities, the largest and the most active market in the world.[20] Not only do such huge flows of funds sloshing around global markets present a powerful and potentially destabilizing element, there is in this movement a distinct chain of causality that emanates from China's currency policies—and those of other emerging economies—and links directly to the volatility in global financial markets, the extreme boom-bust pattern that has so threatened the security of economies and societies in general.

The problem springs in large part from the eagerness with which China and many other emerging economies promote their exports by keeping their currencies cheap, primarily to the dollar. In this way they ensure that their products are priced attractively on global markets. But because their export success induces so many foreigners to buy their currencies in order to buy their products, the value of their currencies naturally faces constant upward pressure. Official efforts to hold down currency values become, therefore, something of a major undertaking, requiring the central banks of these emerging economies to sell their currencies continually into global foreign exchange markets and buy other currencies, mostly dollars. The amounts are vast. Their purchases and sales must offset flows from both their enormous export surpluses and the investment flows heading their way from abroad. In China's case, currency transactions must counterbalance the economy's almost $400 billion yearly trade surplus of exports over imports[21] (more than $250 billion alone with the United States) plus the equally huge, though variable, net investment inflows from the United States, Japan, and Western Europe.[22]

Despite the uphill battle involved, China, in particular, has held rigidly to this currency policy. Between 1994 and 2005 it fought off world demand for yuan appreciation effectively enough to keep the currency's value rigidly at 8.3 to the dollar, month after month.[23] Even when Beijing subsequently came under intense diplomatic pressure from the United States and the European Union to raise the foreign exchange value of the yuan, it kept close control. The People's Bank of China (PBC) allowed the yuan to rise, but kept buying nonetheless to hold the appreciation back. The currency fluctuated a mere 1.5 percent, month to month—low compared with more typical, market-based currency swings of as much as 5–10 percent from one month to the next.[24] The PBC, through these extensive foreign exchange transactions, managed to keep the yuan's rise to less than 20 percent over a four-year period, from 2005 to 2009,[25] a move hardly worth mentioning by the usual standards of currency shifts.

But the complications and distortions of this policy do not end here. Because China and these emerging economies cannot sell the currencies they acquire without risking a rise in the value of their own currencies, they must hold on to the oceans of dollars that they buy. The hoards have reached astronomical size. China's foreign currency reserves have exploded at a rate of 31 percent a year during the last 10 years to reach an astounding total of upward of $3.0 trillion.[26] India, a less active participant in such currency policies, has nonetheless played the game enough to see its official dollar reserves swell toward $500 billion. The pattern of currency management has similarly bloated reserves in other emerging economies as well.[27]

Though typically huge hoards of funds are welcome, especially to emerging economies, these particular holdings can cause problems. Because any flow back into their economies and financial markets could cause inflationary pressures or asset-price distortions, their governments cannot easily use them for domestic development. Even more dangerous to their currency policies, any use of the funds could allow them to flow back onto foreign exchange markets, where they could again shift values and compound the problems of keeping down the value of their currencies. Beijing and these other governments must, then, isolate their dollar hoards from their domestic markets. The larger the hoard grows, the greater control they must maintain over the behavior of their financial institutions and any financial flows into and out of their markets and their country.[28]

Hemmed in domestically in this way, these governments, in another link in this chain of causality, ship their dollar hoards, and holdings of other currencies as well, back overseas to the United States and other developed economies. There they invest in U.S. Treasury bonds mostly but also in European and Japanese sovereign debt.[29] These are the monies that Federal Reserve chairman Ben Bernanke has referred to as "excess savings" in emerging economies.[30] The need to dispose of these funds in this way also explains why China and governments in other emerging economies continue to buy ever larger amounts of U.S. Treasury debt, almost regardless of what else happens. The numbers are striking. The U.S. Treasury calculates that mostly Asian governments already hold more than $3.5 trillion of U.S. Treasury debt and an additional $1.6 trillion of the debts of U.S. government agencies, such as the Federal National Mortgage Association (Fannie Mae). The purchases have left foreigners holding more than 30 percent of all the outstanding public debt of the United States—an unprecedented proportion in almost any earlier period, except perhaps 200 years ago, when the United States itself was an emerging economy.[31]

By flooding American and other developed markets with financial liquidity in this way, those funds cannot help but destabilize. They certainly create financial flows far in excess of the legitimate economic needs of these developed economies. That circumstance alone would cause concern, but the potential harm multiplies as the dynamic nature of modern financial markets carries this dangerous tsunami of financial liquidity into every aspect of global finance, redoubling its effect and, with the techniques of modern finance, its size, too. It is this last link in the chain that stands as the proximate cause of the now familiar boom-bust pattern.

Because of the protean nature of developed financial markets, the already huge Chinese investments and those of other emerging economies become grist for the mill of financial speculation. The pattern redoubles the amount of liquidity available on global financial markets. That flow then naturally lifts asset prices. Eventually, the rising asset prices themselves induce still more buying, reinforcing the upward thrust on asset prices until at last it goes so far beyond underlying economic realities that the situation becomes untenable. Then some event, not necessarily large, calls attention to how far asset prices have diverged from economic reality, and the whole structure collapses. Though the tendency toward boom and bust is inherent in financial markets, the size and independent nature of these emerging-market liquidity flows inflates matters to something much larger and more dangerous than global financial markets have had to deal with for a long time.

Though the boom-bust pattern begins with the currency policies of emerging economies, blame for the destructive cycle certainly has a wider dispersion. For one, the Federal Reserve and central banks in other developed economies have certainly made their contribution by failing to use their powers to counteract the effect of these foreign flows, "sterilize" them in the jargon of central bankers. They could, for instance, withdraw amounts of liquidity from elsewhere in their financial markets equal to the foreign inflows and so neutralize the tendency toward excess. Private financial participants, too, have contributed by permitting the excess of liquidity to wipe away any sense that they may have had of financial prudence, propriety, or even longer-term planning. Regulators and regulations appear feckless because they have not been able to keep up with this fast-moving reality, and in retrospect seem at times not even to have tried. But questions of blame aside, the pattern is clear and clearly associated with globalization. And it explains the whole boom-bust financial volatility that has developed over the last 20 years or more since globalization gained momentum.

Tracking the Destructive Pattern

These basic elements certainly played a role in the first of these cycles, the 1997 collapse referred to as the "Asian Contagion." In the 1990s what were then called Asia's "Tigers"—Malaysia, South Korea, Taiwan, Singapore, Hong Kong, Thailand, and Indonesia prominent among them—attracted more economic and financial attention than China. The initial gains in these economies had roots, as described earlier, in their changing demographics, and so had underlying economic support. But to build on that basic potential, each Tiger realized (as China has since) that exports were a powerful way to accelerate growth. In the now familiar pattern, they ensured attractive global prices for their products by keeping their respective currencies cheap to the dollar. From 1991 to 1997, Thailand, for instance, held its baht close to the dollar within a narrow range of 5–6 percent. Indonesia managed its rupiah similarly, as did Malaysia its ringgit, South Korea its won, and Taiwan its dollar. The Singapore and Hong Kong dollars varied more but still held close to their U.S. counterpart.[32] And the strategy worked. All these Asian Tiger economies grew rapidly[33] on export growth and enjoyed huge trade surpluses with the United States and the rest of the world.[34]

Just as China has done more recently, these economies kept their currencies from rising against the dollar by buying dollars on foreign exchange markets and accumulating hoards. Taiwan's official reserves, for instance, jumped by almost 40 percent between 1991 and 1995[35] and Thailand's by almost 120 percent.[36] And, like China more recently, they could not sell their dollar accumulations without risking adverse currency shifts. So, to protect their own economies from the effects of accumulation, they carefully controlled flows of funds in their domestic financial markets and invested their official holdings in U.S. Treasury securities. Between 1991 and 1998 foreign purchases of U.S. securities jumped by an astounding 26.7 percent a year, with the Tigers accounting for much of the acceleration.[37] Because the Federal Reserve failed to neutralize these flows, financial liquidity in American financial markets jumped well ahead of the economy's fundamental needs. The nominal gross domestic product, for instance—and, presumably, the economy's basic need for financial resources—grew 5.6 percent a year[38] between 1991 and 1995, while the country's monetary base, a key measure of financial liquidity, expanded 7.0 percent a year, and overall borrowing shot up 11.4 percent a year.[39]

As the excess liquidity bid up the prices of U.S. Treasury securities and financial assets in general,[40] investors, flush with an excess of investable funds, searched for opportunities. They saw them in the very place from which the liquidity had emerged: in the fast-growing, export-oriented Asian Tiger economies themselves. American investors began to lend freely to private firms, local governments, and development agencies in the Tigers, effectively transferring to them the reserves that their central governments had accumulated through their currency manipulations and sent abroad. Between 1990 and 1996, lending from America to the Tigers surged $42 billion a year, a leap of 500 percent from the $7.0 billion a year averaged between 1985 and 1989.[41] While initially these loans and investments served the Tigers' legitimate development needs, the excessive flow of liquidity back across the Pacific eventually pushed Tiger asset prices and economic activity far beyond anything that even these fast-developing economies could sustain.

When that fact at last became apparent, the collapse came. Tradition dates the start of the Asian Contagion to July 2, 1997, when Thailand, by then long denied credit by the Americans controlling the funds, could no longer sustain the value of its currency, the baht. But that event was less a cause than a symptom of a collapse that had begun much earlier. The seeds of the Asian Contagion were, in fact, planted three and a half years before the baht fell, at the beginning of 1994, when China decided to go into competition with the Tigers for a share of the lucrative export market and suddenly devalued its yuan by more than 50 percent against the dollar, keeping it rigidly locked at that low level thereafter.[42] Because the Tigers had tied their currencies to the dollar, the yuan's drop powerfully undercut a basis of their rapid growth and the principal motive for Americans to lend into the Tigers.

Matters took time to have their effect. China then was such a new player on the global economic stage that American buyers had few relationships there and, despite the huge price differences, moved only gradually to Chinese connections from familiar suppliers in the Tigers. At the same time the liquidity filtering through American markets was so immense that the flow of funds back to the Tigers alone made those economies seem prosperous. But China's huge pricing advantage eventually told. Between 1994 and 1997 Chinese exports to the United States captured the lion's share of overall sales growth, increasing a powerful 17 percent a year, far faster than the exports of any other Asian economy.[43] American bankers and investment managers, assessing the change, began to rethink the loans and investments they had made in the Tigers.

With the loss of exports to Chinese competition and the flow of lending, demand for Tiger currencies began to slacken. Officials there found themselves in a strange situation. After years of resisting upward pressure on the exchange values of their currencies, they suddenly had to deal with tremendous downward pressure. Market forces were effectively trying to force Tiger currency values down to levels that might compete with China's cheap yuan. But though exporters in these countries might well have welcomed a currency slide as a way to recapture a competitive pricing edge, borrowers there wanted to fight the slide. They desperately wanted to sustain the international value of what assets they had in order to meet their overseas debt obligations. Reversing their old postures, authorities in the Tigers began fighting to hold up the values of their currencies. The market pressure, however, became too great. When Thailand gave up the fight and let the baht fall in the middle of 1997, a panic ensued. Creditors feared that borrowers throughout the region would fail to meet their obligations. Lending from the United States and other developed economies stopped altogether, and lenders, where they could, called in the loans. Tiger currencies fell still further.[44]

Starved for credit and undercut by China, these economies plunged into steep recessions. Thailand's real GDP fell 10 percent in 1998, South Korea's fell 7 percent, and, in a seeming contagion from which the crisis took its name, the economic declines swept through all these former investment favorites.[45] The pain ultimately brought down governments in South Korea, Taiwan, and, most notably, Indonesia. Thailand got both a new government and a new constitution. Malaysia and the Philippines turned out their presidents midterm.[46] All the bright prospects of previous years had turned bleak. It took until late 1999 for matters to stabilize. Then the Tiger currencies settled at lower rates to the dollar, dulling some of China's competitive pricing edge. Tiger exports began to recover, as did their economies, though slowly.[47]

Tiger policymakers took the lesson. To prevent a reprise of this particular disaster they abandoned their former efforts to fix their currencies to the dollar and allowed them to float more or less freely on foreign exchange markets.[48] Since China by that time had come to dominate export flows, that float kept Tiger currencies close to the yuan, for each time one of these currencies rose against the yuan that particular economy lost share in the export market, and the ensuing slack demand for its products and consequently its currency naturally brought its foreign exchange value back into line with the yuan. In the words of Japan's *Daily Yomiuri*, "these nations concluded that the system under which their currencies were pegged to the dollar was ironically a key factor undermining the stability of their currency exchange rates during the crisis."[49]

As this realignment settled into place, the region's export machine, now led by China, grew apace, as did the money flows. Between 1997 and 2000 America's trade deficit with China almost doubled, rising from $49.7 billion to $83.8 billion. After the Tigers underwent their currency adjustments their export growth resumed at a rapid pace, and America's trade deficits with them also widened.[50] Along with China, the Tigers, as before, bought dollars as they were exchanged for their export products. China and the Tigers sent the accumulated funds as official reserves back into developed financial markets, mostly the United States. Foreign, largely Asian, holdings of U.S. Treasury and government agency debt increased uninterrupted during the late 1990s by an average of about 11 percent a year.[51]

As before, the Fed took no action to offset the domestic effects of these flows. Though as early as 1996 then Federal Reserve Board chairman Alan Greenspan worried over the effects of excess liquidity, referring to its power to create what he referred to as an "irrational exuberance,"[52] he did nothing about it. So, once again, money and lending in American markets grew faster than the economic fundamentals required. Between 1997 and 2000 basic American money measures grew more than 7.0 percent a year, far faster than the 5.5 percent pace of the nominal economy and, presumably, the economy's basic need for financial liquidity. The overall pace of borrowing on American markets expanded even faster, by 11.3 percent a year.[53]

The underlying pattern unfolded much as before. The flow of official reserves from Asia raised Treasury bond prices, prompting private investors, seeking higher returns, to move toward riskier assets. This time, chastened by the Asian crash, investors changed their focus and aimed the excess liquidity flowing out of Asia at the exciting computer technologies and Internet applications that were then breaking onto the economic scene. As market leverage redoubled the already massive supply of funds, asset prices in these areas rose disproportionately, as once Tiger asset prices had risen. Technology and Internet stock prices increased so much faster than values on other assets that the technology sector of the benchmark Standard & Poor's (S&P) 500 Stock Index rose from 12.3 percent of the entire index in 1997 to just under 30 percent by 2000.[54]

Even that wonderfully imaginative and exciting sector could not support almost one-third of the economy's market value. Technology was nowhere near 30 percent of the country's overall economic activity or even of its industrial sector. Again, matters under the sway of excess liquidity had gone beyond economic fundamentals. Some at the time warned about the state of affairs, though never in terms of liquidity flows or their roots in Asian currency policies. One "market veteran," according to *The Wall Street Journal* in 1999, worried over the "strain on everybody's systems" from "hundreds of thousands of orders in those stocks" and warned that "on the way down, it's always more extreme."[55] Of course the problems were more fundamental than trading strains, but then there is reason now, in retrospect, to wonder if the *Journal*'s knowledgeable veteran, Bernard L. Madoff, might have had a distorted agenda of his own. Still, it is noteworthy that even he, in his own narrow way, could pick up on the distortions.

The end came not from China, which held its policies constant throughout, but inadvertently from the Federal Reserve. Though the Fed had failed to counteract the effect of these flows of funds from Asia and had done little more than worry over the Internet boom, it began, by late 1999, to act on concerns over inflation, which had by then picked up modestly.[56] Policymakers, responding in a purely economic context, engineered what to them must have seemed like moderate monetary restraint. They slowed the growth of liquidity by raising short-term interest rates gradually from 4.5 percent in early 1999 to, a still low for the times, 6.0 percent by early 2000.[57] But circumstances were not purely economic. On the contrary, financial matters were bloated, resembling a rising hot-air balloon in need of ever more heat just to remain aloft. Markets were so unable to withstand even a modest slowdown in the flow of liquidity that the Fed's seemingly moderate move put the previous boon quickly into reverse. Money measures, which had grown 11.2 percent a year between 1998 and 1999, fell outright in 2000.[58] Asset prices collapsed as well. The S&P 500, led downward by the technology and Internet favorites, tumbled some 40 percent between spring 2000 and September 2001.[59]

Yet for all the financial damage, including that wrought by the terrorist attacks of September 11, 2001, the ongoing interplay between Asian currency policies and American liquidity quickly reemerged, and the next difficult financial cycle began almost immediately. China, in particular, continued to promote exports by keeping its currency cheap to the dollar, as did other emerging economies. Beijing rigidly maintained the cheap yuan peg that it had established back in 1994. Between 2002 and 2006 China's trade surplus with the United States more than doubled, widening from a flow of $103.1 billion a year to $234.1 billion.[60] With the People's Bank of China and other Asian central banks still purchasing dollars, foreign exchange reserves in these economies continued to accumulate rapidly. China's reserves alone expanded by some $780 billion between 2002 and 2006.[61] And, as before, these funds flowed back into American financial markets, where again the Fed failed to sterilize their effect. Liquidity again built faster than the economy's fundamental needs. Though for technical reasons basic money growth during this time remained relatively moderate, actually expanding at a slightly slower pace than the almost 6 percent growth rate of the overall nominal economy, the excess liquidity was clearly evident in the 26.5 percent average annual explosion of total borrowing.[62]

American investors once more used this flood of liquidity to reach for higher returns in riskier investments. This time they skipped both Asia and the Internet, where they had learned painful lessons, and focused instead on residential real estate. Subprime mortgage lending was an ideal lure. Lenders could charge premium rates and at the same time could claim, falsely as it turned out, that tangible real property offered a security beyond the ethereal and seemingly riskier worlds of either Internet applications or far-away Asian dreams.[63] Though such claims and expectations of security turned out to be hollow in the end, they did seem reasonable at the time. Speculation could go still further this time than it had in the past because the flows were that much larger and because the government in Washington, unlike its more or less neutral stance regarding the surge into Asia or the Internet, actually encouraged both lenders and buyers to extend themselves in residential real estate.

Certainly not all the blame should lie with Washington, but its influence clearly helped exaggerate the already considerable influence of Asian financial flows. The government had, of course, long encouraged home ownership, with tax breaks on mortgage interest expenses and capital gains from house sales. But by the time of this boom the authorities had gone much further. Beginning in the 1970s, Washington stepped up support for subprime lending, pressuring lenders more and more to advance mortgage credit to lower-income Americans. After Congress passed the Community Reinvestment Act, in 1977, regulators actually began to deny banks the right to expand their territory unless they also lent in low-income neighborhoods.[64] By the early 1980s the two federally sponsored mortgage finance agencies, the Federal National Mortgage Association, better known as Fannie Mae, and the Federal Home Loan Mortgage Corporation, better known as Freddie Mac, formally dedicated large portions of their ample financial resources to purchase securities made up of loans to subprime homebuyers. Legislation passed in

1992 actually required Fannie and Freddie to devote 30 percent of their loan purchases to such mortgages. In 2004, Congress further extended this support for "affordable housing."[65]

With all the liquidity and the government pressure, the drive to the ultimate collapse proceeded inexorably. As the price of residential real estate in the United States rose 11 percent a year between 2002 and 2005,[66] it far outstripped household incomes, rendering housing less and less affordable.[67] Mortgage lenders sustained these levels of activity, using the superabundance of liquidity to make ever more dubious loans to parties even less able to support them.[68] Borrowers stretched their resources to capture the price appreciation that they came to believe was an immutable aspect of real estate markets. Matters began to feed on themselves. The situation could not persist. As with the Internet bubble, the Fed prompted the turn, again inadvertently.

Ignoring asset markets and the flow of liquidity from abroad, the Fed acted, as before, only on its assessment of the underlying economy. Seeking to slow the pace of expansion a little, the Fed applied what otherwise would have been moderate monetary restraint. It raised interest rates very gradually, by a quarter of a percentage point every six weeks or so, from 2.25 percent in 2005 to 5.25 percent in 2007.[69] As before, what in a purely economic context would have elicited a moderate response had a devastating effect on bloated financial markets, by then highly dependent on excess liquidity. Denied even a small measure of the easy credit flows on which homebuyers had come to depend, new home purchases collapsed, sliding by almost 50 percent between January 2006 and December 2007. Housing prices fell accordingly, by almost 10 percent nationally, much more in some regions. Because lending terms had become so lax, the price erosion pushed the value of many properties below the outstanding mortgages on them.[70]

By 2008 the prospect of widespread losses precipitated a panic. Markets froze and lending collapsed. The growth pace of the basic money supply, the monetary base, fell by half, dropping from a 5.0 percent annual pace of expansion between 2002 and 2005 to a 2.3 percent rate between 2005 and 2008.[71] The pace of total lending in the United States went from an expansion of $2.613 trillion in 2008 to a contraction of

$438 billion in 2009.[72] With no credit available, the U.S. economy tumbled into recession. The third, and worst, boom-bust cycle in just 10 years moved toward its ugly denouement.

These essentially similar financial debacles stand in stark contrast to the conduct of affairs in an earlier, more stable financial world. The harsher employment and income patterns that emerged as a result also contrast to a seemingly more manageable past, before globalization picked up its momentum. Recognition of these differences makes the prospect of still more intensified globalization look threatening indeed. Still, the record of the past suggests that these concerns may be overstated. The history of the last 60 years certainly has revealed some remarkable American successes in dealing with foreign economic threats even as commentators at the time sounded alarms very similar to those commonly heard today.

10

A Record of Relative Success

However legitimate today's concerns, there is no denying that the American economy has in the past dealt effectively with a series of similar foreign challenges. It has always made the necessary economic and business adjustments and, despite all the pressure, managed to raise living standards generally. Still more tellingly, the economy has accomplished this in the face of a steady stream of doubts that arose at each stage in the process and that very much resemble today's warnings. To be sure, this history cannot answer every one of today's concerns. The prospect of much more intense levels of globalization, the effects of aging demographics, a disconcerting income gap between rich and poor, and seemingly uncontrollable boom-bust financial patterns suggest differences. But even if there is little room for complacency, this long, largely successful record does offer an important perspective on today's anxieties, and perhaps guidance for the future.

An Old Story in Many Respects

The United States has adjusted to foreign competition more or less continually since the end of the Second World War. Initially, the challenge came from Europe. Though the war's destruction had left the continent with only a rudimentary productive infrastructure, it, like today's emerging economies, had a relative abundance of cheap labor, though, unlike today's emerging economies, Europe's workforce was highly trained and disciplined. Today, of course, it is hard to see European labor as cheap, but it was in the late 1940s and early 1950s. At that time, manufacturing workers on the continent earned one-fifth the hourly wage of their American counterparts, and British workers made one-third.[1] Even with Europe's poor industrial infrastructure, these low wages gave its producers a considerable cost edge against American competition, at least in certain industries.[2]

That cost advantage took effect almost immediately. By 1947 European products began to replace American output in European markets and choked off a brief postwar surge in American sales there. American exports grew again later in the 1940s and 1950s, with Europe's overall expansion, but they struggled, taking until 1956 to recover their 1947 level. At the same time cost advantages allowed European sales in America to flourish. These rose a strong 7.4 percent a year after 1950, far faster than the 4.1 percent growth pace of the overall American economy.[3] By 1957 Europe signaled its resurgence, building on the European Coal and Steel Community, the forerunner of today's European Union, to broaden trade cooperation.[4]

American anxiety over losses to this foreign challenge waited not a moment. Even while American productive prowess remained fundamentally unequaled, and the balance of American exports over imports about doubled between the mid-1950s and the mid-1960s,[5] Americans watched the flow of European output with anxiety. The congenitally smug American auto industry may have haughtily and foolishly dismissed Volkswagen's 1955 celebration over the millionth car produced at its Wolfsburg plant,[6] but others took a different measure of the trends. By the early 1960s, as the first Hondas and Toyotas arrived in the United States, America's trade representative, W. Michael Blumenthal, warned Detroit that foreign auto sales in the United States had jumped 2,318 percent during the previous decade[7] and were three times the size of American auto exports to the entire world.[8]

While Blumenthal glimpsed Detroit's ultimate decline, most of the period's concerns were less prescient, and in retrospect look highly exaggerated. President John F. Kennedy, mirroring popular anxieties of the time, bemoaned in his 1961 State of the Union address "the failure of [American] exports to penetrate foreign markets," while his later speeches insisted that the country meet the foreign "challenge" by establishing a "reasonable equilibrium in our [clearly deteriorating] balance of payments."[9] Kennedy best caught the time's popular sense of lost economic power when he extrapolated what he saw as America's shrinking global market share and disappearing jobs and spoke of a future haunted by the "dark menace of industrial dislocation, increasing unemployment, and deepening poverty."[10]

By the 1970s the sorts of anxieties first expressed by President Kennedy a decade earlier had become still more common. Steel companies and their unions pleaded for higher tariffs to protect them from foreign producers.[11] George Meany, president of the American Federation of Labor–Congress of Industrial Organizations (AFL-CIO), described free trade as "a joke and a myth" and called for "tighter restrictions on imports."[12] President Jimmy Carter, picking up the same tone, spoke of protecting the steel industry and American jobs in general. He, too, foretold many of today's fears about globalization when he claimed, without much explanation, that America's problems stemmed from the country's "unfair competitive disadvantage in the international market." He wanted trade to remain "free—but fair."[13]

But most of this anxiety was misplaced. By 1980 Europe had lost its low-wage advantage. The continent's previous prosperity and the rebuilding of its industrial infrastructure had fostered wage gains that ultimately caught up with the American equivalent. As the 1970s drew to a close, hourly compensation in West German manufacturing had risen to over 70 percent of American levels. British, French, and other Western European wages were even closer to those in the United States. After accounting for transport expenses, the cost gap had effectively closed.[14] European sales in the United States continued to grow, but no faster on balance than the overall American economy.[15] The inroads had stabilized.

By then, however, a new competitive challenge rose in Japan. Despite a considerable recovery, Japan's disciplined and well-trained workers still earned barely half the hourly wage of their American counterparts during the 1980s.[16] Though Japan's industrial infrastructure fell far short of America's, the country's low-wage structure nonetheless gave Japanese producers a huge cost advantage over their American and European competitors. Exports from Japan rose accordingly, penetrating ever more deeply into the American and the European economies. By 1990 foreign products generally had risen to 11 percent of all goods and services sold in the United States,[17] largely because of Japanese advances. Between 1981 and 1991 the nations of what today comprises the European Union saw a tripling in their foreign account deficit of imports over exports, also largely because of Japanese advances.[18]

Japan's edge showed most vividly in electronics and autos. Especially after the oil price hikes of the 1970s and early 1980s the ability of Japanese industry to offer the world a quality, fuel-efficient product at an extremely attractive price allowed that country, by 1980, to surpass the United States in auto production.[19] By the close of that decade Japan produced 30 percent more cars than the United States.[20] Japanese gains in electronics were, if anything, even more impressive. Here the vastly improved quality of Japanese products, combined with their cost advantages, gave Japanese producers quantum gains in global market share. American firms, which in 1980 dominated 82 percent of the world computer market, saw their global share fall to 38 percent by 1991, while Japan's share rose to 42 percent.[21]

Anxieties over Japan far exceeded earlier concerns over Europe. In the 1980s the Massachusetts Institute of Technology (MIT) produced a study tellingly entitled "The Deindustrialization of America." Inadvertently echoing Kennedy's fear of "industrial dislocation," the study foresaw a transfer of economic power from the United States to Japan, as well as a drop in American living standards.[22] Op-ed writers, columnists, and intellectuals fanned the flames of fear over what Japanese competition would do to America's prosperity. In 1985 Theodore H. White, Pulitzer prize–winning author and longtime reporter on Asian affairs, wrote an article for *The New York Times* entitled "The Danger from Japan," in which he criticized Japan's predatory "trade tactics."[23] A prominent monthly magazine, *The Atlantic*, wondered if America could "contain Japan."[24] Another writer, indicative of the sentiment of the times, entitled his book *The Japanese Power Game*.[25] A more pointed book, *Agents of Influence*, outlined the extent to which the Japanese manipulated trade to their advantage.[26] And these are just a few examples of the fearful outpouring.

Politicians and other public figures, not surprisingly, echoed the frightened and alarming tone. Senator Lloyd Bentsen (D-TX) worried that "American workers will end up like the people of the Biblical village who were condemned to be hewers of wood and drawers of water."[27] Wall Street financier Felix Rohatyn spoke of "de-industrialization" and worried that America would become "a nation of short-order cooks and sales women,"[28] a phrase remarkably similar to more recent descriptions of a nation of "hamburger flippers" and those who work at dead-end "McJobs." The anxiety became so intense that members of Congress, in a remarkable lapse of dignity even for them, smashed apart Japanese electronic products on the steps of the Capitol while simultaneously complaining about (but failing to explain) "unfair" trade practices.[29] In 1990 President George H. W. Bush stressed the urgent need for America to improve its international "competitiveness"[30] and actually traveled to Tokyo to plead for voluntary Japanese export restraints on both autos and electronics.[31]

But, as happened in Europe, Japanese success began to erase that economy's wage and cost advantages. By 1995 average hourly labor costs in Japan actually surpassed those in the United States, by more than 30 percent.[32] Japan, accordingly, began to move much of its production, especially of autos, to the United States. The move has continued uninterrupted since. By 2005 the American operations of Toyota, Nissan, and other foreign automakers had employed more American autoworkers than the big Detroit producers had lost in the previous 20 years.[33] Though America continued to see deterioration in its trade deficit with Japan, the pace slowed as the cost gap closed. Since 1995 Japanese inroads into the American market have expanded at a mere 1.6 percent a year, far slower than the 2.5 percent yearly rate by which they expanded between 1985 and 1995.[34] By this time, of course, China, India, Brazil, and other emerging economies had replaced Japan and Europe as a source of anxiety.

Successful Adjustments

Yet, for all this decades-long concern over American competitiveness and living standards, the economy has managed remarkably well. Undoubtedly many individuals, industries, and regions of the country have lost ground, but for the U.S. economy as a whole the economic adjustments have sustained income growth, job creation, and general prosperity. In nominal terms per capita income has expanded 5.7 percent a year, on average, since 1945 and a healthy 2.0 percent in real terms, after stripping away the distorting effects of inflation. Nor has the pace of growth changed despite the altered source and nature of the foreign competition. Overall real income (measured in aggregate, not on a per capita basis) expanded 2.5 percent a year on average in the 1950s and 1960s, when the challenge came from Europe, at a very similar 2.3 percent a year in the 1970s and 1980s, when the Japanese challenge dominated, and, though it has slowed to 1.7 percent a year since then, much of the difference reflects the severe but ultimately transitory effect of the 2008–09 recession.[35]

Speaking louder still to the economy's ability to respond, this general income growth has occurred pretty broadly among different classes of workers. In the most recent period the bulk of the growth has gone to wealthier people, and the wage gap between rich and poor has widened.[36] But this has not always been the case. From the late 1960s through the mid-1970s, the real income of the poorest fifth of the country grew twice as fast as the incomes of the wealthiest fifth. Accordingly the median income of that poorest group rose from just over 7.0 percent of the best-paid fifth to almost 10 percent. Only later, in the 1980s and 1990s, did the situation reverse, so that recent figures show a return of the relative relationship that prevailed in the mid-1960s.[37] But, however irregularly the relative distribution of income has shifted and probably will continue to shift in the future, the evidence of growing overall national income throughout this time is clear and consistent.

To some extent the broad-based, real income growth has occurred not despite the flow of imports but because of it. Whatever jobs have disappeared, whatever harm the imports have done to regions, industries, and individuals, they also have given the vast bulk of consumers and businesses in the United States access to inexpensive goods. These have held down the general cost of living not only by keeping the cost of those imported goods low, but also by reducing the cost of inputs to domestic producers. On either count the effect has increased the general purchasing power of American incomes, and to that extent has heightened real living standards, in general if not in every particular.

Though such positive effects on living standards are difficult to measure precisely, a comparison of import and domestic price inflation affords some insights. Since import prices over the last 40 years (excluding volatile oil prices) have increased by only two-thirds of the rate of prices generally,[38] they would seem to have held back living costs by a similar ratio. Cumulatively, over this 40-year period, the difference amounts to a significant 15 percent reduction in living costs from what would have prevailed in the absence of imports. This boon to the average American's living standard seems to have become more pronounced in recent years. Since 1990 import prices have actually declined by 1.3 percent a year compared to a 2.4 percent average yearly rise in overall consumer prices.[39] This difference is big enough to have held living costs to half of what they otherwise would have risen to during these 20 years. Measuring the same effect in a different way, the Peter G. Peterson Institute for International Economics estimates that trade and investment liberalization over the same period has improved living standards by somewhere between $1,650 and $3,300 in annual income for every man, woman, and child in the country.[40]

There are, of course, grounds for cavil over such calculations, but if precision is elusive, it is nonetheless clear that trade has done much to raise American living standards. Nor is this general lift in buying power the only way in which trade has helped the many, even as it has hurt in some particulars. Access to cheaper imported steel, for instance, though it undoubtedly has imposed hardships on American steel companies and their workers, has nonetheless benefited those many industries that use steel, such as auto and appliance manufacturers, construction contractors, tool and die works, and the like. The boon first became evident as early as the 1960s. At that time, intense strike activity in the United States forced many steel-using firms to buy from foreign sources for the first time. Their only alternative was to shut down. These lower-cost supplies[41] enabled the U.S. steel-using firms to sell at lower prices than they otherwise might have, enhancing their competitive positions domestically and globally, raising their profits, and sustaining both employment and wage rates in those industries. Indirectly, all these benefits helped raise real buying power generally throughout the country, in spite of the pain imports inflicted on the domestic steel industry.

Though the auto companies and many other steel-using manufacturers ultimately had their own problems with imports, this cost-benefit pattern has persisted. When, for example, President George W. Bush placed a temporary tariff on imported steel in March 2002, it was domestic, not foreign, complaints that made him rescind his decision. The tariffs had imposed insupportable expenses on domestic American producers of machinery, appliances, autos, and other steel-using goods. They forcefully made their plight known to the White House. Even the United Auto Workers saw a threat to its members' jobs and pleaded for repeal of the steel tariff. This overwhelming domestic opposition forced Bush to recind the tariffs late in 2003, two years before they were originally scheduled to expire and long before foreigners could mount their case before the World Trade Organization.[42]

A very similar scenario emerged more recently in response to President Obama's tariff on Chinese tires. Following his campaign promise to "crack down" on imports that unfairly undermine American workers,[43] Obama imposed a 35 percent tariff on these imports.[44] The impact on China's tire sales inevitably helped their American counterparts, though much of the lost Chinese sales went to the European tire maker Michelin and the Japanese tire maker Bridgestone.[45] China, of course, threatened retaliation, but more persuasive were the complaints of domestic tire users, consumers, auto manufacturers, car rental firms, and others. They saw their costs rise with the tariff, and suffered a commensurate decline in their living standards and their profits. They lobbied Washington to lift the levy even more vigorously than China did.[46]

Steel and tires are just two obvious examples of how trade can bring benefits to the economy in general, even as it burdens specific sectors. Cheap imports of chemicals, too, or fabric or machinery or minerals or any number of raw, finished, and semifinished goods have helped keep down costs for the firms and workers in the industries that use them, even as they have damaged those domestic industries that competed with them. But it is more than just general living costs or a balance between winners and losers that accounts for America's success in the face of foreign competition. Beyond simply enjoying access to cheaper goods, the economy has also mounted a more active defense of its living standards by making its workers more productive than others.[47]

Productivity and Staying in the Game

One key factor in this achievement has been the way in which business has offset America's relatively high wages with research and with applications of new equipment and systems. These efforts have raised the average worker's output per hour sufficiently to blunt the effect of high American wages on the cost of each unit of output. In the 1950s and 1960s, technology and research got a special boost from the scientific advances of the Second World War, the Cold War, and the Space Race. Though little data on research and development spending exists for the period before 1960, what was achieved is apparent in business's impressive 4.0 percent real annual rise in R&D spending during the 1960s, much more rapid than the economy's overall growth rate. By spending just as freely on the new equipment, systems, and software that embody the fruits of this research, business effectively brought considerable technology and scientific effort to the workplace. Such capital outlays increased at an impressive 5.0 percent a year throughout the 1950s and 1960s, adding some $2.4 trillion to America's total stock of capital equipment and productive facilities. Even allowing for depreciation and obsolescence, each American worker, by 1970, had an average of $2.7 billion in upgraded equipment and infrastructure at his or her disposal,[48] far more than foreign workers had.

With ever increasing amounts of capital and technological resources at their disposal, American workers enjoyed a huge increase in their output per hour. This measure of labor productivity grew on average an impressive 2.5 percent a year between 1950 and 1970. Even as wages rose, this rise in each worker's output per hour held down the labor costs of producing a unit of output—what economists call unit labor costs—to a 2.5 percent average annual rate of advance.[49] The rise in wages was still too fast for productivity gains to offset all the advantages of cheaper foreign labor, but it enabled many American producers to hold on to much more of their former market share than they otherwise might have.

While the sudden oil price increases of the 1970s confused R&D and investment decision making,[50] the 1980s again brought clarity. Spending on research resumed at an accelerated pace, rising 7.0 percent a year in real terms between 1980 and 1990, and still faster to an average growth rate of 7.7 percent per year after 1990. Capital spending on the equipment and software that embodied the fruits of this research rose 4.7 percent a year in real terms during the 1980s and 6.2 percent a year after 1990.[51] Again, after accounting for depreciation and obsolescence, the effort raised the amount of productivity-enhancing equipment and software in American industry by some $4.0 trillion during this time, effectively putting at each worker's disposal an average of two and a half times more equipment and software than he or she had in 1980.[52]

Worker productivity, in manufacturing especially, rose in tandem. Overall output per hour jumped at an average rate of almost 4.0 percent a year between 1980 and 2000 and has accelerated to 4.6 percent on average since then. Though hourly wages continued to rise, these productivity gains actually cut, by 0.6 percent a year, the average labor cost of each unit produced. Because America's overseas competitors failed to keep up with the strides made in research and productivity,[53] much American industry was able to withstand the low-cost foreign competition—though, as in earlier decades, it did so unevenly, so that some industries, such as garment or shoe manufacturing, lost to imports, even as others, such as chemicals, machine tools, and medical products, held on to or expanded their market shares.

Even manufacturing, which otherwise seems most vulnerable, has continued to do reasonably well. To be sure, it has declined as a part of the American economy. In 1950 it amounted to 27 percent of the country's GDP. By 1965 it had shrunk to 25.7 percent, and by 1980 to 20.0 percent. More recently its share has dropped to just 13.4 percent of the overall economy.[54] But this relative decline reflects less a drop in manufacturing output than faster growth in services and other areas of the economy. In absolute terms, manufacturing has continued to grow through all phases of this foreign competition. In fact, its real value added to the economy rose 3.7 percent a year, on average, in the 1950s and 1960s, in the face of the European challenge, and at that same rate in the 1980s and 1990s, when facing the much feared Japanese competition. It has risen at only 1.8 percent a year since 2000, but this deceleration reflects a shift in the trend less than the ultimately temporary impact of the 2008–09 recession.[55]

Indeed, far from disappearing as a manufacturer, the United States remains a manufacturing giant. Recent calculations put this country's gross annual manufacturing output at over $5.0 trillion. Even after subtracting from this figure all the imports and the services used in the production process, the net manufacturing output—what economists refer to as the value added—exceeds $1.6 trillion a year, led by technology, chemicals, machinery, and motor vehicles, though the autos are not necessarily American brands. By comparison those national economies usually associated with manufacturing strength look small. Comparable figures for Germany put manufacturing value added at the equivalent of roughly $600 billion. Japan and China manage respectively $900 billion and $1.0 trillion in manufacturing value added.[56] American manufacturing clearly still dwarfs its rivals.

Still, there is no denying that, despite the continued, even robust, manufacturing expansion, the country has lost manufacturing jobs. Outright employment declines only started after 1980, but employment growth has lagged throughout. In the 1950s and 1960s manufacturing payrolls grew at only half the rate of manufacturing output, at about 1.5 percent a year. During the late 1960s and 1970s manufacturing payrolls stagnated even as output continued to expand. Then, after 1980, employment in manufacturing began to fall, declining on average 0.5 percent a year to the end of the century. The decline in jobs accelerated after 2000, falling 3.1 percent a year on average to the present, though the still recent, severe recession may have exaggerated the fundamental extent of job losses. Overall manufacturing has lost some 5.3 million workers, on balance, since 1980.[57] Some of the loss, as described earlier, undoubtedly is the result of import competition, mostly in more labor-intensive industries. Much is a reflection of the huge productivity gains that have allowed manufacturing firms to increase output with fewer workers. Whatever the cause of job losses, the economy's reorganization nonetheless has conspired, effectively if not intentionally, to reabsorb most of the manufacturing workers displaced in the process.

Alternative Jobs

Much of this reemployment reflects the shifting product emphasis of American business. It has created new jobs in services and higher-value, more capital-intensive manufacturing, even as industry has stepped away from those areas in which it faced the most intractable foreign competition—largely the low-value, labor-intensive processes. This reabsorption has gone so far that, despite the loss of 5.3 million jobs in manufacturing since 1980, the United States economy overall has created some 25 million jobs, a yearly employment growth of 1.5 percent—about equal to the long-term average annual rate of jobs growth since 1950, a remarkable achievement considering the losses in manufacturing. What is still more noteworthy is that this more recent pace of jobs growth would actually have been faster were it not for the lingering, if ultimately temporary, effects of the 2008–09 recession.[58] The creation of new jobs able to absorb displaced manufacturing workers has, in fact, been so effective that until the 2008–09 recession, a greater proportion of Americans participated in the workforce—some 64 percent of the population—than in 1980, when the figure was some 60 percent, or between 1950 and 1965, when participation averaged about 56 percent.[59]

Much of this reabsorption has actually taken place within manufacturing. During a period of more than 30 years, more than 30 percent of workers displaced from areas of nondurable goods manufacturing—soaps, for instance, cosmetics, drugs, or textiles—found jobs elsewhere in that same area. In the case of durable goods manufacturing—machinery, lumber, tires, and the like—the figure is 40 percent.[60] According to the Commerce Department, many more—indeed half the workers displaced from one area of manufacturing during the past 30 years—have found jobs in trade or services,[61] often created through radical transformations in older industries and the wholesale invention of new industries.

These replacement jobs, so to speak, have emerged across the whole economy, but some areas stand out in particular. One of the most obvious is technology. Of course much of the spur to technological innovation has come from the quest for efficiency and productivity growth in all industry, including manufacturing's efforts to cope with the flow of low-priced imports. In this sense the technology boom is at least in part a product of the import challenge.[62] Whatever the spur to technological advance, there can be little doubt that all forms of technology have grown tremendously throughout this period, and in the process have created jobs, directly and indirectly, at many skill levels, some eminently suitable for workers displaced from more traditional manufacturing industries.

The growth of the technology industry can be described only in superlatives. By the broadest measure its real, inflation-adjusted value added has expanded slightly faster than 20 percent a year over the last 30-some years, almost seven times faster than the overall economy's 3.0 percent yearly growth rate. In the years since 1990, even as the technology industry has matured, its pace of growth has actually accelerated to over 21 percent a year, further widening the gap over the overall economy's 2.9 percent average yearly pace of growth.[63] According to the Bureau of Labor Statistics, this sector's explosive expansion alone has created some 5.0 million new jobs since 1980,[64] almost equal to the 5.3 million jobs otherwise lost in traditional manufacturing during that time.

It would seem, then, that the gains in technology alone could have counterbalanced all but a small part of the jobs otherwise lost in manufacturing. But that comforting calculation would overstate. The loss of manufacturing jobs should, after all, take into account not just the absolute job losses but also the numbers that manufacturing might have employed had it continued to hire at its pre-1980 pace. On this basis the nation could be said to have a shortfall of 11.2 million manufacturing jobs since 1980. At the same time a fair calculation of technology's ability to absorb displaced manufacturing workers should look not at total new employment in the sector but only at the amount above what would have occurred had the sector grown at the same pace as the overall economy. Still, even on that basis, technology has made a significant contribution. Since 1980 it has added some 1.6 million new positions above its former trend, enough to cover 30 percent of the jobs actually lost in manufacturing during these years and more than 14 percent of the manufacturing jobs that would have existed had the sector continued to increase employment at its pre-1980 pace.[65]

Obviously not every displaced manufacturing worker is suited to a job in technology. A middle-aged steelworker does not naturally turn to computer programming as a second career, much less Web site design, though stranger things have happened. Those who can and do fill such places in technology often vacate other jobs that steelworkers and others like them could more readily fill, with relatively little retraining or the improbable motivation they might need to fill other technology positions. However much technology has or has not reemployed these workers, it is only one aspect of the change that has opened employment prospects to displaced manufacturing workers, much of it offering positions better suited to their backgrounds.

The growth of retailing, including restaurants, has laid down one such avenue. Employment opportunities in this area have grown with the increased prominence of large retail chains and the shopping malls that they support, one of the most notable developments of the post–Second

World War period, and particularly of the last 30 years. Though the trend in recent years may have begun to reverse, the visit to a mall established itself as a primary form of entertainment in America. Both contributing to this change and in response to it, retail outlets have worked to make themselves more inviting. Displays have become more lavish, service has become more solicitous, and hours have lengthened to accommodate shoppers' schedules, all changes that have increased the need for staff. The number of employees per establishment has increased remarkably during these last 50-some years. In national chains it has risen from 15 to 25, in regional chains from 12 to 19, and in local chains from 9 to 15. Even as the number of retail establishments increased by some 20 percent during this time, employment—from manager, to cashier, to salesperson—has, accordingly, risen far faster, by some 244 percent overall since 1960 or at a 2.6 percent annual rate, outpacing overall employment and raising the share of total employment accounted for by retailing from about 12.5 percent in the 1950s to 13.5 percent in the 1970s, to about 17.8 percent more recently.[66]

However much intellectuals, city planners, sociologists, spiritualists, and aesthetes deplore such developments, this change in retailing has nonetheless provided considerable employment and income, much for former manufacturing workers, whether displaced by imports or by increased productivity. Though of late this retailing growth has begun to wane, the record shows that it created a cumulative 6.5 million jobs overall since 1980, and 3.5 million more jobs than would have existed in the old structure of retailing. That excess jobs growth alone is enough to have absorbed some two-thirds of the actual jobs lost in manufacturing during this time, or about one-third of the shortfall in manufacturing employment had it continued its earlier pace.[67]

Similarly, innovation in the trucking and shipping industries has absorbed many displaced manufacturing workers. Federal Express led this crucial change. By guaranteeing senders reliable next-day delivery and, what is more, a way to track the progress of each shipped item, Federal Express in effect invented a new industry when it was founded in 1971. Today the company employs some 300,000 people in activities that did not exist some 40 years ago.[68] With FedEx's imitators, the new industry has created in excess of 3.2 million new jobs, or 1.9 million more than would have existed had the shipping industry maintained its old structure. The positions it has offered—from delivery personnel to clerks, sorters, pilots for immense fleets of planes, drivers for even bigger fleets of trucks, mechanics to maintain all this equipment, not to mention office and support staff—have made easy crossovers for many onetime production workers who are willing to relocate and tolerate some retraining. The extra jobs created in the area, above and beyond old trends, alone could have absorbed more than one-third of the jobs lost in manufacturing, and about 17 percent of the jobs shortfall from what manufacturing would have employed had old patterns persisted.[69]

The advent of cable television contributed in an especially interesting way. The industry creates a remarkable array of positions, many well suited to former manufacturing workers. After all, the largest block of employees in the industry includes installers and repairers. In addition to them, there are substantial numbers of technicians, camera operators, photographers, sales agents, dispatchers, producers, directors, clerical staff, executives, and a wide array of support staff, from commissary people to janitors. Not all are glamorous or even especially desirable jobs, at least not in some contexts, but all pay and otherwise would not have otherwise existed. Many offer an improvement on factory jobs, most of which can only seem desirable to those who have never done them. Cable television as a whole employs some 1.5 million people, enough to absorb some 28 percent of the jobs lost to manufacturing since 1980 or just over 13 percent of the shortfall between current manufacturing employment and what would have prevailed had pre-1980 patterns persisted.[70]

Finance, too, has created employment opportunities in ways that were unimaginable 30 years ago. Inevitably the debacle of 2008–09 has discredited the worth of much financial activity, but behind the ugly and embarrassing headlines the industry still provides essential services to millions, most of which have nothing to do with the fraudulent and near-fraudulent endeavors gleefully covered in the headlines. Indeed most of the employment in finance involves activities that are more prosaic, more useful, less questionable, and less glamorous than the activities that have received so much media attention. And this growth has provided much net new employment.

The story of the broker-dealer Edward Jones is indicative. Headquartered in St. Louis, Missouri, this firm has grown to prominence in just the last 25 years or so. It serves not-so-wealthy investors, largely in rural areas, small towns, and the smaller cities of the country, often through single offices, many located in the strip malls of suburbia and exurbia. Its rigorous training and support facilities enable it to offer financial guidance through a staff of advisors who have little financial education beyond their Edward Jones training and claim no special insight besides the ability to apply the firm's carefully constructed investment guidelines. Despite these relative limitations the advisors can fulfill the straightforward financial needs of their client base. Significantly in this context, most of the Edward Jones advisors are involved in second careers. Many are retired military personnel, civil servants, those who have resigned other positions, and many have been displaced from former jobs, some of them in manufacturing.[71]

Like Edward Jones, the entire financial services industry, quite apart from its questionable and glamorous aspects, has grown tremendously during the last 30 years. Technological applications have enabled many less than sophisticated advisors to deliver services to many less than wealthy clients that 30–40 years ago were available only from the most exclusive investment houses and only to the mega-rich. As with retailing, shipping, and technology, these jobs, too, have far outpaced the growth of the economy, offering employment to almost 55 percent more people since 1980 than would have found work in the area had old structures prevailed.[72] Each job may not have been suitable for a displaced production worker, but some have, and for the others, as with technology, those who have stepped up to them have left places elsewhere that would have better been suited to a retrained production worker. Together these additional jobs in finance could have absorbed some 40 percent of the absolute number of jobs lost to manufacturing since 1980, or about one-fifth of the shortfall in manufacturing jobs, compared with what would have existed had old patterns prevailed.[73]

The list of employment shifts and replacement jobs could go on for pages and include, for instance, the employment jump in the travel, leisure, and hospitality industries, and especially the explosion of jobs in medical services, for not just doctors but also nurses, orderlies, physical therapists, and a host of other functionaries, many of whom are in suitable second careers, some of which hardly existed at all 30 years ago, and all of which will increase disproportionately as the baby boom generation ages. These and other such changes have combined, as the overall data show, to create many more jobs than those lost in manufacturing, whether to imports, the industry's reorientation, or productivity increases. Along with all the other adjustments and trade-based benefits, these alternative employment opportunities and the incomes that they have generated have gone a long way toward explaining how the country has continued to prosper even in the face of successive foreign challenges.

While such a backdrop does offer reason to doubt recent dire warnings over globalization's effects, it would be a mistake to become complacent over even so successful a record. Besides the demographic pressure that will characterize the future, and that was absent in this earlier period, much else also will differ, including the nature of the competition offered by emerging economies. The destructive societal impact of a widening income gap between rich and poor signals possibly dangerous unrest ahead, as does the clear link between globalization and ever more severe and destructive boom-bust financial cycles. These matters alone offer considerable ammunition to the antiglobalization feeling that will grow unless the developed economies can ameliorate these and other associated ills. The matter carries a measure of urgency, too. Already, political leadership in the United States and elsewhere in the developed world has begun, ominously, to accommodate the antiglobalization tide.

11

Dangerous Political Responses

In practice, of course, neither the statistical evidence nor the historical record nor sometimes even logic counts. As people feel threatened, whether they are justified in doing so or not, they have increasingly pressured their political leaders to resist globalization, embrace tariffs and other protectionist policies, and impede world trade flows generally. Already an official drift in this antitrade direction is evident. The pattern is exceedingly dangerous, too. Protectionism has always hurt growth prospects and living standards. In the current environment it would also steal from the emerging economies their engine of growth and deny the developed economies their most effective relief from the ills of aging demographics. For the sake of prosperity, then, the world's economies, both developed and emerging, need to do what they can to disarm antiglobalization militancy, preferably by easing the transition strains that have given birth to it.

A Growing Hostility to Free Trade

Politicians have long catered to people's fears of foreign competition. Left- or right-leaning presidents and prime ministers have always voiced sympathy for organized labor's understandable resistance to any product made by people other than its own.[1] But until recently the political authorities offered little more than sympathy and rhetoric. Actual protectionist measures were rare and highly restrained. When, for instance, President Kennedy took up the issue of foreign competition and spoke ominously of "industrial dislocation, increasing unemployment, and deepening poverty,"[2] the government, rather than restrain imports, tried to help American producers by reducing other nations' trade barriers, to "level the playing field," as they said then and have said since. Kennedy's administration, even as the president issued his warnings, initiated what has come to be called the Kennedy round of tariff negotiations, which by the end of the 1960s managed to get 16 of this country's major trading partners to cut their tariffs an average of 22 percent.[3]

Thirty years on President Bill Clinton was following the same script. He, too, was under pressure to restrain trade. When Clinton first ran for the White House in 1992, public concern was great enough to allow a powerful third-party candidate, Ross Perot, to base his campaign in part on opposition to free trade.[4] Perot famously warned against NAFTA, claiming that Mexico would steal American jobs, using the memorable phrase "a giant sucking sound."[5] Yet in office, for all Clinton's public worries about foreign economies "flooding our market and others with much cheaper goods, which makes it a lot tougher for our people to compete,"[6] he promptly signed the already negotiated NAFTA treaty with Canada and Mexico.[7]

More recently, however, official antitrade rhetoric has become much more strident, and policy has begun to follow it. By 2008 Americans no longer needed a third-party candidate to promise protectionist measures. That year's Democratic presidential primaries saw both major candidates Hillary Clinton and Barack Obama decry specific free trade agreements and free trade generally.[8] Neither were their expressions momentary poses for particular interest groups. On the contrary, everything spoke to a genuine turn in sentiment. Both Clinton and Obama, to the chagrin of Canada and Mexico, pledged to renegotiate NAFTA. Obama used particularly militant language, saying he would use "the hammer of an opt out to make sure that we actually get labor and environmental standards that are enforced."[9] Clinton frequently criticized Obama for not going far enough against trade,[10] eventually coming out against a U.S. trade deal with South Korea[11] and calling for a "time out" on new trade deals.[12]

Washington generally has picked up the hostile tone. House Speaker Nancy Pelosi (D-CA) signaled the change even before the 2008 primaries, stating bluntly that new trade treaties would take a backseat in Congress's agenda. Referring to the practice of allowing Congress to vote on such agreements expeditiously without amendments, she told the media that "our legislative priorities do not include renewal of fast-track authority."[13] Though Washington generally, and candidates Clinton and Obama, back-pedaled when Canada and Mexico rebuked the United States and its candidates for their attitude,[14] there was a keen sense among America's trading partners that they had reason for nervousness.[15] And the change was not exclusive to Democrats. The Republican faithful, when surveyed, also showed a strong skepticism about the benefits of free trade.[16] The last two Congresses of George W. Bush's presidency, one dominated by Republicans, the other by Democrats, introduced over 50 pieces of antitrade legislation.[17]

Nor has America made its turn alone. Political threats to globalization have gained momentum across the globe. In 2008, as Clinton and Obama outdid each other to talk tough on trade, then European Union trade commissioner Peter Mandelson noted how "economic nationalism has risen worldwide."[18] European Commission president José Manuel Barroso warned of the increase in "protectionist calls" across Europe that "might be hard to resist."[19] The World Trade Organization worried that the member states of the EU were passing legislation to restrict trade against outsiders at a rate double any measures to liberalize trade. It noted that European requests to the WTO for permission to "retaliate" against trading partners had risen some 30 percent in just the past few years.[20]

Official hostility to free trade has also grown beyond the United States and Europe. The WTO notes that worldwide requests by its members to retaliate against trading partners have risen 40 percent in just the last few years, while import exclusions—from the United States to Egypt to India to France to Russia—have become increasingly common, as have retaliatory measures by other nations against those exclusions.[21] Only a year after the group of the world's 20 largest trading nations (the Group of 20, or G20, which adds 12 largely emerging economies to the developed economies in the G8) made a pledge to halt protectionist measures, 17 of its member nations were found to have erected them.[22] The WTO has complained that its latest negotiations to open up trade, called the Doha Round, after the capital city of Qatar where the negotiations began, became bogged down, due, it maintains, to determined resistance from developed economies, the United States in particular.[23] Matters have become so acute that President Lee Myung-bak, of export-dependent South Korea, rose in front of a G20 meeting in 2009 and implored its members to "name and shame" countries that erect barriers to trade or finance. He got little more than sympathy.[24]

At times protectionist posturing has verged on the brutal. In 2005 Senators Chuck Schumer (D-NY) and Lindsey Graham (R-SC) precipitously proposed a 27.5 percent tariff on all Chinese imports to America, unless China raised the value of the yuan by a comparable amount. The proposal won the backing of 67 of 100 senators. Though resistance by the Bush administration and seeming concessions from China stopped the bill passing into law,[25] it spoke volumes about how popular protectionism had become among the power elite as well as the public in general.

Not long after Schumer and Graham made their threats, the EU also considered duties of its own on Chinese goods, particularly steel imports. Though the Europeans abandoned the idea of blanket barriers, they nonetheless gave a sense of their growing hostility to free trade by loudly reaffirming their stiff textile import quotas and very publicly signing a deal with the United States to cooperate in fighting counterfeit goods made in China.[26] It was, shortly after Europe made its statement, the United States imposed its 35 percent tariff on Chinese-made tires.[27] The following year in 2010, the House of Representatives escalated the matter by officially labeling China a "currency manipulator," a move that eased the legislative path to still more and higher tariffs against Chinese goods.[28]

Nor has China drawn all the protectionist attention. Europe's backlash at Chinese steel stemmed in the first instance from a surge in American complaints against European steel producers.[29] Europe at that time also imposed tariffs on American high-tech electronics and a raft of other products, from shoes[30] to air compressors[31] to frozen strawberries.[32] These trade impediments were severe enough to draw WTO suits from the United States, even as Washington placed a 300 percent duty on French Roquefort cheese[33] and, incidentally, on Chinese chickens.[34] Vietnam, in response to lost trade opportunities globally, imposed tariffs of its own on foreign dairy products.[35] Brazil raised tariffs as much as 100 percent on U.S. pharmaceuticals, music, chemicals, and software. Mexico, in response, it claimed, to American violations of NAFTA rules, imposed duties on U.S. tableware products, grapes, and almonds. Both the EU and Japan have sued the United States at the WTO over its use of duties generally.[36] India has restricted imports of Chinese toys. Indonesia has restricted points of entry for Malaysian products. South Korea, only weeks after its premier's heartfelt complaint to the G20, doubled duties on raw materials, including wheat, flour, and natural gas.[37]

This is hardly a complete list. The media every day bring more news of tariffs and quotas designed to protect domestic industry or to retaliate against another nation's protectionism. Many of the levies and ceilings get repealed or modified soon after they are announced, but they are always replaced, it seems, by new measures. Whether the picture emerges from the comprehensive WTO data quoted earlier or from a revealing flow of anecdotes, the hostile picture is clear. The authorities in most nations are more willing than they have been for a very long time to gratify protectionist sentiments in their populations, often with some of the bluntest tools at their disposal. What is more telling, antiglobalization efforts have pushed well beyond such conventional trade restraints to a wide array of remarkably imaginative, if duplicitous devices.

Subsidies that protect domestic businesses have certainly gained favor. France alone dedicates almost €6.0 billion in government loan guarantees to support its domestic auto industry, a fact that the Germans understandably claim puts their exports at a disadvantage and violates the spirit, if not the letter, of the EU's goal of free trade across all its members.[38] The Netherlands is so generous with subsidies that the

Dutch company Corus, when it took over certain British steel mills, was shocked to discover that Britain was more circumspect. It turns out that the Dutch taxpayer picks up some 70 percent of the salaries of workers if they opt to leave work in the firm's so-called willing layoff program,[39] a significant cost saving for Corus in the Netherlands and a compelling advantage when competing with otherwise inexpensive imports. Meanwhile the United States complains of European subsidies for its aerospace industry, as Europe complains of American subsidies to biofuels. Each threatens retaliation.[40] Every developed nation in the world has research and development subsidies.[41]

Nor are the subsidies exclusive to developed economies. China subsidizes a host of operations, including a flow of tax rebates to exporters generally.[42] Beijing's subsidy to paper manufacturers recently provoked 10–20 percent retaliatory tariffs from the United States.[43] China even takes the subsidies to the regional level. Farmers in the city of Hangzhou, for instance, gain a 13 percent subsidy for buying local manufactures. In the city of Changchun, locals receive a 10 percent subsidy for buying local and are excused normal vehicle inspections on locally made cars and tractors.[44] India, Indonesia, and a long list of other Asian and Latin American states have engaged increasingly in similar practices.[45]

Restraint of trade is never so apparent, however, as in the area of agricultural subsidies. Here the patterns are long-standing but no less real because of that. Europe has attracted the most attention. Its common agricultural policy transfers the equivalent of $70 billion a year from EU taxpayers to farmers, largely through price supports that pay European farmers higher than market prices, based on an administered standard. The policy makes it almost impossible for any but the most efficient foreign agriculture to penetrate European markets. The policy further hurts foreign farmers in other ways as well. Because the price supports encourage overplanting in Europe, they produce a huge food surplus that Europe then dumps on world markets, depressing global prices and the incomes of farmers everywhere outside Europe.[46]

Sugar subsidies in Europe and cotton subsidies in the United States have caused particular problems for farmers in emerging economies. Though the WTO has fought the United States and the European Union on this, neither power bloc shows any sign of yielding, even less now than in earlier years. Brazil has become so frustrated that it now maintains a series of WTO-sanctioned retaliatory tariffs against American and European agricultural subsidies.[47] So committed is the United States to support its domestic cotton industry that, instead of removing its domestic subsidies, it effectively offered to extend them to Brazilian growers, offering to pay some $147 million in compensation. A remarkable gesture that, had it been accepted, would have forced American taxpayers to support growers in both countries as well as pay a higher price for cotton than if they simply had access to the cheaper Brazilian product.[48]

The rising tide of protectionism has managed to leverage questions of product safety, working conditions, and also the environment. Organized labor in particular has looked increasingly to restrain trade when counterparts have failed to impose environmental standards and worker and product protections. Especially as the foreign challenge has shifted from Europe and Japan (which have such protections) to the emerging economies, organized labor has argued that the absence of such rules relieves companies in India, China, and other emerging economies of significant costs, giving them an unfair competitive edge.[49] Though much of what they say is true, an imposition of expensive Western standards on these poorer, much less developed economies would also effectively block them from any commerce with the rich economies of Japan, Europe, or the United States.

Even NAFTA rules have fallen victim to such positioning. Originally the treaty allowed trucks to pass freely over borders between the United States, Canada, and Mexico. But safety arguments, insisted on mostly by America's International Brotherhood of Teamsters, for a long time denied Mexican trucks and drivers license to cross into the United States.[50] Aside from protecting Teamster jobs, the attendant need to offload and reload cargo significantly raised the cost of Mexican products and, therefore, effectively protected many domestic American competitors, though it clearly raised costs to the American consumer and to the businesses that rely on these Mexican products. In much the same way Europe, Germany in particular, has expressed concerns about the safety of American food products, probably the only effective competitor in the face of EU agricultural subsidies. Though Germany's farm minster, Horst Seehofer, stressed fair and safe conditions when announcing the ban,[51] his French counterpart, Michel Barnier, gave away the underlying protectionist motive, calling for curbs on "free market liberalism."

Protectionist sentiment has used social concerns as well. EU bureaucrats, for instance, have sought to exclude U.S. products from Europe because, they claim, the American practice of diverting crops to make ethanol fuel contributes to "global hunger." Of course the European Union has not bothered to explain why it has not caused hunger with its own call for 10 percent of all European fuel to have such a bio-element by 2012,[52] but it is protection rather than any concern about the world's hungry that lies at the heart of the decision. Less obvious, but potentially even more effective, was the fairly recent effort by then French president Nicolas Sarkozy to protect European industry, already burdened by heavy carbon taxes, by imposing comparable duties on goods from places without such taxes.[53] Not all European nations, however, were ready to embrace such measures.[54] Meanwhile, the United States, which does not yet have a carbon tax, is nonetheless clearly ready to follow Europe's example. When the U.S. House of Representatives passed such a levy in 2009 it included duties on foreign products that use a lot of carbon but come from countries that do not have such a levy.[55]

Local content rules, too, have risen with the new official embrace of trade restraint. The United States made headlines in 2009 with the "buy American" provisions of President Obama's huge $800-plus billion economic stimulus legislation.[56] These required any federally funded project to use American-made steel, iron, and manufactured goods.[57] Neither is America alone in the application of such new protectionist tools. Then U.K. prime minister Gordon Brown promised similar rules with his pledge to create "British jobs for British workers."[58] Australia adopted new buy-local policies, while Indonesia has gone so far as to direct its civil servants to buy only locally made shoes, food, clothing, music, and films.[59] Brazil's government-owned oil company, Petrobras, now requires of its suppliers 60 percent local Brazilian content.[60] China takes buy-local policies to the granular level and actually insists that contractors on some public projects source the bulk of their inputs within the region. Anhui province demands that all projects funded there buy their inputs from local firms. Makers of cars in that eastern province must source their steel there, and public projects in the city of Changchun must procure some 50 percent of their equipment locally.[61] Still more recently, New Delhi has legislated measures to force any technology firm to manufacture in India all that it sells within the country.[62]

Piled onto the tariffs, labor rules, environmental and safety strictures, and local content rules is the recent vogue to limit foreign ownership—what some describe as "financial nationalism."[63] Australia, fearful of Chinese financial power, has excluded Chinese buyers, in its mining industry in particular.[64] Germany has only recently tightened its rules, passing legislation that would allow the government to reverse any acquisition of more than 25 percent of any German company by any non-European investor.[65] China has issued regulations that can for "security reasons" block foreign acquisitions in any industry, including a blanket exclusion of foreign ownership in 39 "strategic" sectors of the economy, ranging from natural resources to biotechnology. India has retaliated against China's new ownership strictures by passing comparable rules and immediately using them to block the Chinese purchase of an Indian telecommunications firm. Canada is considering similar legislation.[66] In Japan the government has increased the numbers and types of acquisitions that require official approval and most recently blocked foreign ownership in some of its airports.[67]

This kind of financial nationalism has even risen among EU members. EU treaties make such restrictions difficult, but it speaks to the force of this antitrade trend that officials in the Union's member nations have succeeded in creating barriers anyway. Italy has blocked the Spanish builder Abertis from taking over Italy's 6,400 kilometers of Autostrade highway by drawing on an obscure law that forbids construction companies to own roads. Italian officials made little effort to hide how they used the law as a subterfuge to advance a protectionist agenda. Spain, in its turn, insisted for "security reasons" that before Germany's E.ON could take over Spain's largest electricity firm, Endesa, it would have to sell off one-third of its power stations.[68] Even the United States, which in many respects has the least to fear from foreign ownership, has embraced this behavior, denying, as already mentioned, China's CNOOC 2005 bid for the American oil company Unocal and blocking Dubai Ports World from indirect ownership in six U.S. ports. To facilitate such protectionism Congress has eased the ability of the Committee on Foreign Investment in the United States (CFIUS) to deny any sales to foreigners.[69] China's government investment fund, China Investment Corporation, has complained openly of being blocked by Washington. "Stigmatized" was the word used by its head, Gao Xiqing.[70]

Restrictions on cross-border investments have gathered force so rapidly that not too long ago a group of major American and European banking institutions issued an unusual joint statement warning about the growth of what it called "financial protectionism."[71] Taking much the same line as the bankers, the G8 recently decried the growth of what it called "investment protectionism," noting ominously that at one time some 90 percent of new investment rules eased the path of cross-border investments but that in recent years almost half the new rules and laws have raised barriers.[72]

Since then, financial protectionism has broadened. Seoul, while begging the world to remain open, has put forward a new round of capital controls to stem movements of funds into and out of the country's financial markets.[73] Meanwhile, much of the rest of the world has entered into what can only be described as a low-grade currency war. Japan, after its 2012 elections, instituted policies to drive down the yen's value in order to give Japanese exporters a pricing edge on global markets. China has vocally decried the move, while Brazil, Europe, the United States, Japan, and others have all accused each other of starting the conflict or extending it.[74]

The weight of this protectionist movement, especially set against past, speaks to a noteworthy turn. Whereas once officials coupled protectionist rhetoric with free trade policies, now they couple free trade rhetoric with protectionist policies. Official policy has turned so far against globalization that WTO director-general Pascal Lamy recently warned nations to avoid anything in their financial reform legislation that might facilitate these protectionist measures.[75]

Highly Dangerous Stuff

The protectionist turn is certainly understandable. Not only are the populations of all these nations less enthusiastic about globalization,[76] but the benefits of trade—lower costs of living, greater choice to the buying public, opportunity for producers to concentrate on those areas where their economy has comparative advantages—are more general and less obvious than the sufferings of those who lose out in the process.[77] The remarkable thing in this context is how long officials previously resisted the protectionist impulse.

Understandable or not, the trend is dangerous. Seemingly small losses to the general economy may seem easy to bear for the sake of those who have lost, but multiplied over entire populations they can make a huge difference in living costs and living standards. Protectionism looks still more dangerous against a backdrop of building demographic pressure, since it threatens to block a primary means by which the developed economies can protect their living standards from the ravages of relative labor shortages.[78] If globalization carries significant ills—and it does—attempts to block it can prove a cure far worse than the presumed disease. In the words of WTO head Pascal Lamy: "We know it [protectionism] is a terrible disease at the end of the day."[79] Bundesbank president Jens Weidmann has made similar warnings in response to the recent lapse into currency war.[80]

History firmly attests to protectionism's destructive power. Time and again when nations, for whatever reason, have erected barriers to trade and investment, they have found themselves poorer as a consequence. Sometimes the protectionism creates absolute declines in living standards and lost wealth. At others the protectionist nation, to its chagrin, simply falls economically behind its more open neighbors. But the message is clear nonetheless that these barriers, however erected or justified, hurt economic growth and living standards. An extensive study made by the National Bureau of Economic Research (NBER) used American data to conclude that heavy American tariffs during the late nineteenth century, averaging 30 percent of the value of the goods involved, retarded overall growth rates by a full percentage point a year, a "dead weight" that dissipated almost entirely as the country reduced its tariffs into the mid-twentieth century.[81]

A comparison between Britain and France in the nineteenth century affords a classic illustration. At the beginning of that century, both nations were heavily protectionist. In 1815, to protect local agriculture, Britain passed the first of its Corn Laws, imposing heavy duties on a number of products, food imports in particular.[82] France went one better and in the same year imposed what is called the "prohibitions," which effectively banned foreign goods.[83] Though in the 1820s both nations began to liberalize, France, unlike Britain, quickly relapsed into protectionism by the 1830s.[84] France's protectionists made all the classic arguments for tariffs, those still heard today. One political pamphlet could have been issued by a modern protectionist, in its sentiment, if not in the old-fashioned language. "What does it matter if the wealthy man pays an extra five or ten centimes for an ell [45 inches] of fabric," it argued, "if, in exchange for this minor expense, he allows the people to survive without the shame of begging?"[85] Easy as it is to sympathize with such sentiments, protectionism, as always, failed to deliver on its promise. France fell behind Britain. From 1840 to 1870 per capita incomes in Britain outpaced those in France by a wide margin, and what evidence exists suggests that the British gains were broadly based throughout society.[86] A smaller proportion of Britons had to suffer the "shame of begging."

Still more compelling is the evidence left by America's infamous Smoot-Hawley tariffs of 1930. Senator Reed Smoot (R-UT) and Representative Willis Hawley (R-OR) were troubled by the economic dislocations that followed the stock market crash of late 1929 and set out to protect American jobs and industry by raising a tariff wall against foreign competition. Their bill raised duties on some 20,000 imports by an average of 20 percent.[87] The law might stand as a study in unintended consequences, for it protected no jobs and destroyed many. If not all economists and historians agree that the tariffs caused the Great Depression, all agree that they contributed mightily to the economic devastation.[88]

The tariffs hurt immediately, as do all tariffs, by keeping the cost of living higher than it otherwise would have been had less-expensive foreign goods flowed into the country. Because at the time American wages were already suffering, any such resistance to a general decline in overall price levels added considerably to the working person's burdens. If some jobs were saved—and that is questionable—American living standards generally declined. The legislation compounded economic problems further by provoking retaliatory tariffs abroad. Some of those foreign tariffs were aimed specifically at American goods, others were more general, but all clearly rose in response to the Smoot-Hawley legislation. The League of Nations at the time noted the trend with dismay, writing in its *World Economic Survey* of 1932–33 that Smoot-Hawley was "the signal for an outburst of tariff-making activity in other countries, partly at least by way of reprisals."[89] The net effect detracted meaningfully from economic well-being across the globe.

There is even evidence that the tariffs reversed an incipient recovery that had begun in 1930. Though a recession started right after the stock market crashed in 1929, economic conditions by 1930 had begun to stabilize and even point toward recovery. Business activity began to show tentative signs of life. The unemployment rate had fallen from about 9 percent of the labor force in January 1930 to 6.3 percent by June. But once the tariffs went into effect the economic slide renewed with a vengeance and unemployment began its rise toward one-quarter of the workforce. The stock market anticipated the problems, falling some 10 percent on June 17, 1930, the day President Herbert Hoover signed the legislation into law.[90] The market's implicit forecast of an ugly economic impact was if anything mild. As foreign nations retaliated with tariffs of their own, markets for American exports disappeared. World trade fell some 67 percent from the bill's passage in 1930 to the lows of 1932. The United States, export-dependent at the time, actually suffered worse than most. Though American imports fell 40 percent during that period, exports fell more than 75 percent.[91] American farmers lost 20 percent of their wheat sales, 40 percent of their tobacco sales, and 55 percent of their cotton sales.[92] Industry suffered even more. The tariffs, according to some research, reversed the entire integration of world markets that had occurred in the prior 40-plus years.[93]

Though a lot has changed since the 1930s, and certainly since the nineteenth century, there is ample reason nonetheless to suspect that a rise in protectionism now could have comparable ill effects. Certainly it was just such a prospect that prompted EU trade commissioner Peter Mandelson's critical response to the protectionist rhetoric embraced by several American presidential candidates during 2008. "It is irresponsible," he said, implicitly alluding to the pain of Smoot-Hawley, "to be pretending to people you can erect new protections, new tariff barriers around your economy in the twenty-first century global age, and still succeed in sustaining people's living standards and jobs. It is a mirage, and they [the candidates and other politicians] know it."[94]

There is no doubt that recent protectionist moves by the United States and other trading nations have already elicited the kinds of retaliation that Smoot-Hawley did. In 2009, for instance, when the United States persisted in blocking Mexican trucks from crossing the border, the government in Mexico City not only protested under NAFTA rules, but it also placed duties of between 10 and 45 percent on 89 American products. So while American consumers and the firms that use Mexican inputs had to pay for the higher shipping costs imposed by the policies of their own government, Mexico's retaliation cut into the sales of American exporters. Christmas tree growers in California and Oregon lost respectively 90 percent and 65 percent of their markets. Washington state fruit growers lost 25 percent. Other farming interests recorded comparable losses. Even New York's jewelry industry noted the effect, as did those previously mentioned, who make their living from selling plastic table- and kitchenware. All found themselves priced out of the Mexican market.[95]

Neither have the retaliations emerged entirely as straightforward tit-for-tat measures. The buy-American provisions included in America's 2009 stimulus spending evoked more than grumbles from trade officials in Canada, Europe, and Asia. Though few governments were quite ready to up the ante with tariffs of their own, provincial and local governments in regions that depended on exports retaliated with boycotts of American goods.[96] In 2010, when Senators Schumer and Graham escalated the protectionist posturing by again threatening a general tariff on Chinese goods, Beijing officials responded by threatening American firms that did a lot of business in China, suggesting that they might ease their own circumstances by pressuring Washington to change its posture.[97] When the United States imposed the previously mentioned 35 percent tariff on Chinese tire imports, Beijing immediately struck back with tariffs on American auto parts and on agricultural products, mostly chickens.[98] China expanded the retaliatory pressure by also hinting loudly that it would consider selling part of its massive holdings of U.S. government bonds.[99]

This strike-counterstrike pattern has already become remarkably convoluted. Sometimes it is difficult to know where the protectionism began and where it will end. In 2008, for instance, Beijing reacted to EU duties on its exports by tightening its rules on European investments in China. Concurrently it denied several American and European takeovers. The European Chamber of Commerce countered China's reaction by demanding that EU authorities punish China with additional trade barriers.[100] A still more obscure pattern developed when China denied Coca-Cola the right to buy the Chinese beverage maker Huiyuan, ostensibly on antitrust grounds. The company took the rejection gracefully, but Washington seized on the matter, accusing China of dressing up economic nationalism in terms of antitrust concerns and threatening substantial retaliatory measures. The government of Australia then escalated the tension still further. Though it had suffered nothing in the Coca-Cola rebuff, it used the incident to promise China that it would treat its bids in Australia as China had treated Coca-Cola's bid in China.[101]

No matter how the exact patterns of action and reaction have arisen in the past, and might arise in the future, it is nonetheless clear that if protectionism gains momentum all countries would suffer, just as Smoot-Hawley and the other tariffs have caused widespread suffering. Living costs would rise, and living standards would fall concomitantly. Much of industry would suffer from increased costs in their inputs and supplies. More fundamentally, nations would lose out on the maximum output that can be achieved when they can divide labor around the comparative advantages described by David Ricardo. However many specific industries and regions have legitimate complaints, the protectionist route would, as ever, present a solution that itself becomes an even bigger problem.[102]

The demographically challenged future makes nations even more vulnerable. Because protectionism could deny them the use of trade and global investments to relieve the strains imposed by their aging demographics and the relative labor shortages it brings, an antitrade trend now would, if anything, cause more harm than protectionism has brought in the past. Rather than suffer such a setback, leadership in these countries needs to dispel antiglobalization demands by smoothing the adjustment to globalization, and in the process finding ways to mitigate the pains it imposes.

12

Helping the Economy and People Cope

Protectionism poses such a dire threat, and de- mographics such a compelling need for globalization, that complacency has no place. Either America, Europe, and Japan will find ways to disarm protectionist sentiment, largely by easing the transitions imposed by globalization, or their economies will decline. The old ways of simply ignoring the adjustment pains or disguising them with subsidies will no longer serve. Trusting past success to continue into the future is too risky. These economies must do more.

Using past successes as a partial guide, Europe, Japan, and America would best deal with the situation by pursuing three courses of action. To sustain their competitive edge, as well as create new, replacement jobs for those lost to globalization, they must intensify their emphasis on research, development, and innovation. To provide their innovators with the skilled employees that they need, and at the same time smooth the transition of workers displaced from jobs elsewhere, training must improve radically. To support both these efforts, these nations must also upgrade general educational standards. Success on these fronts can relieve globalization's strains by using the process to best advantage even as it disarms dangerous protectionist sentiments. It will not be easy, but there is little choice if these three—Europe, Japan, and America—want to sustain their high living standards.

Promoting Innovation

Developed economies have long toiled to promote innovation. Although the record is patchy, both the successes and the failures make one thing clear: the process cannot be forced and demands subtle combinations of sometimes contradictory elements. On the one hand it needs considerable funding and concerted, top-down direction. The grand projects of huge government-related research, such as the Space Race, capture these aspects of the process. On the other hand research has its best economic effect when diverse players have the freedom to experiment and pursue applications never envisioned by the original designers. This more chaotic, bottom-up aspect of the process requires a diversity of players, some large, some small, some sophisticated, some not, each acting from his or her own perspective, exchanging ideas and guessing at what might work. Because these aspects of the process differ so radically, one can at times hamper the other. Striking the right balance to allow both full play is essential.

The historical record makes clear the need for concentrated funding and direction. The Manhattan Project, which developed the atomic bomb during the Second World War, the Space Race with the Soviet Union in the 1960s, and the technological advances associated with the long Cold War[1] all clearly show how expensive and time-consuming research and development is and how often it asks those funding it to wait a long time for sometimes dubious practical results. Only large concentrations of wealth, either in government or industry, can afford that kind of expense or take on the associated risk of loss, much less wait the often long periods for a commercial payoff. No doubt the great economist Joseph Schumpeter, who popularized the phrase "creative destruction," had just such considerations in mind when he called for economic and financial "concentrations . . . to increase innovation and progress," and went so far as to recommend the creation of "monopolies" to give firms sufficient resources and security from market ups and downs to assume the risks involved.[2]

Such concentrations certainly can produce results. The statistical work makes clear that larger, more profitable corporations do most of the R&D spending, often spreading the risk and expense in partnerships with universities and government. It also makes clear that, because so much money is involved, R&D benefits flow most freely when firms can reasonably expect to secure for themselves the additional profits from the research.[3] To attract this participation, corporations and government must have a fair measure of the control and discipline as well as an ability to profit from their advances.[4] It follows that strong patent protection plays an important role here, as does a profit-friendly attitude among government authorities.[5] When, for instance, Europe limited the profit potential of its pharmaceutical firms by imposing price controls on drugs, European drug firms immediately and dramatically cut back research from spending 24 percent more than the Americans to spending 15 percent less. Analysts concluded that the shortfall cost Europe some 46 new drugs.[6]

But size, concentration, and exclusive access to profits cover only part of the need. Economy-wide innovation, the record also shows, calls for that additional, less directed, element in which large numbers of diverse economic players work on applications. All the scientific and engineering effort in the world will produce limited innovation without this more chaotic dimension, in which firms and individuals, some larger, some smaller, combine new technologies and practices with old and apply them to a wide range of commercial opportunities, some high-tech, some low-, most having little to do with the original research or technology. As much as the process demands some way for researchers to keep their findings to themselves, it also needs flows of information to foster the efforts of this diversity of market innovators, which, as they strive to outdo each other, build on insights gleaned from a wide variety of unrelated and often unscientific parties—entrepreneurs, suppliers, customers, even competitors.[7]

Innovative success, then, can only emerge from a marriage of these opposites, the directed R&D and the more chaotic "lateral" developments,[8] as they are called. These "spillovers,"[9] some analysts contend, are the main means for technological advances to spread into every aspect of economic endeavor and do more to promote efficiency and productivity and help the economy cope with changing economic environments than the R&D itself.[10] The failure of the once scientifically advanced but highly centralized Soviet Union speaks loudly to this point. If the system fails to support a tension between these powerful countercurrents, the innovative effort will fail either to produce basic technological advances or to benefit from them commercially or in productive efficiency.

Even an area as prosaic as the development of cable television illustrates. The basic research work for television technology occurred in the laboratory during the 1930s and 1940s. Large corporations, in concert with government, made the first applications for the mass market. But it took individuals and smaller firms, using much lower-tech applications, to solve the problem of bringing the broadcasts to remote, difficult topographies. They captured the electronic impulses with a well-placed tower, then cabled them into remote valleys in mountainous regions. The practice was established for literally decades before others, even less technically oriented, saw that cable had many richer commercial applications by allowing an operator to control programming and charge for it separately.[11] By applying long-existing technology in a new way they expanded a simple idea into a huge industry that met a previously unanticipated consumer need and, importantly, provided new sources of employment to millions otherwise displaced from jobs in older, less viable industries.[12] The commercial insights offered by cable then prompted others to apply existing advances in radio technology to challenge the cable model with satellite TV.

The same pattern emerged from the extremely high-tech, defense-based research efforts of the Cold War and of the Space Race. Miniaturization was one aspect. The well-financed, top-down efforts turned to miniaturization to reduce the weight of payloads for the relatively weak rocket boosters of the 1950s and 1960s. It was, however, much lower-tech business and production people who found the commercial applications of this new technology to consumer electronics, to reduce physical bulk, and therefore the cost of shipping, and for productivity innovations never considered by the National Aeronautics and Space Administration (NASA) engineers who did the original work.[13] Combined with applications of other space-based efforts to send and receive a clear radio signal, miniaturization permitted the telecommunication revolution, which then, with further unanticipated applications, led to mobile telephones.[14] Other aspects of defense and space research also found a remarkable array of commercial spillovers unintended and undreamed of by the R&D effort—lasers, for instance, hundreds of uses for microfibers, even a transfer of torsion bar suspension systems from tank design, for which it was originally developed, to trucks, buses, and railroad cars. Even the Internet originally aimed exclusively at defense research.[15] And these are only a few examples.

The saga of Japanese-American semiconductor competition offers a different perspective on the same patterns. Though the United States invented computer technology in the late 1940s, and dominated the industry for the first three decades of its existence, the Japanese in the 1980s gained ground by making new applications of existing technologies. By the end of that decade they dominated half the global industry, while the American share had shrunk to just 35 percent. The government in Washington responded with calls to adopt what it thought was the Japanese approach of top-down government direction. But the Japanese had never really made a major research effort. Their success came from new applications of existing technologies. The eventual American response had the same character. While Washington fulminated, smaller American firms, with no explicit intention of beating the Japanese, used their close relationships with their customers to capitalize on the growing interest in chips designed around specific needs. The Japanese, stuck in their original applications, lost out to this newer, more tailored American effort. By the end of the 1990s American firms dominated more than half the global industry again, while the Japanese retained barely 20 percent.[16]

Of course different business cultures manage this innovative tension in different ways. America has experienced its greatest success through a plethora of small firms and start-ups that can spot the great variety of market applications that are often overlooked by the larger firms and government efforts that do the essential original research. It seems that in America, once the innovators grow large enough, they become complacent,[17] and however much research they do, their approach often actually encumbers the process of finding applications, a task that largely falls to smaller firms.[18] The Germans, by contrast, seem capable of achieving this dispersion of ideas within industrial conglomerates. They depend heavily on state assistance for basic research and development,[19] but manage nonetheless, through different divisions of large firms, to make the wide range of productive and commercial applications. The Japanese seem to have found a middle way. They pursue the research and innovative path along separate branches of a single firm, sometimes located in distant parts of the globe. In America alone Japanese firms have 174 stand-alone research operations.[20]

Evidence of this diverse process emerges even within individual firms. A study of a large multinational pharmaceutical firm (that the researchers kept nameless) uncovered a centralized, concentrated, top-down R&D effort. Much like government-coordinated programs, it brought together the best available talent from both its American and European operations. To gain the most from the myriad potential applications that management knew existed (but knew that they could not identify at headquarters), the firm presented the advances, whether in new products, distribution, or production techniques, to all branches, leaving their application to local managers. Whether located in Europe or in the United States, those branches that kept to the hierarchical, centralized model used for the basic research made fewer applications than those branches that cultivated a more networked, open environment that was receptive to communication among management, professionals, researchers, and workers. So, too, the branches that advanced this cross-fertilization through good and open relations with suppliers and customers showed more innovation than those with less open and controlled relationships. Even interchanges with competitors, the research showed, helped advance innovation.[21]

Applying These Lessons

This oft-repeated picture, sometimes with different specifics but always with the same general features, can guide future efforts to promote innovation. Because centralized, top-down direction, whether from government, large firms, or universities, is critical, government can do much through coordination and straightforward allocation of research monies. In addition to targeted grants it can further promote the process through tax incentives, low-cost loans, administrative relief, and other such inducements. All these incentives are well known. In a less active but equally critical way, government can further encourage firms to take the risks implicit in research by ensuring that it does nothing to deny innovators the profits from their private efforts. In this regard it should actively protect intellectual property and patent rights, avoid confiscatory tax regimes, price controls, and anything that mandates the sharing of technologies.

But when it comes to the networking and applications side of the process, the picture changes radically. Here government and sometimes large, centralized corporations can often misdirect or block progress. The naturally concentrated, centralized nature of government and larger firms is, more often than not, ill suited to recognize the always diverse and often elusive array of commercial and productive opportunities.[22] At this stage the authorities would do best to step back and try not to interfere but instead avoid practices that might impede the communication and commercial experimentation that is integral to it. In particular the authorities need to resist the heavy direction and regulation to which they are prone and which, often unintentionally, stand in the way of this admittedly chaotic process. Of course a complete list of regulations and policies that might facilitate or impede would go far beyond the scope of this or any single book, but the record offers general guidelines, nonetheless.

In this regard licensing rules and regulation become areas of danger. Often designed with no thought to innovation, but simply to keep track of business or ensure certain levels of competence or capitalization, they can frustrate the development of new commercial applications or approaches to production. In particular licensing and regulation can block commercial experimentation by limiting entry into some industries sometimes so thoroughly that they constitute the grant of near monopoly to already established firms. Environmental, labor, safety, and financial regulations can also impede this desired innovation. Obviously such licensing requirements often serve critical societal needs that government cannot and should not abandon. The idea is to maintain these protections but at the same time avoid interfering with innovation by crafting and administering the regulations to allow as much networking, commercial development, and experimentation as is feasible.

The biggest difficulty here is that most of these obstructions are inadvertent. They aim, appropriately, to protect people, the environment, disadvantaged classes of society, and so forth. They seldom consider the effect on innovation. But intentions often mean little to practical effect. Environmental rules, for instance, might impede the establishment of a wind farm for electricity generation, perhaps because the turbines injure migrating birds, or their preferred location is the habitat of a small, endangered species. The same holds true for any number of regulations, national and local. The needs of innovation, of course, do not necessarily trump environmental or other legitimate concerns, but the economy's needs should at least weigh into the calculations of regulators, especially as the pressure to cope with globalization intensifies.

Some instances are remarkably simple, making them seemingly easy to remedy. Take the example of a businessman who sees an opportunity for gain by placing a nail salon in an airport waiting lounge or railway station. To establish his business this entrepreneur must deal with at least three layers of government: the licensing authority that has jurisdiction over nail salons, the port authority that runs airports or railway stations, and their respective security authorities. Each has a valid desire to protect the public. But though the salon may raise no fundamental issues, these authorities have the power to make this commercial idea a reality quickly or slowly or block it altogether. To be sure, the salon may seem trivial to the economy's general innovative needs—certainly it has no association with the advance of technology—but it would nonetheless provide a superior service to eating junk food out of boredom, which would remain in place anyway. It would also create additional jobs, perhaps for those who lost theirs to foreign competition.[23]

Often unintentional impediments grow out of labor regulation and custom. Flexible labor practices are a great asset to innovation. They allow business to adjust more readily to changing economic conditions and foster change within the workforce to suit the needs of the unfolding economic environment. Inevitably cultural differences among countries and regions leave much in this area inaccessible to policy. American workers, for instance, are far more willing to relocate than their European counterparts,[24] a factor that has facilitated America's more complete adjustments to globalization.[25] But if culture changes only slowly, effective policy and practice can still promote some of the desired flexibility. For a start, protecting workers' rights without resorting to rigid rules on hours, hiring, and firing can maintain needed and desired humanitarian safeguards yet still encourage flexibility. The difficulty that, for instance, European employers have in laying off workers makes firms there reluctant to hire, keeping Europe's underlying unemployment problem more severe than America's and its businesses less willing or able to experiment with new products and techniques that might demand new hires.[26]

French retail zoning rules shed an entirely different light on this same matter. When France imposed strict restrictions on large-scale retail establishments in the 1970s, they no doubt only intended to protect the visual aesthetic of the rural environment and the livelihoods of small proprietors on the French equivalent of Main Street.[27] Whatever their intent, these rules also cut France off from the retailing innovation that in America made it possible to absorb many manufacturing workers otherwise displaced by globalization.[28] Even much smaller compromises than those made in America could have proved significant. One study concluded that France could increase employment 10 percent simply by reverting to the original pre-1970 rules.[29] No one would want to disfigure the exquisite French countryside with strip malls or the Gallic equivalent of Walmart, but it is doubtful that the authorities in Paris even considered the ill effects of the retailing rules on commercial innovation and employment. As with the other rules and regulations, the innovative requirement should not trump aesthetics, but it does warrant consideration in the policy equation.[30]

Hindrances to innovation can weigh heaviest when governments extend subsidies. Always well intentioned, sometimes aimed at individuals, sometimes at firms, industries, or geographic regions, subsidies come in all shapes and sizes across different countries. There are tax abatements, wage supplements, low-interest loans, regulatory relief, price supports, and even the granting of monopoly rights. Invariably these are justified on the grounds that they help rectify the impact of some economic reverse, often the adverse effects of globalization. Regardless of their specific nature or their justification, subsidies interfere with innovation on at least two counts. By allowing firms and individuals to avoid needed adjustments and innovation they reward intransigence and passivity. By taxing the rest of the economy to finance the subsidies they burden those people and firms in the economy that have shown themselves willing and able to make the needed innovations and adjustments.[31] Because the uneconomic, inefficient operations that subsidies support raise costs generally, they burden the economy overall. What makes all the effort still more regrettable is that it often comes to nothing, since other nations often retaliate when faced with subsidies elsewhere, and wipe out any advantage.

A detailed list of the many subsidies across the globe is hardly necessary to illustrate their negative effects. Just a few will serve. One prime example is the huge support Europe gives its exporters by excusing them value-added taxes. Because this tax otherwise falls on the value added at each stage of production, Europe's tax subsidy allows its exporters to sell at prices significantly below those in the domestic market, a meaningful edge against foreigners who have no way of avoiding the taxes imposed by their own governments. This concession, however, also relieves these exporters of the motivation to seek those efficiencies that would enable them to compete otherwise. The concession also burdens Europe's other taxpayers, who have to make up the deficiency in government financing to the tune of several billion euros a year.[32] And for all this misdirected support, the Americans have erased much of Europe's export sales edge by giving loan guarantees and by excusing their exporters U.S. taxes equal to those that they pay abroad, also at a cost of billions a year.[33] Each, then, has discouraged innovation while canceling the other's hoped-for advantage and at such significant cost that both sides presently are battling over their respective subsidies at the WTO.[34]

Making subsidies still more unsatisfactory is the fact that the little good they do comes at huge expense to the rest of the economy. Agricultural subsidies, for instance, according to the Organisation for Economic Co-operation and Development, cost the world's developed economies the equivalent of some $300 billion a year in taxes alone. Because these subsidies typically come through price supports, they also burden household budgets with higher grocery prices. That burden is estimated at 10 percent in the United States, 42 percent in Europe, and 100 percent in Japan.[35] In the European Union this combined cost amounts to a dollar-equivalent expense of $200,000 a year for each agricultural job presumably saved by subsidies. America's sugar subsidies cost an exorbitant $800,000 a year for each job saved.[36] And the pattern repeats with more or less drama for the long list of other subsidies on grains, fabrics, metals, petroleum, and exports generally. Even if the strain were less extreme the justification in jobs saved would still leave unanswered questions about whether the monies might be better used to help people and firms adjust.

Humanitarian concerns complicate assessments of subsidies to individuals. But understandable as it is to want to help workers hurt by economic reverses, including foreign competition, money flows from the government nonetheless do just as much harm as subsidies aimed at companies and industries. However the worker assistance arrives, it still allows recipients to avoid or postpone making necessary adjustments to their skills and, to that extent, it delays the economy's innovative response to unfolding economic circumstances.[37] No one advocates turning a blind eye to the legitimate needs of such people, most of whom were hardworking, tax-paying citizens before their circumstances changed. As with industry, however, the counterproductive nature of subsidies raises questions about whether the funds might be better spent in ways that facilitate personal innovation and adjustment.

The record on such endeavors is decidedly mixed. It does make clear that blanket, long-lasting unemployment and welfare benefits do harm on two counts. Not only do they postpone worker adjustments or excuse them altogether, but by effectively encouraging extended periods of debilitating idleness they also do considerable social and individual harm.[38]

The United States has tried to avoid these shortcomings with its trade adjustment assistance (TAA). This program provides generous assistance to workers and firms set back by foreign competition, at least by some standards, including direct cash supports, tax credits for unemployed workers to buy health insurance, and wage supplements for workers over 50. But unlike past subsidies, TAA tries to encourage personal innovation and adjustment by insisting that its beneficiaries use the retraining and relocation services it also offers.[39] Well short of the "revolutionary" answer to the ills of globalization, to which some of its more ideological proponents refer,[40] the program has nonetheless contributed materially to advancing America's adjustment to globalization.[41]

Denmark, and to some extent Germany, too, have made similar moves in a European context. Noting both America's relative success and the expense involved in Europe's generous, blanket unemployment and welfare subsidies, the Danes, who have pioneered the effort, have made an effective compromise with their "flexicurity" program. Flexicurity offers generous support for displaced workers, but to ensure that it does not substitute for efforts either to find alternative employment or retool skills better suited to the new economic environment, it maintains stricter eligibility standards, reduces the duration of benefits, and includes workfare elements. Further, flexicurity encourages workers to find other, even low-paying jobs by subsidizing their wages for as long as they also remain in training programs where, presumably, they will gain skills suited to unsubsidized, higher-wage employment.[42] Though also well short of revolutionary, Denmark's approach appears to reinforce the arguments in favor of the sort of humanitarian relief that also encourages people to gain new skills, helping both them and the economy adjust.[43]

Training and Education

Removing or reducing needless impediments is, of course, no easy task. Each nation, province, state, and locality will need, within its own cultural and historical milieu, to review its tax system, its regulatory structure, its subsidies, and its benefits programs, not to abandon those policies but to weigh their benefits against the costs to innovation and adjustment. Even if such efforts were to achieve great success, however, they would only partly meet the challenge faced by these economies. Each nation, province, state, whatever needs also to ensure that its workers, the young and those displaced from older industries, acquire skills suited to the future—for their sake, obviously, but also to ensure that business has the workforce it needs and, just as important, to disarm protectionist impulses. Such efforts must be sufficiently attractive to overcome workers' natural tendency to remain attached to industries in which they have spent their formative years and in which they would like to remain, even though those lines of work have become obsolete or have changed beyond recognition.[44] And since this future will demand a generally more sophisticated workforce,[45] these economies, in addition to training, will need to educate their populations more effectively at all levels.

In some rudimentary ways markets throughout the developed world have already begun to meet these needs. Japan, for instance, has gradually let go of its once seemingly universal lifetime employment.[46] The growth of employment agencies in a nation that once appeared not to need them has been nothing short of miraculous. Japanese who have lived abroad universally note, on their return, the ubiquitous presence of advertisements for such agencies in newspapers, on billboards, and in the Tokyo subway.[47] The United States, and to a lesser extent Europe, have seen a marked rise in what are called producer service industries, which provide skilled or semiskilled labor to firms on a short- or long-term basis, allowing firms to adjust staffing as market demands dictate and quickly find the skills they need. In the United States over the past couple of decades such services have grown almost three times faster than overall employment.[48] Meanwhile the American National Association of Manufacturers has pushed to upgrade training schools, going so far as to try to standardize curricula at community colleges.[49]

Ultimately training efforts will have to go much further. They will need to involve corporations, singly or in partnership with government, colleges, universities, community colleges or their equivalent, and private technical schools. All should have an increasing incentive to step up to that demand: government, to relieve the strain on the public purse; business, to create a pool of employees with useful skills; and individuals, to enhance their career opportunities and incomes. The direction, fortunately, is clear. Employers, at least outside each economy's subsidized sectors, have made their needs known through lobbying, chambers of commerce, and direct pressure on schools.[50] Guidance also emerges in the United States from the 3.4 percent average annual growth rate in new patents during the last 20 years and the 8.6 percent annual growth in new trademarks.[51] The needed skills are also evident in the 1.6 percent average annual growth in new business establishments, especially since, as the Census Bureau notes, each has a more specialized focus than in the past. The change is so powerful, in fact, that the bureau during the last decade has increased its catalogue of major occupations almost 20 percent.[52]

But while these clear changes indicate which skills are needed, the actual training will prove more difficult. There is, however, guidance in past training programs, both the successes and the failures. Certainly the developed economies have tried a wonderful diversity of training programs over the years and decades. The United States has made efforts on both the federal and state levels, as well as through independent vocational schools, many with considerable pedigrees, smaller community colleges, and a raft of specific company programs—all with varying results.[53] Germany, Austria, the Netherlands, and the Scandinavian nations are known for well-established apprenticeship programs to equip workers with marketable skills.[54] Japan seems to rely mostly on company-sponsored training programs, no doubt a relic of the nation's original commitment to lifetime employment,[55] though that commitment has faded in recent years, as have the once omnipresent and successful vocational training schools that were a part of company-sponsored training.[56]

The findings relating to this vast array of strategies are decidedly mixed. Some statistical work has discovered a positive impact of training, or retraining, on ultimate wages.[57] Other research points to the low proportion of displaced workers who secure additional employment, coupled with the probability that such workers ultimately have to settle for much lower wages than they earned in their former jobs.[58] In many countries private vocational schools have produced results, but not all researchers think the returns to the effort are satisfactory.[59] Even the great successes of the German, Dutch, and Scandinavian apprentice programs seem to have been restricted to the young. Though these programs have gained credit for their more equitable income distributions than exists in the United States, for example,[60] they have exhibited very limited success in retraining more mature, displaced workers. Nor have Germany's once highly praised retraining efforts, through union and local chambers of commerce, done very well[61] or Japan's nonresponse to the training setback delivered by the demise of the lifetime employment system.[62]

In the United States much of the success to date seems to lie with much narrower, company-based efforts. Carrier Corporation, for instance, has garnered accolades for the high percentage of workers that it placed from a retraining effort it established on closing its air-conditioner plant in Syracuse, New York.[63] Grumman similarly had success with its retraining after closing plants on Long Island,[64] as did General Electric when it has closed plants.[65] Some state efforts in the United States also report good results. South Carolina's retraining program has seen a demonstrable rise in the ultimate earning power of its participants,[66] and even the chronically beleaguered auto and general manufacturing state of Michigan has had success retraining laid-off auto and other manufacturing workers.[67] For all these successes, a detailed Canadian study of results across several countries found so many shortcomings that it recommended a complete reorientation of Canadian policy away from training of any kind.[68] Still, even the most discouraging failures can offer insight into what does and does not work.

Two important contributory factors to successful outcomes, the record seems to show, are scale and consistency. On this count the United States and Japan will need to correct the paucity of public funds that each dedicates to training and retraining, certainly compared with those of Europe.[69] But it is not just overall funding that matters. The highly politicized nature of training seems to create a destructive on-again, off-again pattern in public programs. Still more destructive is how political interference seems to keep much of the allocated funds from actual training, because of bloated administrative overheads, sometimes related to overbearing accountability rules, or even unrelated, politically favored projects that anomalously get attached to the authorizing legislation. Typical is a state-run training effort in California that, despite a seemingly lavish budget, had such a paucity of monies for actual training that its modern airline mechanics course used vintage Second World War aircraft.[70] The OECD reports that such problems are widespread and impair the success of training programs in all its member countries.[71]

The record of the past also indicates a need for focus. Commonly throughout the developed world, training efforts, particularly when publicly funded, undermine themselves by trying to do too much for too many at once. They strive, for instance, to assist displaced workers in the same program that also tries to improve the lot of society's disadvantaged. Though both efforts have legitimate social purposes, the two groups of people have such fundamentally different needs, objectives, and contexts, making joint training inappropriate for either group. One group or both fail. Studies that parse the results in these mixed groups according to race, age, past education, and past job experience typically reveal startling success among the retraining enrollees but an overall record of failure because the disadvantaged seem to get little out of the courses.[72] Taking each group separately and tailoring the effort for it surely would help. Indicators suggest also that future programs for displaced workers might achieve still greater success by focusing on still more particular orientations. Older workers, for instance, seem to respond better when training programs aim to keep them in work without having to relocate, even if it requires them to shift industries, whereas younger workers respond better to the opposite stimulus.[73]

Motivation, too, the record shows, has played a crucial role. Results, invariably and not surprisingly, are best where enrollees attend regularly and stick with the program to its conclusion. They acquire genuine skills, and the programs indicate success by any number of measures.[74] The motivation to inspire such diligence is explained, in part, by the fact that some of the most successful training efforts are run by companies for their existing employees. There, with particular job advancements in mind, workers commit themselves to the effort with less ambiguity than in more general programs. Obviously, displaced workers cannot fit directly into such employer-specific operations. Still, programs established for displaced workers could devise comparable ways to motivate their enrollees, perhaps with penalties for poor attendance and dropping out, and rewards for those with good attendance who finish the course.[75]

General education is a supplementary consideration. The evidence from existing and past programs, their successes and their failures, shows a clear link between education and motivation and, consequently, successful training,[76] probably because better-educated workers with presumably a better understanding of the broader picture are more realistic about their circumstances than their less well-educated kin. Along with other motivational tactics, then, future training and retraining programs might do well to concentrate on better-educated workers or, alternatively, to include a general educational upgrade along with the more technical aspects of a course, an enhancement that might also meet business's expressed dissatisfaction with the general cognitive and educational skills of graduates from public school systems.[77]

The more successful efforts clearly incorporate these various guidelines, if sometimes unintentionally. Denmark's flexicurity, for instance, has produced superior results, no doubt through the link in the program between wage subsidies and continued enrollment in training. A half-dozen New Jersey community colleges and technical high schools have devised other ways of achieving results by focusing on students with common objectives and backgrounds and motivating them by teaming with local industry to design curricula with direct links to specific potential jobs. They have increased scale, too, by getting the associated firms to enhance funding for the training programs. Similar efforts have proved successful in California. IBM has developed its own national program along these lines.[78] In North Carolina, Guilford County motivated its enrollees and focused its effort by linking its community college's training programs with the entry of new industry into an area, registering high placement rates at higher salaries.[79] Canadian policymakers were so impressed with these successes that they have linked all future retraining to regional development plans that include general schooling, community development, and the in-migration of business.[80] Since most community colleges and technical schools still pay little heed to employer needs,[81] there would appear to be ample room for further improvement along these lines.

If the outcomes of these experiments have created a somewhat blurred blueprint for future training efforts, the needs in higher education are even subtler. Here, the obvious call is for more scientists and engineers. Washington, other governments, and the commentariat have made it frequently,[82] no doubt drawing on memories if not the nostalgia for great research efforts in the past.[83] Typical is Washington's recent call to "train many thousands more scientists and engineers."[84] Government frets over the low level of interest in science and engineering among the nation's youth, and expresses concern that developments in science education in China and India will staunch the flow of engineers and scientists who come to study and stay in the developed economies,[85] plugging the gap in the domestic workforce. Such an emphasis is clearly reasonable, drawing, as it does, on the huge advances created by the great government, university, and industry partnerships of the past, and the powerful research centers that they built—Bell Labs, RAND, and DARPA (Defense Advanced Research Projects Agency) to name just three of the most prominent.[86]

But this scientific emphasis, as should be clear from the earlier discussion on innovation, meets only part of innovation's requirements—an important part to be sure, but only a part. Because innovation across the economy also requires parallel, lower-tech, diverse applications, the whole process also demands educational support of a very different kind than that associated with scientists and engineers. Instead of the intensive study, knowledge, and thought demanded of the technically proficient, a more extensive way of thinking suits those who would apply technologies of all vintages to previously unimagined commercial and production applications. For innovation's sake the universities need to support this kind of lateral thinking as well.

These considerations would seem to support frequent arguments for the practical value of liberal as well as technical education. Doubtless this debate will never reach resolution. If innovation is to flourish, however, universities will need to produce broad-based graduates, as well as scientists and engineers. Innovation needs executives, entrepreneurs, and managers who can at once grasp the broad character of technologies but also can ferret out the needs and tastes of their existing and future customers. These graduates will possess what researchers in the area of innovation call "life skills," such as communication, critical thinking, and an ability to cooperate,[87] what others characterize as "non-cognitive" skills.[88] Perhaps, in the broad analysis, studies in literature, history, art, and other traditional liberal arts subjects support the innovative process as much as those in physics, chemistry, and electrical engineering.

This amorphous but critical demand on higher education may well play to America's incredibly diverse system. No doubt inadvertently, it may have given America some of its innovative edge over Japan's or Europe's more hierarchical and focused efforts.[89] Even America's government-funded research allows for more room for diversity. Because the governments of Europe and Japan provide their universities with blanket subsidies, they tend to pressure the whole curriculum to accommodate public objectives. Because Washington funds specific projects, its control extends only to them, leaving more latitude to the university as a whole.[90] Still more generally, America, with more than 2,600 accredited colleges and universities, and 1,800 community colleges, some private, some state-supported, each with a different charter, vision, and mix of programs,[91] cannot help but create the diversity of thought that is essential to innovative progress. Of course it takes great wealth to support such a system—something, perhaps, only possible within America's vast economy[92]—but even so the returns to this seemingly chaotic mix are clear.

Even if efforts to promote innovation, adjustment, and retraining were wildly successful, they would still prove inadequate to meet all the challenges of globalization. To begin to do that and more thoroughly dispel protectionist pressures, efforts must also seek financial reform that can tame the destructive boom-bust cycle to which globalization has so thoroughly contributed.

13

Helping Finance Cope

Even more urgent than the economic adjust- ments is the need to break the link between globalization and destructive boom-bust financial patterns. Aside from wrecking the prosperity of every economy, developed and emerging, these cycles inflame ever more destructive protectionist impulses. The dreadful fallout of 2008–09 may make financial problems seem almost intractable, but remedies in this area are actually more straightforward than in the areas of innovation, training, and employment. Some will emanate from regulatory change, but, because regulation can only go so far, the most promising remedies lie in changing the way in which central banks make monetary policy.

Hope Is Not a Strategy

Quite aside from steps that the United States and other developed economies might take to mitigate financial volatility, there is always the hope that China and other emerging economies will obviate the need for such steps by changing their currency policies. If they were to cease their seemingly tireless efforts to keep their currencies cheap to the dollar, as described earlier, they would no longer have to buy dollars in the volumes that they have to date and still do. Since they would then have less need to shift a huge volume of funds into developed markets, a major cause of this volatility would lift, and neither regulators nor central bankers in the developed economies would need to work so hard to offset the effects.[1]

Efforts to promote such a change have, in fact, characterized American and European policy toward China for years now. Separately and together, diplomats from the United States and the European Union have leaned on Beijing to allow its yuan to appreciate. Admittedly most of the diplomatic pressure was aimed more at trade than at alleviating financial pressures. It is not even apparent that American and European negotiators realized that there was a financial dimension to China's policies. They wanted primarily to blunt China's export prowess. In their desired scenario, a rising yuan would increase the price of China's goods on global markets and thereby enable domestic producers in America and Europe to compete more effectively with Chinese imports in their own markets, and perhaps find more opportunities for American and European exports in China and other emerging economies. Whatever their motivations, their efforts have borne little fruit. China's fundamental need for exports has prompted a remarkable degree of intransigence on Beijing's part toward any serious suggestion of yuan appreciation. Even when China has appeared to yield and allow the yuan to rise on foreign exchange markets, its actions have had more of a cosmetic than a substantive character.

The historical picture certainly leaves little reason to expect a substantive change in Chinese policy anytime soon. In fact, Beijing has made its position painfully clear over and over again for almost two decades. The extent of Beijing's commitment to a cheap yuan first became evident early in the Clinton administration. When treasury undersecretary Larry Summers publicly sought yuan appreciation in 1993,[2] Beijing, instead of yielding, did the opposite. Only six months after Summers made his plea on behalf of President Clinton, China devalued the yuan massively and then established a policy of holding it rigidly at that low value. Even as that decision led ultimately to the Asian crisis of 1997,[3] Beijing refused to move and made no secret of its intention to hold the yuan relentlessly at that low level opposite the dollar for the foreseeable future.

Despite Summers's conspicuous failure, President Clinton kept up the pressure on Beijing, but to no avail. The best that he and his celebrated treasury secretary, Robert Rubin, got was Beijing's promise not to devalue the yuan further during Asia's crisis in the late 1990s. China clearly never even considered an upward yuan revaluation[4] and continued to hold the yuan cheap to the dollar.[5] Far from acceding to Clinton's or Rubin's importuning, Beijing actually got Rubin to persuade Tokyo to keep up the value of its yen and so sacrifice some Japanese export advantage to China's benefit, making it that much easier for China to compete globally with Japanese products. Chinese premier Zhu Rongji no doubt enjoyed the humiliation of American policy when he publicly thanked Secretary Rubin for his efforts with Japan,[6] as though he were an agent of Chinese policy. As Clinton left office, in 2000, the yuan still had not moved.[7]

George W. Bush picked up the frustrating effort where Clinton left off and met with the same Chinese intransigence. Two treasury secretaries failed. First Paul O'Neill demanded yuan appreciation. Beijing stuck to its cheap yuan peg. Some even suggest that O'Neill's failure led to Bush's so-called Friday Morning Massacre, in which he summarily fired O'Neill and National Economic Council chairman Larry Lindsey.[8] But Bush's next treasury secretary, John Snow, met with no more success, at least at first. In 2003 he made the administration's policy clear, stating bluntly that American policy toward China sought "the establishment of a flexible exchange rate regime."[9] Beijing simply held firm to its cheap yuan peg.[10]

The president and Secretary Snow did, however, make some small progress after 2005. Bush started that year by describing China's currency policy as "highly distortionary," calling for a "substantial alteration" within six months.[11] This time his rhetoric received unwanted but nonetheless substantive support from congressional threats. When Senators Lindsey Graham and Chuck Schumer threatened to impose a 27.5 percent tariff on Chinese imports unless Beijing made some currency accommodation,[12] it got Beijing's attention. The People's Bank of China finally allowed the yuan to rise from its rigid, cheap peg to the dollar. But Beijing's action did more to disarm the two aggressive senators than change anything fundamental. The yuan rose only very gradually, so slowly, in fact, that a frustrated Secretary Snow complained loudly about the "disappointing pace of reform of the Chinese exchange rate regime."[13] Underlining how little China intended to do, then Chinese premier Wen Jiabao responded to Snow's criticisms with his own blunt statements, asserting that China would adjust the yuan's value only according to "an independent, controllably gradual process."[14]

Even in the face of tariff threats Beijing probably only conceded this little bit because its competitive position in Europe had improved. By the time Snow, Schumer, and Graham threatened in their respective ways, the dollar had declined some 14 percent against the euro from its inception.[15] Because the yuan fell along with the dollar, China had gained enough of a competitive pricing edge in Europe to substitute export sales there for any lost in America to a modest yuan appreciation against the dollar. Of course the change also brought European diplomatic pressure that intensified as the euro continued to rise against the dollar and the yuan. In 2007 an august European delegation, including French president Nicolas Sarkozy, European Central Bank president Jean-Claude Trichet, and other EU luminaries, visited Beijing to press for active yuan appreciation. Beijing did not say no, but neither did it move from its very gradualist policy.[16] China's leadership maintained its position as Bush's third treasury secretary, Henry Paulson, echoed everyone else's demands.[17] Then, under economic pressure during the 2008–09 recession, Beijing underscored its continuing commitment to its cheap yuan policy when it stopped all further yuan appreciation, resorting for a time to a rigid peg only slightly above the original one.[18]

When the Obama administration came into power in 2009, it picked up right where Bush had left off. Treasury Secretary Timothy Geithner actually took a rhetorical step beyond previous administrations and labeled China a "currency manipulator" in written testimony during his Senate confirmation hearings. Though for diplomatic and legal reasons he withdrew his blunt language, the mood of his position lingered.[19] China, however, did not relent and continued to hold firm to its new and effective, if informal, currency peg of the time. Even months into the new administration, when President Obama traveled to Beijing to meet China's leadership and, as he said, "raise the [yuan] issue,"[20] Beijing refused to budge. Indeed, rather than concede, a spokesman for the PBC described American importuning particularly, and Western demands generally, as "ridiculous" and an example of "gangster logic."[21]

Meanwhile Beijing continued to work hard to keep the yuan remarkably cheap to the dollar. Indeed, after all the pressure from three American presidents, at least four treasury secretaries, and a phalanx of European leaders, the yuan in 2013 remained more than 10 percent cheaper against the dollar than before China's initial 1994 devaluation,[22] giving Chinese exports, for all the rhetoric, pressure, and maneuvering, that much more of a competitive pricing edge than they had 16 years earlier. Since the yuan, even back then, was cheap to the dollar, some have put its present competitive edge at 25 percent[23] and some, especially in Europe, have argued that the yuan's undervaluation verges on 40 percent.[24] Even as Beijing has recently resumed yuan appreciation, its very gradual path will take a long time indeed to relieve the situation.

Regulation

If China, then, is unlikely to make a substantive move, control of this cycle will fall to domestic means. Beijing, and by implication other authorities in other emerging economies, can be expected to continue keeping their currencies cheap to the dollar to one degree or another, and, as in the past, continue buying dollars on foreign exchange markets, and continue investing them in the American and, to a lesser extent, European financial markets. And those liquidity flows will continue to feed the boom-bust financial patterns unless something is done. In seeking alternative remedies, developed economies will inevitably turn to market regulation. Particularly popular in the aftermath of the 2008–09 financial crisis, regulation is a perennial favorite with government. But it has limits and can only do the job, so to speak, in concert with an altered approach to monetary policy.

The claim for regulation hinges on its ability to constrain the excesses of financial players. This is a tall order in any financial environment but especially in the face of the continuing, massive liquidity flows from overseas. The inevitably blunt character of regulation and law can no more create ethical or prudent financial behavior than it can ensure such behavior in any other aspect of life. Prudence and ethics may be even harder in the financial realm, where they are not only hard to enforce but also difficult to define. So while regulation is essential to discourage fraud and abuse, to ensure that banks and other large financial institutions have a sufficient cushion of easily accessible financial capital to sustain smooth operations in the face of losses, and to promote a degree of confidence that facilitates financial dealings, regulation as an answer in this circumstance has severe limits. No matter how strictly applied, it can neither identify where dangers lie nor block excesses when markets become awash with liquidity, as they have done and would continue to do under the influence of foreign currency policies and foreign financial flows.

It speaks volumes about regulatory failings that so many of the financial excesses exposed during 2008–09 were already illegal and were ultimately exposed only by the crisis, not by regulators. Ponzi schemer Bernard Madoff, after all, broke laws of very long standing, yet grew his illegal business to over $100 billion under at least four presidents and many more chairmen of the Securities Exchange Commission (SEC). Madoff might still have his illegal business today had not the financial collapse prompted his investors to try to withdraw funds, thereby exposing his fictions about their investments. The SEC and other forms of government oversight were so far from uncovering and preventing his and other such abuses,[25] that Madoff, even as he built his illegal business, was frequently consulted by Washington on financial developments, quoted as an expert in the financial media, and for a time was president of the American Stock Exchange.[26] It hardly seems likely that new laws that make already illegal activities doubly illegal would do more to prevent such behavior in the future.

Rules to keep financial institutions within prudent limits, though a welcome addition to market safeguards, also can only do so much. In

2006, for instance, the Bank for International Settlements (BIS), in consultation with regulators in 120 countries, laid out 25 new, stricter rules for bank regulation and supervision. These included carefully crafted limits on licensing, ownership, capital adequacy, risk management, consolidated systems, ways of dealing with problem situations, divisions of tasks, and cross-border responsibilities.[27] Called Basel II, after the headquarters city of the BIS, this raft of new rules and regulations was heralded as a bulwark against financial disaster.[28] Yet less than two years later the whole elaborate structure failed even to slow the financial panic of 2008, though every major financial institution in the world at the time had fully complied with it.

Even something as seemingly straightforward and universal as capital adequacy ratios have severe limitations. Such rules appear in almost every regulatory regime. They insist that banks and investment firms set aside a portion of their assets in a safe, easily accessible form so that these institutions can draw on them to meet their obligations in difficult markets. That access, regulators argue, can help these institutions maintain smooth operations through market fluctuations and so sustain confidence. These are necessary and reasonable strictures, but in practice they can guard only against the most minor and routine reverses. To function adequately and to provide credit to support economic growth, financial markets have to process such vast flows of funds that even seemingly modest market reverses can wipe out even hefty amounts of ready cash holdings. When, for instance, Bear Stearns failed in 2008, then–SEC chairman Christopher Cox noted that the company complied fully with all regulatory standards and was in fact $2.0 billion overcapitalized by the Basel II standards.[29] To enlarge capital ratios sufficiently to guard against any eventuality would force financial institutions to idle so many assets that they would lack the resources needed to support economic activity—hardly a palatable policy option.

The regulatory solution to this boom-bust problem has still more general drawbacks. Rules, by nature, are inevitably shaped by past experience. Though that past may offer a general guide to the future, its specifics seldom do. As is already clear, each bout of financial excess has carried very different specifics, even if it has had the same general contours.[30] It simply asks too much of anyone to anticipate what particulars will surround the next boom. Even ex–Federal Reserve chairman Alan Greenspan, a man who clearly enjoyed cultivating a wizardlike persona, nonetheless acknowledged: "Identifying a bubble in the process of inflating may be among the most formidable challenges."[31]

A glance at the last three cycles of boom and bust makes Mr. Greenspan's point. Regulation responded to the Asian Contagion crisis by stressing floating exchange rates, because the Tigers, with their fixed rates, were caught out by China's sudden devaluation. That regulation also expressed suspicion of the intimate connections among firms, and between them and governments. Such "crony capitalism," as it was called, had been prevalent before the Asian Contagion (and still is today) and was considered somehow responsible. Because the Tigers had trouble getting new credit when their short-term loans matured, the regulatory response stressed the use of longer-term loans.[32] All this might have prevented the next unfortunate cycle, if it had these same specifics. In the event, such safeguards did little to temper the next boom's focus on technology and the Internet. When in response to that bust regulatory emphasis adjusted yet again, it stressed investment diversification to avoid the excessive concentrations that had just hurt so many investors.[33] To thwart overoptimistic corporate reporting, Sarbanes-Oxley rules actually made it a criminal offense for executives to overpromise.[34] Though all this regulation was desirable, in principle, none had any applicability to the specifics of the subprime crisis and the consequent calamities of 2008–09.[35]

The regulatory solution suffers in a similar way to the infinitely protean nature of financial arrangements. The greater the access to liquidity, the greater the temptations for financial people and institutions to sidestep regulatory niceties or even the broader dictates of financial prudence. The fertile imaginations of financial firms and their employees, without a thought of lawbreaking or deception, find ways around rules, regulations, and even the principles that they themselves espouse. Though most financial players conservatively steward the monies in their charge, even in the face of all the enthusiasms associated with excess liquidity, it only takes a small minority to feed the destructive boom-bust cycle. For the regulatory agencies to guard against such behavior they would need almost as many investigators as there are financial actors, and each regulator would need to be at least as clever as those that he or she investigates. Even then such regulatory and investigative legions could do little if financial firms manage, as many do, to evade the spirit of the rules without actually violating their letter.

Sometimes regulations that are a help in one environment make matters worse in another. The Basel II rules, for instance, deserve some of the blame for problems that arose in the 2008–09 meltdown. Basel II reasonably required banks to hold more financial capital against riskier loans as does its successor, Basel III. In the circumstances of 2008–09, however, when loans that formerly looked secure suddenly began to look precarious, this rule forced banks to raise additional monies to add to this safety net of reserve capital.[36] Under normal circumstances such a requirement would demonstrate reasonable prudence for a single institution. But when the rule forced hundreds of financial institutions to sell assets suddenly—and almost in unison—into an already chaotic market, it put asset prices under still greater downward pressure, creating still more losses, and weakening already precarious institutions still further. In their desperate attempt to get the most from their asset sales, financial institutions raised the capital demanded by Basel II by selling their most salable and hence best assets. But then, to cover the new, lower average quality of their loan portfolios, they had to raise still more capital, forcing still more asset sales, putting still more downward pressure on markets, and imposing still more losses in a rule-enforced downward spiral that for a while fed on itself.

The only way that a regulatory regime could overcome these diverse difficulties would be to shift from explicit rules and give its administrators and investigators the flexibility to cope with new situations. But while such a regime might overcome some of today's inadequacies, it would nonetheless bring a different set of problems. Having dispensed with defined rules, the discretion given enforcement agents would invite an inconsistent application of oversight and, by implication, an inequitable application. Indeed, it would be remarkable if a group of investigators so empowered could apply oversight consistently, either from one investigator to the other or from one case to another, even with the same investigator involved. And since it would necessarily be run by human beings instead of saints, discretion would inevitably risk considerable abuse as well. Even in ancient Rome, Juvenal (55–130) asked, *Quis custodiet ipsos custodes?* (Who is to guard the guards?),[37] a question always applicable to those with even well-circumscribed power.

Even if regulators were incorruptible, it is questionable whether they would have any greater ability and motivation to identify risk in uncertainty than do the managers of financial firms. After all, those firms, having invented the products, know them well, and it is they, not the regulators, whose existence hinges on a successful navigation of the risks. Indeed, most regulations implicitly admit that practitioners have the greater insight. When, for instance, the U.S. Treasury made suggestions for risk-control guidelines, it asked the financial firms themselves, not the government agents, to "identify firm-wide risk considerations (credit, business lines, liquidity, and other) and establish appropriate limits and controls around these considerations."[38] The Treasury warned firms to avoid "incentives that could threaten the safety and soundness of supervised institutions,"[39] but left it to company managements to determine what those incentives were. While such guidance sounds eminently reasonable on the surface, it says little more than that firms should know their business, keep track of risks, and proceed carefully. Most firms, even when taking horrible risks, believe that they are doing just that. There is, then, no more control now than most firms always thought they had.

On a still more fundamental level lies the question of what many risk-control experts refer to as "moral hazard." Many financial institutions, particularly the larger ones, are confident that regulators, on guard to protect the system, would help them work out problems when they arise rather than risk financial collapse. This kind of government support achieved prominence with the bank bailouts in 2008–09, but it was in operation even earlier. Such confidence however, tempts financial firms to proceed with less regard for risk than they would have had they no expectations of support and feared bankruptcy.[40] An elaborate regulatory regime may banish other, even more fundamental cautions by convincing the consumers of financial services that government protections against fraud, inadequate funding, and other such risks relieves them of the need to do the research for themselves, something they would do otherwise to assure themselves of the financial health of the institutions and individuals with whom they do business.[41] In this effect on both business and finance, the regulatory oversight increases, rather than decreases, risk.

None of this is to suggest, of course, that the authorities abandon all oversight, much less that they cease their efforts to expose or prevent fraud or other abuse. Their rules offer important guidelines. And just the threat of an investigation is embarrassing enough to discipline most firms, not to mention the prospect of legal action. The whole array of capital and leverage ratios, risk-weighted assessments of bank assets, background checks on employees, licensing issues, and many more standards too numerous and too detailed to list here,[42] remind managements of the elements of sound financial management that they should never forget. For all these virtues, it should be apparent that even the most carefully wrought regulations would prove inadequate in the face of the boom-bust cycle stoked by globalization during the last two decades. Even Harvard Law professor, now senator, Elizabeth Warren, once chair of the Congressional Oversight Panel for Economic Stabilization, member of the Executive Council of the National Bankruptcy Conference, first head of the new Financial Consumer Protection Bureau, and major proponent of government oversight and control, admits "regulations, over time, fail."[43]

Monetary Management

In the face of regulation's severe limitations, and Chinese intransigence, only the management of monetary policy remains as a viable mechanism for controlling globalization's contribution to the harmful boom-bust financial cycle. Here there is real promise, since it is clear that the want of remedial action by the Federal Reserve and other central banks has played a significant role in past crises.[44] With sufficient will, central banks and monetary boards all over the developed, and indeed even the emerging, world have the ability to control overall levels of liquidity in their markets. They have the power, after all, to create and destroy the underlying amount of money flowing through their financial systems, and with that power have long had the ability to offset, or "sterilize," any excess funds flowing from abroad. Indeed, this ability is so widely recognized that even undergraduate economics and finance textbooks discuss sterilization actions, sometimes at length.[45] Of course each central bank has its own preferred mechanisms to inject or withdraw liquidity, but the technicalities mean less than the objective and the will to secure it. International Monetary Fund research suggests that even the central banks of smaller economies with much smaller financial markets can control such matters to a remarkable degree.[46]

Given that this ability to sterilize foreign funds flows has always existed, and given the severe damage done by the boom-bust pattern in the past, questions naturally arise as to why the Federal Reserve and other central banks have failed so far to employ this capability. Without knowing the inner thoughts of central bankers, any answer is by nature speculative. Perhaps the urgent need for such sterilization is only now clear in retrospect, or central banks cynically have bowed to political pressure to keep economic and financial booms running. More likely, the past failures to sterilize foreign funds flows have stemmed from a misplaced and exclusive focus among central bankers on economic conditions, most particularly inflation, to the exclusion of financial considerations.

Such biases are certainly understandable. Though the boom-bust cycle associated with globalization has lasted for some time now, it is nonetheless a relatively recent phenomenon in the grand scheme of things. Most of today's central bankers and other policymakers spent their formative years fighting destructive bouts of inflation during the 1970s and early 1980s, when at times general price levels rose at rates over 18 percent a year and contributed to near-stagnant growth as well as major increases in unemployment.[47] They have naturally looked for danger from those quarters instead of from financial volatility. But if the world's economies are to avoid boom-bust cycles in the future, each central bank will need to shed such biases and conduct monetary policy to take such liquidity flows seriously into consideration.

The record of former Federal Reserve chairman Alan Greenspan offers an ideal illustration of the common policy biases and where they have led. Though in 1996 he alluded to the "irrational exuberance" of financial markets, he did nothing about it and went on to ignore the Internet boom entirely. Rather, he consistently shaped monetary policy and explained it solely in terms of inflation. In 1999, for instance, just before the implosion of the Internet stock bubble, Greenspan made no mention in his congressional testimony of the overwhelming liquidity then sloshing through the financial system,[48] or to the dangerous rise in stock prices. Instead he explained the Fed's decision to raise interest rates entirely in terms of how continued rapid "gains in employment" would "engender inflationary pressure."[49] What is remarkable was not that he considered inflationary pressure but that it was his sole concern. Years later, as the real estate bubble began to expand, Chairman Greenspan again ignored the liquidity flows emanating from China. Instead his anti-inflation focus led him again, in congressional testimony, to paint a uniformly benign picture of global events, arguing that "the integration of China and India into the global market" would "tap" the "world's productive capacity" and so create a "favorable inflation performance."[50]

Neither was Greenspan alone in his biases. The first president of the European Central Bank (ECB), Wim Duisenberg, began his term, and the ECB's existence, without a mention of international liquidity flows but with great stress on the need to "build a track record of low inflation."[51] Again there is no faulting his inflation concern. The fault was that it was his only concern. Indeed, the founders of the ECB shared this singular focus, making its sole mandate to control inflation, ignoring even the health of the real economy, let alone a consideration of foreign liquidity flows.[52] Similarly the Bank of England states bluntly, in its major public descriptions of itself, that it "sets interest rates to keep inflation low," and, though it also talks about a "stable financial system," it makes clear its regulatory approach in this regard has little to do with any obligation to control overall levels of liquidity or the effect of foreign funds flows.[53]

Whatever the reason or excuse for past neglect, it will have to end. Central banks will need to take a new approach or risk still worse boom-bust cycles as globalization intensifies. If the tools for maintaining fundamental liquidity levels are straightforward enough, the change will require a new, broader way of thinking about monetary policy that not only maintains the sensitivity to inflation and economic conditions but also adds a consideration of market actions, including liquidity flows. More than just broader thinking, however, the new approach to policy will also require new decision-making rules.

Until recently the almost exclusive inflation focus of central bank decisions made policymakers depend heavily on forecasts. Central bankers had to assess the unfolding economic situation in terms of its inflation prospects. They then had to fine-tune policy according to those forecasts, raising and lowering interest rates according to whether that situation might result in more or less inflation one, two, or more years distant. Not only does such an approach entirely ignore the control of current market liquidity and the boom-bust cycle, the reliance on forecasting even makes the inflation control problematic. It demands an almost godlike prescience. Such demands may explain why so many central bankers cultivate an Olympian demeanor, but the need nonetheless makes policymaking parlous, even in the best of circumstances.

Against such a problematic background an attempt to replace this approach with one that focuses on fundamental liquidity levels could offer several benefits. Primarily, of course, it would help with the crucial need to control market liquidity directly and thus the ill effects of globalisation and international capital flows. But beyond its ability to calm financial volatility, such an approach might also do a better job on inflation control as well. Since inflation is essentially a monetary phenomenon, tending to rise when the system faces an excess of money and liquidity and abate when those excesses abate, the focus on fundamental liquidity levels might ultimately do a better job on controlling inflation than the present, forecast-based approach. Further, a commitment to manage liquidity would make policy decisions more transparent and predictable than in the present, forecast-based approach. By helping those in finance and business plan more effectively, this greater transparency would add both to market and to economic stability as well as efficiency. Still further, by reducing the vagaries of forecasting in policy and putting it on a more technical, measurable basis, the change would also make central banking less vulnerable to political pressure. If the changes deprive central bankers of that wizardlike status that they so clearly enjoy, the loss would be a small price to pay for the potential benefits.

Without such change there is little that can moderate the boom-bust financial cycles that have come to plague developed and emerging economies alike. On the contrary, intensifying globalization will only exacerbate these destructive cycles, harming all economies and adding force to the dangerous protectionist backlash. Even if some interpretation of these suggestions manages to forestall or at least blunt the effect of these financial problems, reform in the emerging economies could improve matters still more, for them and for the developed economies.

14

Reform in Emerging Economies: China

Emerging economies will have to make still more fundamental changes than will the developed economies. Their export-driven growth models, though hugely successful so far, and in many ways essential for continued prosperity, will nonetheless face increasingly severe limits, forcing them to seek alternative, domestically based growth engines. They will need in the process to broaden their economies, integrate their various parts in untried ways, and raise wealth and income in huge regions and segments of their populations that to date have hardly experienced the efficient, trading aspects of a modern economy. China, in particular, needs to make such alterations, broadening its economic efforts to include its so far neglected hinterland. The effort will require radical and difficult adjustments in Beijing, including an increased openness to imports, a relaxation of centralized direction, the promotion of more fluid and open financial markets, and, if only for economic reasons, a turn toward a more liberal political order.

An Urgent Need to Change

It might appear from the remarkable strides made to date, by China and other emerging economies, that change is unnecessary. After all, export-led growth in an increasingly globalized environment has during the past 20–30 years lifted some 500 million people out of poverty in Asia alone, reduced, according to the United Nations, the proportion of the world's population living in extreme poverty from 30 to 20 percent, and raised to an impressive 90 percent the proportion of the world's children now attending primary school. The migration that has accompanied globalization has raised the flow of remittances from immigrants back to their poorer homelands to levels that now exceed all official international aid flows by a factor of three.[1] China has already surpassed Japan as the world's second-largest economy after the United States, and India may soon surpass the United States as the second-largest trading economy after China, two developments that the media have viewed with much alarm.[2]

Amid these triumphs, the emerging economies remain needy. China, for all its impressive absolute size, still has depressingly low per capita income flows, the equivalent of only $7,600 a year, less than one-quarter of Japan's, and only about one-sixth that of the United States.[3] Some 36 percent of China's population lives on the equivalent of $2.00 a day or less. And China is by no means alone in these sorts of disappointments. More than 75.6 percent of India's population still lives in comparable poverty. Brazil, which by many standards has integrated the sectors of its economy far more thoroughly than other emerging economies, still has 12.7 percent of its population at this oppressive poverty level.[4] By comparison, Singapore and Hong Kong, both of which have effectively completed the kind of economic integration now needed by emerging economies, have brought their per capita incomes up to, and their poverty rates down to, levels of Japan and the developed West.[5] Continent-sized China may have little in common with the city-states of Singapore and Hong Kong, but their success nonetheless should alert Beijing to the great advantages of broader economic integration.

Even if Beijing were uninterested in its people's economic welfare and so chose to ignore the poor per capita income picture and other such deficiencies, its export-based approach to growth faces clear limits that will force China to broaden its economy anyway. The model, simply, is no longer sustainable. To continue producing rapid growth, as it has, China's exports would have to make impossibly large further inroads into foreign markets. China already commands some 12 percent of global exports. Further growth, at even a fraction of its past rapid pace, would require that China gain command of upward of 20 percent of global exports in just the next few years.[6] Even if the developed world were not already resisting Chinese export dominance, such an outsized command of markets would certainly generate considerable resistance. It would also undermine itself, since dominance over such a huge percentage of foreign sales would take so much production, wealth, and income from these other economies that they could no longer afford to buy China's output.

China's heavy export dependence is already facing troubles of a different kind. Like so many low-cost producers before it, the Chinese economy's remarkable export success has begun to undermine its own foundation by putting upward pressure on wages.[7] China's failure to integrate the rest of its economy with the coastal export effort has only exaggerated the pressure by leaving large portions of the population more or less isolated from these coastal industries. Factory wages generally have risen 8 percent or more a year,[8] far faster than America's nominal wage gains of 2–3 percent.[9] Adding in new mandated benefits that Beijing hopes will quell social unrest has increased overall worker compensation at an annual rate of 10 percent.[10] Matters are still more intense in export industries, where Chinese industry reports 9 percent more vacancies than there are job applicants. The competition for workers has pushed up wages in the sector at an annual rate of 17.8 percent in just the past couple of years. More skilled workers have done even better. Honda Motor Company's operation in China reports 24 percent pay rises, while Foxconn, an electronics maker, reports a doubling in labor costs at its Shenzhen complex.[11] Toy producer Hasbro expects the cost of the goods it sources in China to rise 14–15 percent a year.

If the rise in Chinese costs still leaves a huge wage gap between China and developed economies, it presents a problem nonetheless. China's rising wages already have tipped the competitive edge toward other, still lower-wage emerging economies, such as Vietnam, Pakistan, Bangladesh, and Indonesia, where wages average about one-third those in China.[12] Governments as well as producers in these economies are more than eager to gain market share at China's expense. This low-wage competition is expected to close 60,000–70,000 factories in China's Pearl River Delta.[13] China's labor-intensive and once profitable shoe manufacturing industry has all but closed.[14] Rather than gain the export share that its growth model demands, China seems set to lose a portion of it to other, still lower-cost, emerging economies.

China's peculiar demographic trends will compound these problems. Because Beijing has insisted for years, in fact since Mao Zedong's premiership, that families have only one child,[15] the economy will ultimately face a general shortage of younger workers. The flow of 15- to 24-year-olds into the workforce will slow by 30 percent over the next 10 years.[16] Of course China will avoid the demographic extremes faced by Japan and the developed West. Even 20 years from now China will have almost 4.5 people of working age for every person aged over 65, compared with 1.8 in Japan and 3.0 in America.[17] But if China's aging population fails to constrain its economic growth potentials as sharply as the aging process will in Japan, Europe, and America, it will still have an adverse impact. China could, by some estimates, have added a cumulative 10 percent to its economy's growth rate through 2030 if it had pursued a two-child policy. What is more, these strict demographic averages doubtless understate the coming labor supply and wage problems of China's export machine, as older people are less likely to migrate to the coast.[18]

Well aware of these difficulties, Beijing has begun to rethink the one-child policy. The city of Shanghai already actively encourages its residents, when they can within the law, to exceed the one-child limit.[19] As an offset, Beijing has begun a program to encourage older people to remain in the workforce,[20] much as was discussed earlier as a path for the aging economies of Japan and the developed West.[21] But so far Beijing retains the one-child rule.[22] Such demographic considerations, on top of already eroding wage cost advantages and China's inability to command the kind of dominance in export markets that its former growth path would demand, make a policy shift away from export-led growth and toward economic integration and broadening a stark imperative.

Beijing has other, equally important reasons to pursue a broader economic integration. Bringing China's hinterland into its economic mainstream, thereby exposing it to modern business efficiencies and, more thoroughly, to trade within the country as well as with the rest of the world, would enable China to use its natural, financial, and, especially, human resources more completely and efficiently than it does now. As economist David Ricardo explained, open trade and financial flows, whether between countries or within countries, allow each sector or region to focus on what it does best and so maximize the total value of its output. Incomes and wealth follow that value upward.[23] Even beyond generally improved living conditions, especially in China's presently impoverished hinterland, a diversification of economic endeavor away from its present export emphasis would also offer a welcome corrective to the widening income and wealth gap between the exporting coastal cities and the rest of the country.[24] The social tension that has emerged as a consequence already forces Beijing to spend more now on internal security than even on its military.[25] Meanwhile a broader-based economy would also have greater stability and resilience than the present export-based economy has, while increased wealth would raise China's geopolitical stature, something that Beijing clearly desires.

A brief backward glance at the trauma of 2008–09 illustrates at least some of these potential benefits. Had China had a broader, more integrated domestic economy at the time, one that depended for income and growth as much on domestic consumers and businesses as on exports, it surely could have coped better than it did. When the global recession of the time dried up export markets, export workers, who lost their jobs, instead of finding themselves without options, could have turned to more domestically oriented occupations. Those who returned to their hometowns would have found more attractive employment opportunities than was the case. At the very least a broader-based economy would have left China in a better position to offer displaced export workers a safety net that, at least temporarily, would have sustained levels of consumption and permitted them to stay where they were, in the coastal cities, instead of having to return to the interior, as many did, with all the attendant hardship, social discord, and further economic disruption that movement caused[26] Overseas recessions would still have had their impact, but this would have been less acute than was the case while China's economy was so heavily export-dependent, as indeed it remains.

China's 2008 emergency economic stimulus demonstrated from yet another perspective the huge potential of broader-based development. When Beijing initiated its huge 4.0 trillion yuan spending program, largely on infrastructure, it aimed to stabilize the faltering economy by creating substitute jobs for those lost in exporting.[27] To a degree it did that, though not enough. Still, in other important respects the stimulus program exceeded expectations. By improving roads, bridges, rail links, and public spaces across the country, it connected previously isolated villages and regions with the coast and with the world generally, and in so doing it opened, no doubt inadvertently, previously unexplored commercial opportunities across China. Each dirt road that received a macadam surface literally opened a path, previously blocked, over which outlying regions could bring to market their agricultural produce, handicrafts, and other products in which they had some comparative cost or other advantage. As income rose in the wake of such improved opportunities more local business developed as well. Multiplied over countless towns and districts, the economic response went far beyond the initial jobs at which the stimulus aimed, surpassing even official, typically optimistic expectations.[28]

What China Needs to Do

Beijing knows it has to change. No less a figure than former premier Wen Jiabao has characterized the country's export-led economy as less strong than it seems on the surface, using expressions such as "unbalanced," "uncoordinated," and "ultimately unsustainable."[29] The premier began to plan for needed adjustment by building on the 2008 stimulus with more infrastructure spending in the interior hinterland, including an additional 19,000 new rail miles by 2015.[30] Then-President Hu Jintao connected land reform to the needed broadening effort. He pointed out that by consolidating China's 730 million tiny farms (with an untenable average size of only 1.5 acres) the country can improve agriculture's commercial viability and raise incomes in the interior[31] while at the same time freeing labor to work in industry of all kinds. By improving agricultural efficiencies and consequently reducing food costs, the move aims also to relieve strains on household budgets and offer consumers a more expansive, if not necessarily lavish, lifestyle. Beijing wants also to see more domestic production of the components used in its export industries. Though this effort clearly still has an export focus, the development will invite some domestically oriented efforts as well and reorient the country's capital spending flows in ways that can eventually support entirely domestic ventures. Already this broadening of industry has begun to sever the close link that previously existed between China's imports and its export effort.[32]

China's new leadership, when it came to power in 2013, endorsed these plans and was, if anything, still more explicit then the previous administration. Its plan, released in February of that year, set out point by point how government proposed to divert economic effort away from exports toward domestic development, with particular efforts to bolster the consumer sector by improving wages for workers, especially in the provinces. Premier Li Keqiang made clear that prosperous urbanization would drive "domestic demand."[33] Under this new plan, farmers would get greater property rights and state-owned firms would divert 5 percent of their profits to finance a social safety net. The expectation is that 1–2 percent more of China's economy would shift to consumption by 2015, the income gap between the wealthy and poor would narrow, while Beijing would go on a campaign to root out corruption. Statements by China's new president, Xi Jinping, in March, shortly after the report's release, gave it and its general effort his important stamp of approval.[34]

But Chinese policy will have to go much further than these plans. Since such changes will demand that China abandon long-established policies, the effort will not be easily. People will only reluctantly abandon practices and perspectives that once worked so well, propelled double-digit annual rates of real growth, brought China's GDP to second place in the world, and sparked speculation over when it would overtake the United States and move into first place.[35] Though the need for change is nonetheless evident, China's government functionaries and business interests will only reluctantly turn away from such success. Those many who benefit from today's pro-export policy biases will fight to keep them in place, while the consumers and smaller businesses across the country that would benefit from change will remain a diffused group with little direct power.

Making change even more wrenching, the application of the export-based model during the last 20-plus years has made China's economy more export-dependent than ever. China today, by some estimates, dedicates fully 80 percent of its economy to exports and to the development of export-oriented industrial infrastructure.[36] Even the country's more general infrastructure spending concentrates mostly on port facilities, rail links, and other shipping support for exporters. Meanwhile the restraints imposed on Chinese consumers and on domestically oriented economic endeavor have kept consumer spending to a mere 33 percent of the economy,[37] a remarkably low proportion for any economy. Even Japan's consumer sector accounts for 57 percent of its economy, while in the United States the consumer sector dominates upward of 70 percent of the economy.[38]

Beijing seems to know that it will have to make the adjustment regardless of how painful it will be and however much internal resistance it will face. The plans to date are only the most tentative first steps. To accomplish its goal, China will have to go on to remove the outsized benefits long enjoyed by Chinese exporters, the special enterprise zones near major coastal cities, the pro-export tax rules, and the administrative as well as credit biases.[39] Beijing will also need to end today's political control of credit, which inevitably directs it to export industries. In its place, China's leadership will need to allow freer credit flows that can support promising domestic projects, and perhaps even consumers, in addition to effective exporters. Perhaps most challenging of all, Beijing will need, at least gradually, to abandon its long-established, export-oriented practice of keeping the yuan cheap on foreign exchange markets. The objective of such change would not be to penalize exporting. Exports should continue to dominate in China for a long time to come. Many of them need no special support and can compete effectively without currency manipulation. Rather, the intention would be to allow economic resources of all kinds to flow unfettered and on an equal footing to the Chinese consumer and to domestic development, as well as to exporters.

Government would also need to remove long-established impediments to consumer spending and domestically oriented enterprise generally. Like Japan's export-oriented economy before it, China's devotion to overseas sales has led it to view both consumer spending and domestic development as competitors to exports for economic and financial resources, and, like Japan before it, has suppressed both sorts of activity. In addition to the effects of the cheap yuan policy, China has also blocked imports of consumer goods through an array of tariffs, quotas, and spurious health and safety rules. By shielding local operations from external competition, these actions have allowed domestic operations to remain inefficient and less than customer-friendly. This array of influences has discouraged the consumer and purely domestic development by at once degrading what is on offer domestically and by making travel, retail shopping, and other such consumer activities expensive, inconvenient, and unattractive. Little wonder, then, that the consumer side of China's economy has failed to develop. Policy has reinforced the effect by limiting the size of retail facilities and by discouraging other means to make retailing efficient and attractive.[40]

Lifting import restrictions would do much to unwind these biases. Simply allowing a greater flow of products from abroad would promote consumer spending by increasing the choices available to China's consumers. And by inducing an expansion in retailing to meet that demand as well as inspiring domestic producers to rise to the competitive challenge, China would find yet another engine of economic growth. Beijing could further enhance the effect with more general infrastructure development across the entire country, not just to support exporting from the coastal cities. As with the 2008 stimulus program, such an initiative would create commercial and productive opportunities in the hinterland, where previously these were neither attractive nor even feasible. Such changes would build on themselves, too. As incomes increase in these regions, they would spur still more such development and, what is more, convince China's business talent, which to date has had a singularly export focus, to include domestically oriented opportunities in their calculations. Flows of credit by state-owned banks to domestically oriented enterprises would reinforce the process, as would the development of private lending institutions.[41]

Beijing's effort to broaden and integrate the economy would also want to encourage a more expansive nature among China's famously thrifty population. Freer consumer spending would at once provide a new element to the growth equation. And, as business moves to accommodate the new, more expansive Chinese consumer, the new pattern would also encourage the development of domestically oriented business across the country. At present Chinese households save an enormous 25 percent of their overall income,[42] far more than the 3–4 percent or so of American households and slightly less in Japan.[43] But even if part of this tremendous savings rate is clearly culturally driven and therefore unlikely to change very fast, policy shifts can still have some effect. Undoubtedly the greater variety of attractively priced goods that would follow from an easing of import restrictions would direct some savings into the spending stream. Improved infrastructure would encourage more travel and more expansive lifestyles, as would a freer flow of credit to households and the retail sector. But Beijing could promote an even more profound change by fostering a greater sense of personal security among Chinese households, financially as well as generally.

Greater access to financial services would help in this regard. Though far from the whole story, part of the root of China's high savings rate lies in the paucity of financial services available to the population. With limited sources of credit or insurance,[44] certainly compared with their counterparts in Japan and the developed West, Chinese households must maintain a relatively large pool of savings just to cope with life's contingencies—the new roof after a major storm, the sudden expense involved in taking advantage of a child's educational opportunity, a temporary period of unemployment. Because households in Japan, Europe, and the United States can meet such contingencies with insurance or credit, they need to save less. If Chinese households had even a small proportion of that kind of access to financial support they would in time see less need to maintain such large savings flows and feel a lot freer to spend from current income. Equally, a more effective pension system, offered by the state, private firms, or both, as in the developed economies, would further nourish a sense of personal financial security, as would a better social safety net, either through a welfare system or unemployment insurance, or both.[45]

A better, broader education system also would contribute to a sense of security as well by giving people the confidence of having career and income options. Here, China already has achieved a great deal, sending some of the country's best students abroad to study in the West's best universities, and raising the number of undergraduate and graduate students at their own schools more than 30 percent since 1999. The authorities in Beijing clearly intend to build on this effort, to help the Chinese consumer and for other reasons. Every five-year plan emanating out of the Communist Party's annual National People's Congress includes more for education at every level, primary, secondary, and tertiary. But for all these efforts most of the population in China's hinterland has only limited access to education,[46] as it does to pensions, public or private insurance, or financial services generally. This huge shortfall suggests that even modest remedies have great potential to produce results in increased consumer spending and in domestic commercial development.

Political change, too, would do much to further such possibilities, though it most certainly would create a special challenge for the authorities in Beijing.[47] At the simplest level the government could crack down on the corruption and petty tyrannies of local party officials. Resentment against such people, the party that supports them, and the sense of helplessness in the face of this corruption and arbitrary power featured large during the rioting 2008–09. Much of that violence centered on party officials, including assaults and murder, and even lynchings.[48] Much of this feeling remains near the surface. Even in recent, relatively more placid times official Chinese sources admit to two or three significant incidents a month.[49] But more important, Beijing could cultivate a fundamental sense of personal security were it to encourage its officials to show greater respect for the rule of law and for human rights as well as minority rights, and allow more representative government.[50] All would ease the perception among people that they live in an arbitrary universe that demands from each individual as large a financial cushion as is feasible. Though a tonic for society as a whole, for the consumer, and for domestic development, such political shifts would prove problematic indeed in today's China, and are at best a long way off.

A change in China's currency policy would be much less difficult from a political perspective but probably even more beneficial to the ultimate objective of broadening and integrating that economy. China has held to the cheap yuan policy for years not only to promote exports, as described in earlier chapters,[51] by pricing Chinese goods attractively to the rest of the world, but also to impede the flow of imports by making the rest of the world's products expensive to the Chinese consumer. If Beijing were to allow the yuan to strengthen on foreign exchange markets, it could have the same effect as removing tariffs and other import barriers. Not only would foreign goods be less expensive to Chinese people and businesses, prompting a more open outlook in the Chinese consumer, but by introducing foreign competition, an upward move in the exchange rate would induce domestic producers to seek efficiencies and, importantly, assume more customer-friendly business practices. Still more, a dearer yuan, by allowing Chinese incomes to go further in the global marketplace, would reduce living costs for Chinese households as well as general costs to domestic businesses, thus further enhancing the vitality of the domestic economy.

Helping even more, a change in China's currency policy would enable the country to lift controls on its capital markets and so gain greater ability to underwrite economic broadening and integration. Beijing's present yuan policy forces it to intervene in currency markets to accumulate dollars and so also forces it to control China's financial markets tightly.[52] None of this would be necessary if Beijing were to abandon this currency policy. China would need neither the interventions in foreign exchange markets nor the tight financial controls. With the constraints on finance lifted, lending could support activities throughout the economy according to their commercial promise instead of according to their political suitability, which to date has focused almost exclusively on exports. Especially if Beijing were also to allow foreign firms entry into its financial markets, something it could readily do once it no longer needed tight control, still more credit would flow toward opportunities for domestic commercial development and perhaps even consumer finance.

Such an array of measures would not only help the Chinese people and their economy's overall strength and stability but the rest of the world would benefit as well. Political leaders in the developed nations might well feel some anxiety about a general strengthening in China's economic base and the political and military power that it would bring to Beijing, but the economic returns would more than outweigh such concerns. Business in Europe, Japan, and the United States could only gain were China to liberalize its import policies around its potentially huge consumer market. Indeed, by opening sales and business opportunities in such a vast market, a Chinese economic broadening would address today's destabilizing division of world economies between huge net exporters, such as China, and huge net importers, such as the United States. In so doing the policy change would alleviate much of the trade tension current in the world today, most especially between the United States and China.[53] Prospects of such relief no doubt explain why the world generally—from emerging economies in Latin America, Africa, and the Middle East to the International Monetary Fund—has stressed the need for China to "swing its economy away from exports" and increase "domestic consumption."[54]

A change in China's cheap yuan policy would extend these benefits to global financial markets. China's currency policy, as already described, has contributed significantly to the destructive boom-bust pattern that has so plagued global financial markets.[55] But without a desire to hold down the yuan's value and the attendant need for Beijing to make huge dollar purchases, the flow of dollar investments back to the United States and other developed financial markets would slow. The government in Washington might then lose a ready buyer of its debt, but it cannot continue in recent budget patterns anyway. Meanwhile the changed Chinese policy would spare American and other financial markets the destabilizing floods of liquidity that, as described, have from time to time so contributed to financial volatility. If such a change would spare the monetary authorities in the United States and elsewhere the need to offset such flows, they cannot, as is also already clear, wait on Beijing to alter its currency policy. They need to take immediate steps to control such flows of liquidity.[56] But a Chinese change ultimately would relieve the urgency and much of the strain.

In this connection, the world can welcome China's recent effort to put forward its yuan to replace the dollar as the world's reserve currency.[57] China, of course, has no intention of actually pursuing such a role for the yuan, at least not anytime soon. Because a reserve currency is held universally by governments, banks, and businesses as a store of value beyond the normal needs of trade and finance, it habitually trades at a premium to the price at which it would otherwise settle, keeping up the global price of its goods and services and making export sales difficult.[58] As much as China needs to broaden and move away from its export dependence, and as much as a gradual rise in the yuan's value would help that prospect, China will remain too export-dependent to withstand the shock of a suddenly overpriced yuan for some time to come. Beijing therefore will need to wait an equally long time until its broadening transition is sufficiently advanced for it even to consider a reserve role for the yuan. But if Beijing's talk of reserve status for the yuan is premature, even a little silly, the gesture itself at least hints at Beijing's recognition that in some way and at some time an unwinding of its cheap yuan policy will become necessary, even desirable.

For all that Beijing realizes this fundamental need for economic broadening and integration, its record so far with this transition remains understandably mixed.[59] China's consumer sector and its domestically oriented industry remain underdeveloped. The authorities and the economy clearly can respond only gradually. If China fails to make its gradual change, its growth will first slow and then stall, as rising wages erode its competitive edge globally and its exports experience increasing difficulty enlarging their market shares. A successful transition, even if gradual, will permit continued prosperity, offer relief from festering social problems, lift global trade tensions, and relieve global financial volatility. For similar reasons, and to avoid similar pitfalls, other emerging economies must make comparable changes. They, of course, will make them in different economic, geographical, social, and historical contexts.

15

Adjustment in Other Emerging Economies and the Curse of Oil

However much China differs from other emerging nations, each similarly has to broaden its economy and integrate it more thoroughly, within itself and with the rest of the world. They must do so for the same fundamental reasons, too: it is the only way any of them can maximize their economic potential, sustain growth over the long term, gain stability, avoid social unrest, and contribute to the balance of global trade and financial flows. Some of these economies will have a harder time adjusting than others. The oil exporters in particular will struggle, as oil, in this critical context, is less a blessing than a curse. Other emerging economies, India and Brazil most notably, face less imposing challenges, but even in the best of conditions, they, too, will face difficulties.

The Same Uneven Development

For all the fabulous growth many of these economies have exhibited to date, most, like China, show remarkably uneven patterns of development. All the advances have occurred in the coastal or export areas, where these economies have begun to enjoy huge productive efficiencies and accordingly have seen their incomes and wealth grow 10-fold in a generation. But vast regions and sectors of these populations remain separated from their modern, developed regions and, by extension, from the rest of the world. They often suffer dire poverty, live by subsistence agriculture, even lead nomadic lives, and have little or no economic opportunity.[1] Just as in China, their peoples subsist on a dollar a day or less and remain closer to their country's undeveloped past than anything resembling a modern economy.[2]

Mexico is typical. Though different from China in so many ways, it looks very similar in this respect. It has none of China's intensifying demographic pressure, but its economy, just like China's, is highly uneven. Long before the North American Free Trade Agreement, Mexico had established its own special economic zones along the U.S. border. These have enjoyed special administrative and tax breaks, much like China's special enterprise zones, but whereas China aimed to set up its own firms, Mexico aimed to lure foreign firms. These *maquiladora* industries, as they are called, are, however, functionally the same: they produce for export and are entirely outward-looking. The regions where they have located have become comparatively rich, like China's special economic zones, while the rest of Mexico's economy remains largely undeveloped and effectively isolated. Incomes in these neglected regions have lagged, if they have grown at all, and the people living there continue to suffer the grinding poverty that has long characterized them.[3] Much of Latin America exhibits these same characteristics. Only the parts involved in trade benefit, while the rural populations suffer as though globalization had never occurred.[4]

And, as with China, such grossly uneven, export-driven development is ultimately unsustainable. The potential for social discord is obvious. Even if these emerging economies could repress social problems indefinitely, their export-dominated economic models can only propel rapid growth for as long as they can enlarge their share of global markets. Though easy to do early on in the development process, and with small economies, such relative gains in market share get harder as these exports gain prominence.[5] To the extent that these economies can diversify and generate domestic growth engines, they can expand the limits of their development more reliably than their export dependence allows and secure for themselves the same significant benefits already described for China. The humanitarian motivation for such change is obvious and worth the effort for its own sake, but a broader, more domestically oriented economy would also offer greater stability by removing what today is an outsized relative dependence on foreign markets and foreign economic policies. Still more, success in such an endeavor would realize the economy's full potential by bringing all its economic resources, especially its human resources, to bear, allowing its political leadership to enjoy greater power and stature.

The Case of India and Another Glimpse at Latin America

Though all emerging economies have problems in this regard, some are either luckier than others or more aware of the virtue of economic broadening. India in particular has made more progress in this direction than most. Though only about one-quarter the size of China's economy, and actually slightly smaller than Brazil's,[6] it remains a critical model, since its huge land area and population give it great potential, not least because it is not hampered by China's demographic problems.[7] More than most, then, the direction that India has taken is significant for global trade patterns and the success of globalization. Here, the country's atypical development trends and more open government have already advanced its necessary broadening changes beyond those of most emerging economies, and certainly those of China. Statistically India looks a lot poorer than China, with lower per capita incomes and higher poverty rates,[8] but statistics, especially averages, can be misleading. There is much else about India's development that shows how much further it has moved toward a broad, well-integrated economy, and indicates which directions these other emerging economies need to proceed.

Indian growth and prosperity depend less on exports than China's does. To be sure, India, like China, has promoted exports as a growth engine,[9] but it has not done so nearly as thoroughly. Whereas exports have generated almost 50 percent of China's growth,[10] they constitute only some 10 percent of India's GDP. The 45 percent of China's economy that is involved with trade would show impressive integration with the global economy if that figure reflected an interchange of exports and imports across many economic sectors, but as it is, the whole of that figure reflects exports and only the imports needed to support the export effort. Very little of this global connection benefits China's consumers. By contrast the 20–25 percent of India's economy that is involved in trade does cut across all sectors.[11] The greater Indian balance also shows in its larger consumer sector, some 56 percent of total GDP, compared with China's meager 30-some percent. Though China dedicates far more of its economy to the acquisition of productive equipment and the construction of productive structures than India, 48 percent compared with 34 percent, China's larger effort aims largely at exports,[12] while India's spending encompasses far more domestic industry.[13]

To be sure, India could accelerate its growth rate were it, like China, to focus more on exports and spend more on export-oriented capital goods. It might then lift its already impressive 8.5 percent real yearly growth rate of the past 10 years toward China's nearly 11 percent average real growth pace.[14] But India's slower pace of expansion, by being more diffused, has sown the seeds of more sustainable development once the export growth engine slows, as inevitably it will. Especially since India's development extends into the interior, although in pockets, the country has developed a solid middle class, admittedly alongside its huge underclass, and a comparatively vibrant and widespread consumer sector that also has begun to drive broad-based domestic development. If India's poverty rate is still distressingly high, the country has at least begun to secure the benefits of development and globalization more broadly than has China.

Part of India's advantage in this sphere lies in its unusual development path. Typically development follows the patterns pioneered by Great Britain during the late eighteenth century and by the United States and Germany during the nineteenth and early twentieth centuries. In all these cases the growth of mineral extraction and manufacturing drew surplus labor from agriculture, which enjoyed great efficiency gains from the same sorts of technological advances that propelled mining and manufacturing.[15] Services developed only after the great strides of industrial development were well established. China is repeating this pattern. There service-based growth has hardly made an appearance. Other newly emerging economies show parallels. But India—because the prevalence of the English language allows its citizens to deal directly with the global business community and because of the superior technical education of many of its young—has focused much less exclusively on manufacturing and goods exports than China has, or Britain did so long ago. Since electronics makes it feasible for services to locate away from ports and major railroads, the Indian economy's relatively large services component also has managed to shift development away from the expensive coastal areas, where firms would have had to locate had India followed China's emphasis on goods exports.[16]

It is in large part India's ability to move the modern economy into the interior that has spread the benefits of global commerce across more of the country and promoted relatively more domestically oriented business than in China. The Indian city of Hyderabad is a good example. Some 200 miles from the coast, the city has become a favored location for call centers and other sorts of consulting, both Indian-owned and foreign. The income flows from these businesses have, in turn, lifted commercial activity in the region generally, both consumer spending and the development of locally oriented business. Furthermore, the natural communication and movement between Hyderabad and the capital, New Delhi, both inland cities, as well as outward to the obvious coastal cities, has promoted commercial development along the rail, and especially road, links. Much of it has a domestic, largely consumer focus that is much less evident in China, where the vast majority of modern commerce is coastal and outward-looking and where the workers, mainly migrants, promote little domestically oriented development.

The pattern has already begun to build on itself. Because call centers and other services located in the interior cities have cost advantages over those in the more expensive coastal locations, the firms located there, largely Indian-owned, show greater profitability than comparable operations in the coastal cities, where foreign-owned "captive" outsourcing operations have naturally located.[17] As the competitive edge has become better known, still more Indian firms have either moved altogether to interior locations or have set up branches there, extending still further the spread of modern commerce throughout the country and, along with it, the income growth and the domestically oriented economic endeavor that invariably follows it.

Ironically a part of this head start on broad-based, domestic development may well have emerged as an unintended legacy of India's past, failed development programs. India's old way, which it followed for decades after independence in 1947, took a strict, anticolonial approach. Fearful of foreign economic hegemony, the nation's policy aimed to minimize interaction with the global economy through both high tariff walls and subsidies to encourage firms to develop the usually more sophisticated, capital-intensive industries that India lacked. The approach failed. The nation wasted its limited economic resources on industries in which India simply could not compete. At the same time it needlessly isolated labor-intensive, low-value-added industries that otherwise could have coped well with foreign competition. Worse, these policies discouraged the efficiencies that would have developed in the face of import competition.[18] The effort ran so counter to where natural economic advantages and markets would have taken India that government planners in New Delhi had to impose tight centralized controls to sustain the structure. These, in turn, introduced still more economic ills into the system, including rigidities, bureaucratic abuses, and petty corruption—what the Indians came to call the "permit Raj." The whole ungainly structure so held back the economy that people sarcastically referred to the poor record of that time as the "Hindu growth rate."[19]

When India abandoned this approach, in the 1980s and more completely in the 1990s after the Cold War ended, memories of its failures kept New Delhi from steering industry as actively as Beijing did China's. Though the government looked to exports as an engine of growth, it was reluctant to twist the economy on their behalf, at least not to the extent that Beijing did. Grateful to throw off the permit Raj and all that it meant, India has allowed producers to pursue opportunities more freely and allowed Indian finance to support purely domestic development across a broader geographic area, certainly more than Beijing has permitted in China. Although slower, less focused and directed, growth in India has consequently proceeded more organically than in China. To be sure, the opening of trade prompted India to narrow its economic efforts in some respects and abandon areas where it was ill equipped to compete.[20] Accordingly, the Indian economy increasingly has imported those sophisticated products that once it had tried, ineffectively, to make for itself. Even so, the greater freedom has brought commercial development over a broader geographic region than in China.

This past legacy has no doubt informed an Indian currency policy that has itself contributed to broader development. India, like China, has tried at times to promote its exports by keeping its currency, the rupee, cheap to the dollar. Its rapid accumulation of foreign reserves, especially dollars, during the past 20-some years[21] speaks to active dollar purchases of the sort that would keep the rupee cheaper than it otherwise would have been. But New Delhi clearly has refused to go to Chinese extremes. The rupee has fluctuated over a much wider range than China's yuan, moving some 11 percent up and down from its average, a narrow range by the standards of freely traded currencies but much wider than the rigidly controlled yuan.[22] India's willingness to accept bouts of currency appreciation has periodically brought down the price of foreign imports and, in so doing, improved the population's living standards, contributed to a more vibrant consumer culture, and indirectly encouraged domestic development in retailing in particular but also more generally.

No doubt India's democracy has helped drive this more balanced approach to development. Representative government, for all the political factionalism for which India is famous, or maybe perhaps because of it, has created a strong incentive among the powerful to extend the benefits of development and globalization to as many voters as is possible. Government documents, such as the ruling coalition's *Report to the People,* make that impulse explicit with its aim of "inclusive growth." Moreover, the government has outlined the kind of structural reforms that India needs in order to extend its broad-based development and economic integration. These reforms target the petty corruption and market interference left over from the permit Raj and promote four other critical supports for the broadening effort: improved health care, increased spending on education, the expansion of India's still stunted financial sector,[23] and efforts to refurbish and expand its infrastructure.[24] The first two of these commit to the integration of India's massive underclass into the modernizing economic mainstream. The third aims to give business the wherewithal to capitalize on such steps and turn them into higher incomes and greater wealth.

Some of these efforts are already well established. The previous government more than doubled health care spending, and official plans call for a five-fold increase over the next six years.[25] On higher education no emerging country has had greater success than India. Its graduates have supported the economy's more service-oriented growth model, one noteworthy aspect of which is the remarkably successful Bangalore high-technology area, which, though directly a product of private investment from both domestic and foreign firms, would have been impossible without India's investment in advanced education.[26]

For all this success, further development demands that India make more strenuous efforts with more general education to raise the country's horribly low literacy rate, at "sub-Sahara African levels," in fact.[27] The financial elements of the plan—to put this healthier, better-educated population to work—would benefit if India were to open its doors to foreign firms. These not only would bring financial capital from abroad to bear directly on development, but they also would introduce best practices into India's financial community and so help upgrade it generally. Whether or not such plans can meet India's broadening and integration needs, they at least point India in the right direction.

Some South American economies, Brazil and Chile most especially, have, like India, made strides broadening and integrating their economies. This is hardly surprising, since these countries also began their most recent phase of development after a period of failed anticolonialist policy. From the 1950s to the 1980s development policies, fearful of dependence on the United States, also tried to block interaction with the global economy through high tariff walls and support for heavy, capital-intensive industries for which these economies had little comparative advantage. As in India, these policies ran so counter to market signals that they required heavy, top-down government control of economic activity and investment flows. They failed, as did India's, leaving in many of these countries, Brazil in particular, a legacy of suspicion against the control, economic isolation, and excessive government interference that characterized them. Accordingly, many of these South American countries, though certainly not all of them, have enjoyed a broader, better integrated, more open, less controlled pattern of development than China certainly.[28]

Obviously, there is much that differentiates them from India. Latin America lacks the higher education available in India to promote service exports and to help with broader development in other ways. But like India, these Latin American economies permit businesses to pursue domestically oriented ventures and allow them to procure the credit to support such projects. These economies have also adopted a generally more liberal attitude toward currency management. In Brazil's case, its currency, the real, during the last 10 years has fluctuated over a wide range, from a low of 3.8 to the dollar to a high of 1.6.[29] Certainly compared to China's yuan, this pattern has allowed foreign goods to flow into the country at prices sufficiently attractive to promote a consumer sector and, through its concomitant activity, domestically oriented businesses as well. But there is much still to do. The three steps that India has outlined for itself—health care improvements, education spending, and financial depth—would help these economies, too, but the process has at least started.

The Curse of Oil

If India and parts of Latin America have outpaced China on broadening and integrating their economies, those economies that export natural resources, especially oil, have fallen seriously behind. Though often in possession of great wealth, and therefore seemingly positioned to pursue all sorts of development, they nonetheless seem to face the greatest impediments to developing their future potential. They are consequently the weakest and, ironically, given their power over such a vital resource, the most vulnerable component in the global economy.

Saudi Arabia is archetypical. For all the options that its monumental wealth presumably brings, it has done little or nothing to broaden or diversify its economy or integrate its various elements domestically or with the rest of the world. Instead Saudi Arabia's entire economy revolves around oil. Exports of crude oil account for just about all Saudi sales overseas. Imports have little to do with economic development outside the oilfields, the military, and a few luxuries.[30] The population lives almost entirely off oil, much as the beneficiaries of a trust fund live off their bequest. There is little genuine economic opportunity or incentive to develop talent. The government, which controls the oil, is by far the largest employer. The backward, poorly paid private sector has trouble attracting local talent and needs to import workers from abroad. More than half the labor in Saudi Arabia is performed by non-nationals, largely Filipinos and Pakistanis, while on a more professional level,[31] except for a few titular local hires, European and American "experts" manage the oil inheritance and the financial wealth that it produces.[32]

The result of this thoroughly distorted picture is a fundamentally weak and vulnerable economy. When oil prices are low the Saudis and other oil exporters have no recourse but to cut back on spending of all sorts. When prices are high, they do little to build themselves up but rather live large and, usually, wastefully. Extensive research commissioned by the Gulf States on themselves shows that excess revenues when oil prices rise seldom get directed to genuine economic development but instead get channeled into dubious, if grand, construction projects that, in the report's words, give a "superficial impression of affluence."[33] These projects offer little or no additional economic return. Meanwhile these economies suffer remarkable volatility, rising and falling with the price of crude oil. Consider the disruption to nations dependent on oil sales as the price of a barrel rose from about $50 in 2005 to over $140 in 2008, only to plunge back down to $35 in 2009 and then turn up again.[34] No economy can cope well with such income volatility. It certainly can neither plan nor build effectively for the future. The United States, for all the decades it has decried its oil import dependence, suffers much less because so much of its economy generates income from unrelated sources.

Testifying to their lack of genuine economic development, productivity in these oil-rich economies, despite their great wealth and seeming investment advantages, has suffered. Worker output per hour in Saudi Arabia and the Persian Gulf States, including the oil sector, has grown a mere 1.0 percent a year since 2000, compared with 1.5 percent in both Europe and the United States, 5 percent in India, and 10.5 percent in China. The richer the oil exporter the worse the productivity record, presumably because these economies are the most unstable. Saudi Arabia, the United Arab Emirates, and Kuwait have productivity growth barely above zero, while less well-endowed Bahrain, Oman, and Qatar, though they have had low productivity growth by world standards, have enjoyed advances more than five times those of their better-endowed neighbors.[35]

Even when these oil producers realize that the oil reserves, vast as they are, eventually will run out, they still have trouble embracing broad-based development. Their answer for such an eventuality is government-controlled investment funds, the so-called sovereign wealth funds (SWFs), which place a portion of today's oil income into overseas investments on which they plan to draw at some future date when the oil runs out, like a national retirement program. Though seemingly far-sighted, the approach only substitutes one form of inherited wealth for another. No real economic activity, no effort to develop the means to produce for themselves, seems even contemplated.[36] Indeed, the behavior is antithetical to economic development, much less broad-based development. Switching one endowment for another still leaves the country with no production of its own and all but entirely dependent on the output of other economies for what it needs.

If instead these states were to use their wealth, or a portion of it, to invest in their own economic development beyond oil, they could do much better for themselves than such overseas investment funds. They would, in fact, secure for their populations the same long-term economic benefits that broadening in China or India or other emerging economies can: realization of their full economic potential, relief from a major source of social discord, and greater economic stability. To be sure, some of these economies, even with the best will and insight in the world, would have fundamental problems with broad-based development. Saudi Arabia maintains a closed culture for religious reasons, making it difficult to relinquish the control offered by a single product in government hands. Beyond that, Middle Eastern climate and geography present impediments. Agricultural possibilities are limited. The oppressive climate hardly encourages enterprise generally. Such physical constraints no doubt have held back even the Gulf States, which have much more open and enterprising traditions than Saudi Arabia. Dubai, for instance, has had only middling success with the billions it spent on tourism.[37] (It did not help Dubai's plans to create a glamorous, romantic getaway that its laws forbid kissing in public.)[38]

Many of these countries also face huge political impediments to economic broadening efforts. Beyond religious matters, the authoritative regimes typical of many oil exporters need the control offered by a single source of wealth in their hands alone. Because that arrangement gives them immediate and direct access to their economy's income and its wealth, it excuses them from ever having to court their people. They hardly even need taxes. The government finances itself through oil sales. An economic broadening would threaten their singular power on at least two fronts: First, it would create private interests separate from those of the government and force the authorities to consider at least one class in society other than themselves. Second, the education demanded by broad-based development would risk the creation of potentially effective political opposition, as would the inevitable foreign contacts that would result. A consideration of such effects no doubt explains why Dubai, with its relatively more open culture, was more interested than, say, Saudi Arabia in alternative economic endeavors.

On a still more basic level, human nature surely also gets in the way. The easy wealth offered by oil must surely lure governments and peoples away from the huge effort and determination required to pursue genuine economic development. The existence of such a stress-free option could convince even the best-intentioned men, women, and governments to rationalize simple oil sales as the best route to national prosperity. When confronted with the hard work of genuine domestic economic development, it is easy to believe also that sovereign wealth funds prepare for the future, when all they do is keep these nations dependent on others. Such depressing reflections make a huge endowment of oil truly look more like a curse than a blessing.

Russia's Sorry Failures

Among the oil-rich nations the example set by the Russian Federation is the saddest of all. Unlike the desert states of the Middle East, Russia has no excuse, in either history or geography, to neglect broad economic development and integration. On the contrary, it is naturally rich and inherited from the Soviet Union an effective education system and a fully functioning, if remarkably inefficient, industrial infrastructure. But Russia's leadership, after a chaotic transition, remarkably began to undo the broadening trends that it had inherited and that emerging economies need. Instead of leveraging Russia's existing industrial base to modernize itself and make its economy more efficient, productive, focused, and competitive, Russia, under Vladimir Putin and Dmitry Medvedev, has consistently narrowed its economy to become primarily an oil exporter, embracing, it seems, all the ills associated with much less developed economies.

To be sure, the economy that passed to Russia's present leadership from the Soviets was largely closed to the rest of the world. The Soviets exported minerals, including oil, and sold industrial supplies, machinery, and military equipment, largely to their Cold War allies. Nor was Soviet Russia a big importer. It produced almost everything for itself and, in the words of the CIA, was "globally isolated."[39] This inward approach was highly inefficient and failed to use the nation's economic resources, including labor, as effectively as it could have had the economy sought a more thorough integration into the world trading system. Nonetheless the economy that passed to Putin and Medvedev had a broad industrial base on which to build. Inevitably globalization would have forced Russia to cede to foreign producers those industries developed under the Soviets that lacked comparable advantages. Where those advantages did exist, the global competition would have spurred the Russians to increase their economic effectiveness, allowing this otherwise well-endowed economy to engage world markets on a broad front.

Russia's leadership, however, betrayed this productive prospect. First, the government under Boris Yeltsin, in the 1990s, succumbed to the temptation to live off its inheritance by selling off state-owned assets to foreign and domestic buyers and running itself on the proceeds.[40] The chaos that behavior engendered understandably stalled the desired broadening and integration, and though the corporate buyers might eventually have moved in the direction of efficiencies, Putin, when he seized back the assets, effectively blocked that path.[41] Instead he and Medvedev chose to de-industrialize Russia and focus its economy more and more narrowly on oil and natural gas.

Today this unfortunate regression is nearly complete. Oil constitutes some 80 percent of Russian exports.[42] The income from those sales finances half the government's budget.[43] Petroleum exports amount to more than 30 percent of the country's entire GDP. Since oil and mining as a whole amount to about 35 percent of Russia's economy, petroleum clearly dominates. The general economic damage is already apparent. On a per capita basis Russia's economy ranks in the lower half of the world, with an income equivalent of only $9,000 a year, a figure that falls to a mere $6,100 if oil exports come out of the equation.[44] This smaller figure is probably the more accurate, as the oil revenues flow more generously toward the Kremlin than to the Russian people. Indeed Russia advertises its own negative assessment of its development prospects when its sovereign wealth fund invests some 70–80 percent of its take from Russia's oil revenues in overseas assets[45] instead of using the funds to develop Russia's otherwise vast economic potential. It is little wonder, then, that the World Bank puts Russian investment opportunities at 96th out of a list of 175 countries.[46]

Russia's experience during the recent 2008–09 financial crisis and recession is itself an illustration of the ill effects of such shortsighted behavior. Because of the economy's unnecessary concentration on oil exports, Russia's stock market (a crude measure of investor assessments of the economy's worth) fell in the recession much faster than stock markets in the rest of the world. The 75 percent drop in the price of crude between 2008 and 2009[47] saw a 68 percent plunge in Russia's popular MICEX index (Moscow Interbank Currency Exchange), a far more severe adjustment than the global average stock decline of 45 percent during that period. The country's official currency reserves shrank by almost 40 percent, and industrial activity fell at an annual rate of almost 60 percent, far worse than in the United States, for instance, where industrial production fell 17 percent from high to low.[48] Worse still, the Russian government's heavy dependence on shrinking oil sales abroad left the authorities bereft of means to mitigate the economic and financial pain. The best that they could do was hope that other nations would take effective steps to repair their respective economies and return to their former level of oil purchases. Russia, in effect, has rendered itself a completely passive economic player.

Now Iraq seems to have succumbed to the same curse. It, too, has more natural options for development than the Gulf States and Saudi Arabia. It has agricultural potential, a remarkable geographic presence that offers natural transportation links, and, most important of all a relatively well-educated, urbanized population that can function within modern economic arrangements.[49] But oil now provides 95 percent of its government revenues and constitutes more than 60 percent of the nation's GDP. Few other economic interests exist. Although oil directly employs only 1 percent of the workforce, the bulk of the population depends on the money earned from the sale of this single, government-owned product. Almost 90 percent of employment in Iraq is government-related, while the Iraqi government owns 90 percent of the land.[50] For all the opportunities with which Iraq could potentially broaden its economic base, it seems content to expose its economy to the volatility and vulnerability implicit in oil export dependence. Iraq has chosen to reject all the advantages and efficiencies that otherwise would have been available to it and instead to remain helpless in the face of the foreign economic vicissitudes.

Oil export dependence seems to go beyond economic distortions to skew thought as well. When oil prices were rising in 2007–08, for instance, Russian president Dmitry Medvedev floated the idea that the Russian ruble could replace the U.S. dollar as the world's reserve currency.[51] At the time, the ruble had risen some 20 percent[52] against the dollar in tandem with a 175 percent rise in the dollar price of oil between 2006 and 2008.[53] Whether Medvedev was overcome by the ruble's rise, simply wanted to slight the United States, or genuinely believed his proposal was feasible, his suggestion was nonetheless preposterous on its face. Strong as the ruble was then, any reserve currency, as the repository of central bank and corporate wealth, must offer relative stability, a trait distinctly absent from an oil-based currency that cannot help but rise and fall with the price of crude. By late 2008 this point came home. Oil prices tumbled in the world recession to lows below $35 a barrel,[54] and the Russian ruble followed, collapsing more than 60 percent against the U.S. dollar.[55] Though Medvedev raised the matter once more, in 2010, when oil price increases enabled the ruble to regain some strength,[56] mostly he was shrewd enough to avoid further embarrassment and let his earlier proposal drift off the headlines in silence.

Actually, Medvedev was not the first oil exporter to embarrass himself in this way. Iran's former president Mahmoud Ahmadinejad blazed that trail. Eager to hurt the United States, he threatened to price oil in euros and have Iran take over global oil trading at a facility on Kish Island, in the Persian Gulf.[57] For some reason, even in this electronic age, he seemed to think that a trading center physically close to the oil would have an advantage over others more distant from the wells. But Iran could neither command other trading centers to move from London, New York, or Tokyo, nor could it direct global trading. Iran simply did not have the leverage. As important a supplier as it is, Iran nonetheless constitutes only 5.4 percent of world supplies.[58] And certainly Tehran is in no position to keep its oil off world markets, since sales of crude amount to 20 percent of the country's GDP and 65 percent of government revenues.[59] Iran needs to sell its oil more than the world needs to buy it. Once the oil is sold on the global market, it trades where the global markets want and in the currency the market chooses. Iran can do little about it.

Ahmadinejad, however, did show himself a touch more realistic than

Medvedev. He looked for the euro, and not Iran's own currency, the rial, to supplant the dollar as the world's oil currency and, by implication, its reserve currency. The euro, at least at the time, looked like a viable candidate. Even with the recent sovereign debt problems of some of its members, the euro has a large, broad-based, and stable productive area behind it, with well-developed financial markets that can handle the understandably huge trading flows demanded of a global reserve currency.[60] Because Iran does most of its buying in Europe, certainly more than in the United States, it also had good reason to want to match the currency of its income to the currency of its outlays. Even so, it is the buyer, not the seller, especially not Iran, who will determine the currency in which oil is priced. If the Iranians insist, they may have prices quoted in euros, but that is less a matter of the value of the resource than mere currency conversion arithmetic.

With such a backdrop of economic and financial ineptitude, there would seem to be little hope that the leaderships of the world's oil exporters will manage to diversify their economies or, sadly, even see the need to do so. There is, however, good reason to expect that China, India, and others, more in touch with economic and social realities, will make the effort. Either they are already doing so or they have clearly stated their intention to do so. Still, it remains to be seen whether these nations can make the necessary changes, especially since, as in China's case, the effort in part demands difficult political concessions. Given the difficulties involved, global leadership on issues of trade and finance would seem essential, not just to help the emerging markets with their transitions but also to contain protectionist impulses in the developed economies and help them with their difficult adjustments. The United States, even now facing reduced relative economic power, still stands as the only viable candidate.

16

Leadership

The notion of international leadership is harder to support than it once was. The end of the Cold War has made most nations less amenable to the idea than they were in the face of a nuclear threat. Many Americans, after decades of strenuous international effort, would like their country to become just another nation. But if this global system is to continue to prosper, it will need leadership. The elements of sustained prosperity may, of course, fall into place of their own accord without the need for conscious political direction. After all, the needed elements—the globalization to cope with aging demographics, the pursuit of innovation and training, the broadening among emerging economies—reflect self-interests. Even so, only disciplined domestic and international guidance can ensure that the global economy avoid populist protectionism and continues down these necessary paths. In a different world that direction might come from the United Nations or the World Trade Organization. Since neither of these organizations has either the influence or the power to do the job, nor the European Union, nor Japan, nor China, the United States, despite its diminished relative dominance, will have to rise to the role and ensure that policy focuses on the essential interdependence of economies.

An Attractive Record

Custom and momentum surely favor America in such a role. The United States has long championed open trade, freer financial flows, and broad-based development. At least until recently it has done so through the multilateral arrangements that support the system best. Perhaps it was the lessons of the Great Depression, not least the devastating effects of the Smoot-Hawley tariffs, that prompted America to come out of the Second World War with a powerful commitment to open interactions among economies and the maintenance of multilateral rules to sustain them. The United Nations was the signal institutional expression of that commitment,[1] and no doubt the quick onset of the Cold War, in the late 1940s, added to Washington's motivation. Policymakers could see clearly that open trade brought prosperity and so was the best way to thwart communist ambitions.[2] But, whatever the specific motivations, the American push for free trade was clear and served as the basis of the great surge in global prosperity that followed.

In fact, American leadership in this area predates the country's entry into the Second World War. In 1940, when President Franklin Roosevelt signed the Lend-Lease Agreement to support Britain against the Nazis, he included a provision stipulating that any recipient of such aid cooperate with the United States in the construction of a liberal, open, postwar world economic system, a goal later incorporated into the Atlantic Charter, agreed to in 1941 between Roosevelt and British prime minister Winston Churchill. As early as 1943 Washington had devised plans for the yet to be established United Nations and in those seminal documents laid out as part of its mission the need to promote an open, free-trading world order, including provision for an International Trade Organization (ITO), the precursor of today's WTO, to reduce trade restrictions of all sorts and set global "rules for commerce."[3]

After the war, Washington pushed hard to put these plans into practice. It established the General Agreement on Tariffs and Trade (GATT) as, in the words of one observer, a "transcendent international trade organization" to remove trade restrictions. It moved quickly in what came to be called the Annecy Round (1949) of treaty negotiations to expand the number of countries acceding to GATT.[4] In that same spirit, Washington promoted the 1946 Monnet Plan for European economic integration, which began as the European Coal and Steel Community (1952), became Europe's Common Market in the late 1950s, and finally the European Union. Behind all this effort Washington held to the conviction that, in the words of postwar undersecretary of state for economic affairs William L. Clayton, "economic advancement and political freedom would benefit from the liberal principles of free markets."[5]

The United States remained remarkably stalwart in this commitment for decades. Sometimes it bullied other nations to support the vision. In 1947, when France resisted tariff reductions, President Harry Truman bluntly told French prime minister René Pleven: "High tariffs have not worked for the U.S. and they will not work for France."[6] Though President Dwight Eisenhower adopted a lower-key style, he continued to insist on international free trade. His secretary of state, John Foster Dulles, had at the time warned against even occasional backsliding in favor of trade restrictions, claiming that it seriously damaged American leadership in international affairs and was viewed by other countries as a "retreat into economic isolationism." Eventually American leadership, in what has come to be known as the Dillon Round of GATT negotiations (1960–62), exacted 10 percent tariff reductions out of the international community, despite considerable European resistance.[7] President Kennedy kept to the same internationalist principles after he entered the White House in 1961 and initiated what became known as the Kennedy Round of GATT negotiations (1964–67), which produced substantial further tariff cutting, as did the Tokyo Round (1973–79) that followed and took effect in the 1980s.[8]

American leadership was not entirely consistent. President Richard Nixon played partisan hardball with Japan and Germany on currencies and seriously disrupted the multilateral trade system when he ended the dollar's gold convertibility in 1971.[9] But even during that great lapse, Washington's bias still leaned toward the principles of free trade. Nixon only resorted to his bold move after Japan and Germany had rejected his multilateral efforts at accommodation. And even as he imposed his currency solution the Nixon administration continued to endorse the European Common Market's promotion of economic integration among its members.[10] Throughout the episode the U.S. Congress continued to show bipartisan support for free trade and global development and the conviction that it served America's and the world's long-term interests.[11] When faced with tariffs or other such impediments to free trade, the United States never retaliated but instead sought to remove the foreign trade restrictions.[12]

Still Only America

No doubt in those days Washington had an easier time leading than it does today or will in the future. American economic and political hegemony were never so pronounced as in the second half of the twentieth century. At the end of the Second World War, when the United States began its push to open global trade and free financial flows, its economy accounted for more than 35 percent of the world's total output of goods and services, and the financial assets of its capital markets verged on 50 percent of the world's value.[13] Whereas the rest of the world staggered under huge wartime debts, the United States had become the world's great creditor. The dollar was the world's undisputed international reserve currency. Indeed the world complained of a "dollar shortage."[14]

This kind of overwhelming dominance has long since disappeared. By the end of the first decade of this new century, the American economy accounted for less than 25 percent of the world's output of goods and services, while the European Union had long since surpassed America's GDP.[15] Though U.S. financial markets, even after the great crisis of 2008–09, remained the largest and most active in the world, London could justifiably claim parity. Other financial markets also had grown, so that as the second decade of this new century began, American markets accounted for only about 37 percent of global assets.[16] America had slid from a substantial trade surplus of exports over imports to a deficit of some $500 billion, almost 3.5 percent of the overall economy.[17] The country's public finances had fallen into chronic deficit as well.[18] Nor could America claim the status of the world's great creditor. On the contrary, America had become its debtor, mostly to Japan and especially China, which, along with other foreign interests, owned more than 35 percent of outstanding U.S. government debt. Matters have gone so far that talk of an American default emerges frequently, and the country's debt has suffered a downgrade.[19]

But despite the clear ebbing of relative American power, the country remains the only viable source of global leadership. To be sure, many have presented the euro and Europe as natural successors to the dollar and to American leadership, and up to 2010 much research weighed the possibility as real.[20] But if Europe has a large enough economy and sufficient financial depth for the job, it has other, significant drawbacks. The severe sovereign debt problems of some of its members, more severe than in the United States, certainly weigh against Europe's assumption of such a role, as do the fundamental contradictions of its still young union. China has even more failings in this regard. Its closed, immature financial markets render leadership impossible, while Beijing's still highly partisan trade policy[21] makes risible any suggestion that it take the world toward more open trade and freer financial flows. Nor does Europe or China have America's global presence, and neither claims America's historical record of leadership on trade issues. Meanwhile the dollar, despite America's slide from dominance, remains as the world's clear reserve currency, accounting, for instance, for almost 90 percent of global transactions,[22] whether Americans are involved or not.

For all the weakness of the United States and its finances, there simply is no alternative to its dollar. Europe's most significant drawback is a fundamental lack of unity. The problem was clear years ago in the failure of plebiscites over union. Voters in France rejected the European Union's new constitution by a wide margin, and Irish voters rejected the watered-down but still unifying Lisbon Treaty.[23] Since the effort aimed at "strengthening the EU's ability to act as a united force on the global stage,"[24] the no votes loudly demonstrated the EU's inability to fill such a role. Indeed, after the Irish vote the European Union even had to abandon plans for tax harmonization within itself.[25] Then French president Nicolas Sarkozy had gone so far as to refer to the continent's "identity crisis." If that condition were not enough to disqualify Europe as a leader on trade issues, Sarkozy's maiden speech to the European Parliament, in 2007, rallied a receptive audience around the notion of removing the "taboo" surrounding "protection."[26] Swedish officials subsequently pointed out the lack of European leadership by noting how nobody approached Europe for support during the 2008–09 financial crisis and recession, turning instead to "the Middle East, Singapore, and China, for loans if not for guidance."[27]

Nor can the European Union easily resolve its disqualifying ambivalences. They truly are fundamental and are part of an ongoing confusion over where the power of Brussels's bureaucrats ends and that of each member nation's elected assembly begins. Complaints of a "democratic deficit" are common.[28] Against such basic disagreement it should hardly come as a surprise that Europe has difficulty mounting a concerted policy on anything, much less global economic policy. Indicative of the problem is the euro's status as "a currency without a state,"[29] hardly a recommendation for it to replace the dollar's reserve status. No less a personage than Czech president Václav Klaus has highlighted this lack of common purpose by pointing out how differently EU members react to economic shocks, including foreign competition.[30] The European Commission itself has admitted that the European Union lacks a "strong voice" globally or a "clear international strategy," and has concluded that the union lacks sufficient weight in itself to seek a seat of its own in any "global institution."[31]

Rather than assume a global role, much less supplant the United States, Europe's divisions seem to have impelled it to take an inward, regional focus. Singapore's prestigious Lee Kuan Yew School of Public Policy spoke for many in Asia when it dismissed Europe as a "geopolitical dwarf" that is "slavishly following the U.S. lead," effectively "free riding on U.S. power" and failing even to contemplate "badly needed strategic initiatives." The EU's narrower focus during the latest Doha Round of world trade talks, the Asians contend, has shrunk "Europe's footprint on the world stage,"[32] and consequently disqualified it for leadership. Some commentators, even within Europe, have described the continent as a "giant Switzerland," suggesting that it, like that perennial neutral, offers a rich haven but has no significant influence outside its borders.[33] If such accusations are unfair, their prevalence nonetheless detracts from Europe's ability to supplant the United States as a global leader on any front, especially world trade and financial matters.

These failings came into especially sharp focus during Europe's recent financial troubles. Debt problems among several EU members—Portugal, Ireland, Italy, Greece, and Spain—first came to public attention in spring 2010. Greece then admitted that it had misled the union about its public finances. Bond buyers reacted to the news by abandoning Greek debt and forcing up the cost of borrowing for Athens and for many of these other governments. Greece, already precarious, could not stand up to the increased costs and faced default.[34] The European Union, embarrassed by its inability to monitor or control the public finances of its own members, naturally faced questions about its ability to lead itself, much less the world. Such questions become even more pointed when it became apparent that Brussels had no way of dealing with the situation. For months major European powers dithered about what to do, arguing about where the financial burdens of a rescue should fall or, indeed, if the EU was even ready to rescue one of its members.[35] Eventually the member nations managed to establish a fund to rescue Greece and act as a backstop to other vulnerable nations, but even then the union had to turn outside for help, to the IMF[36] and even to the U.S. Federal Reserve, to produce some of its needs for financial liquidity.[37]

Shedding still more doubt on Europe's competence to lead is how its debt crisis has exposed fundamental weakness in its underlying structures. Even after rescues were put in place, its inadequacies and the lack of commitment of member states were apparent. Many inside Europe and outside observed the distinct lack of unity and questioned the euro's future existence, not to mention its fitness to act as a global reserve currency. Critics, officials, and commentators wondered about the union's viability.[38] All in all, Europe's recent sovereign debt crisis made clear that the United States, whatever its economic and financial troubles, still retains a tremendous edge in any competition for leadership.

In the event, Europe's crisis indirectly highlighted China's and Japan's inadequacies as global leaders as well. Had they had anything near a leading role in world trade and finance, they would have had a presence in Europe's deliberations, maybe consulted, certainly considered. Yet while Europe's troubles threatened the stability of world financial markets, these nations remained absent in every way, either as support or as economic participants. Their regional or internal focus persuaded them that European problems were not their concern, a view reinforced by the Europeans, who hardly even considered China or Japan for assistance or for guidance. Nor did the rest of the world consider them.[39]

China's behavior elsewhere on the globe only reinforces such dismissive conclusions. It is of course prominent within Asia. Beijing has played a key role in Korean tensions,[40] vied for regional dominance with India,[41] and has aggressively pursued sometimes outrageous claims in the South and East China Seas.[42] It has, none too subtly, sought leadership of the Association of Southeast Asian Nations (ASEAN).[43] But elsewhere, however impressive the economy's growth rate, size, dynamism, and promise, Beijing has shown little, if any, diplomatic prowess. Beijing does make many trade deals in Africa, the Middle East, and Latin America, but outside Asia its diplomacy is purely commercial. It has no diplomatic presence of note in Africa or Latin America and certainly not in the Middle East, where China's exclusive focus lies in procuring oil supplies. In sharp contrast to China's absence, the United States, for all its loss of relative stature, still plays on a world stage. Even as it exerts considerable influence in Europe, Latin America, and the Middle East, it also stands as China's chief rival in all these Asian disputes, even in ASEAN, half a world away from Washington.[44]

How to Proceed Now

If, then, it falls to the United States to lead on world trade issues, Washington needs to set aside any plans to become just another nation. Its own prosperity and that of the rest of the world depend on it. To ensure that the world can secure necessary trade and financial flows, especially in the face of building demographic pressure, Washington must use a position of global leadership to ensure that the world avoids destructive protectionist temptations and focuses on its longer-term needs. Though circumstances have changed radically since the last century, Washington should still take its cue from that time. It may no longer have the ability to bully as thoroughly it once could, but it can and must return to its earlier emphasis on a multilateral, multinational, rules-based system. Only through this approach can it effectively promote world trade, free financial flows, and hence facilitate the adjustments needed to secure prosperity. Since the nation has lost its former hegemonic position, Washington will have to pursue these former goals in a more consultative, collaborative manner than in its past.

The first order of business in this effort demands that the United States resolve its budget problems. Even without today's already urgent fiscal problems, the pressure of aging demographics on Social Security and Medicare would cause budget concerns.[45] As it is these demographically linked matters will exacerbate already severe strains. Washington's seemingly uncontrolled deficit spending, aside from raising questions about the country's solvency, also raises serious concerns about future inflation, the dollar's foreign exchange value, and ultimately its position as the global reserve currency.[46] This is not the place to weigh all the various deficit reduction proposals—whether the government should meet its goals more through spending cuts or through tax increases, and exactly where these should be made. But it is clear, even so, that the reform effort generally will force major changes in the way that the U.S. government finances itself and manages its outlays. Any solution, even if enacted tomorrow, will take years to implement and bear fruit. Fortunately for America's ability to lead, however, a credible plan for fiscal order can secure influence long before actual deficit figures come into line.

America must also deal with recent questions about the dollar's status. Because the United States has lost its once overwhelming global economic and financial stature, and because Washington faces severe economic and financial problems, many have begun to question, even in the absence of a viable alternative, whether the dollar can sustain its position as the world's only reserve currency. The last chapter showed the preposterous character of some of the proposals for replacing the dollar as the world's reserve currency, but others are more thoughtful and reasonable. The old palliatives of ignoring alternatives and simply assuring the world that Washington seeks a strong dollar will no longer serve.[47] Rather than pretend that nothing has changed, Washington would do better to recognize that the relative position of the United States and the dollar has declined and acknowledge that nations, firms, and individuals have legitimate reasons to rethink the dollar's former singular role. If the United States fails to deal with these considered proposals realistically, it will only further detract from its global stature.

Take, for example, an alternative Russian proposal to President Medvedev's embarrassing suggestion that the ruble replace the dollar. This one asked the Shanghai Cooperation Organisation (SCO), a group of nations including Russia, China, and four other Central Asian republics, to consider a number of dollar alternatives as a reserve currency,[48] including a proposal from Russian deputy finance minister Dmitry Pankin that a group of regional currencies might serve.[49] Similarly, China, apart from its unlikely recommendation of its yuan as a dollar replacement, reasonably asked a meeting of the G8 to consider ways to diversify the reserve currency system away from the dollar.[50] Beijing even went so far as to establish a pilot program for Chinese companies to settle trade orders in yuan, and began talks with Russia and Brazil to settle bilateral trade in each other's currencies.[51] India, without commenting on any replacement for the dollar, admitted that it was diversifying its official foreign currency reserves away from dollars.[52] Rumors have circulated about conspiracies among China, Russia, France, and the oil-producing states of the Middle East to stop using dollars to trade oil,[53] though the oil-producing states later denied these.[54]

Even the World Bank, often seen as a creature of the United States, has warned Washington not to take the dollar's reserve status for granted.[55] World Bank president Robert Zoellick went so far as to predict that within 15 years the yuan could offer an alternative to the dollar as a global reserve currency.[56] Given such a long time horizon, his comments are not entirely unreasonable, even if they no doubt were intentionally incendiary. Both the IMF and the United Nations have offered to create an international currency to replace or supplement the dollar as a global reserve. Most popular are proposals to elevate to reserve status a synthetic currency developed by the IMF decades ago to help central banks deal with temporary foreign exchange problems and to settle accounts.[57] Called special drawing rights (SDRs), their value is determined by a basket of major currencies, but, since the dollar already dominates the basket, it is hard to claim that SDRs really are a substitute.

In dealing with all this speculation and maneuvering, the United States must proceed with the certain knowledge that the dollar's fundamental status is not necessarily threatened by the rise of an alternative. On the contrary, history demonstrates that two or more currencies can coexist in international reserve status for decades. Certainly that was the case when the dollar began to supersede British sterling in the reserve role. Though the process started in the mid-1920s, it took until the 1960s for the dollar to eclipse sterling completely. During that 40-year interim, the two currencies functioned side by side as reserves and mediums of exchange for central banks and international business. In the words of one prominent researcher, the competition for reserve currency status is most definitely not "a winner-take-all game."[58] If realistic consideration raises a viable rival to the dollar, Washington would do well to take the development in light of history. Petulant resistance can only embarrass and undermine the country's stature. In the years or, more likely, decades that it would take for the new arrangements entirely to eclipse the dollar, if they ever do, the dollar's continued special, if not unique, status would still support America's efforts to exert leadership on trade and financial matters.

Currency, however, is just one aspect of the picture. The dollar's key role only ever served as a backdrop to Washington's more active trade negotiations and diplomacy. This trade and diplomatic activity can continue even if the dollar ceases to enjoy singular status. And since U.S. efforts to promote trade must continue, if the world is to avoid the pitfalls of protectionism, Washington needs to abandon its more recent efforts at bipartisan trade deals and individual negotiations and return to its earlier internationalist posture. If anything, circumstances demand that Washington intensify that earlier approach.

It was in the 1980s that the United States began to move away from its original, multilateral approach to trade issues. The move no doubt reflected the great fear of Japan that swept political and business circles at the time. Since then Washington has become more partisan in its attitude and increasingly prone to squabble for position with its trading partners. Pointed currency disputes, earlier with Japan and more recently with China, have often dominated discussion.[59] Under these influences, Washington has migrated from a multilateral to a bilateral, or specialized, approach. Even NAFTA has this new quality, as do recent pacts with Latin America and with South Korea. The problem with these arrangements is that they advance open trade only for the signatories. They exclude those outside the deal. To this extent they are in many ways antithetical to America's original and successful global approach, and do as much to thwart free trade as to advance it. Worse, by casting the United States as a partisan maneuvering for position, they also detract from Washington's ability to exert global leadership in a broader pursuit of open trade and free financial flows.

The long-standing trade tension between China and the United States is a case in point. American frustrations with Beijing's currency policy are understandable. As already described,[60] Beijing, at least since the mid-1990s, has sought a special export advantage by artificially depressing the yuan's value against the dollar. Repeated American efforts to elicit change have met with only the most modest success. But the retaliatory tariffs that the United States has repeatedly threatened[61] contrast sharply with earlier multilateral efforts to remove trade barriers. The threatened tariffs clearly go in quite the opposite direction. Rather than close itself down, America should work to open China, and it has options other than tariff threats that might more effectively move Beijing and remain closer to the multilateral spirit of Washington's earlier approach.

One course of action would organize resistance to China's policies among the members of the G20 group of the world's largest trading nations. Many of its members, the Europeans especially, object to Beijing's current currency posture. If, instead of threats, Washington could confront China with concentrated pressure from all or some G20 members, Beijing might more readily yield than it would to an imposition of

American tariffs. These only insult China's already ridiculously inflated sense of national pride and invite a dangerous game of coup-countercoup that would do more to frustrate trade and economic growth than advance either.[62] In contrast, a negotiating partnership among the United States, members of the European Union, India, Indonesia, and perhaps Japan would have more impact on Beijing than complaints from Washington alone.[63] Alternatively or additionally, the United States could pressure China through the IMF, insisting that Beijing become more cooperative before allowing it any of the elevations that China covets within that international body or others.[64] Washington might even seize on the dispute as an opportunity to advance global rules for freer trade already proposed by others at the IMF that would act directly on China's currency position by for instance, forbidding any nation to buy another's liabilities until it opened its financial markets for reciprocal purchases.[65]

Though there are no guarantees that such multilateral efforts would move Beijing, the likelihood is greater and certainly carries less risk of trade war than this country's current partisan approach. What is more, a multinational multilateral approach would cast the United States in the light of international leader rather than partisan squabbler. In a similar way Washington would become generally more effective if it abandoned its by now well-established pattern of fighting for position through bilateral trade arrangements, a policy, as already indicated, antithetical to its former multilateral approach.

Though not widely discussed in the general or even the financial media, such preferential trade agreements, or "PTAs" as they are called, dangerously undermine the needed multilateral approach to trade.[66] They threaten global trade as much as they promote it. Renowned trade economist Jagdish Bhagwati has gone so far as to describe America's recent enthusiasm for PTAs as the position of a "selfish hegemon," pointedly referencing the equally renowned international economist, Charles Kindleberger, who described the United States at the height of its multilateral free trade leadership as an "altruistic hegemon."[67] Charles A. Kupchan, a senior fellow of the Council on Foreign Relations, has stated flatly that in matters of trade or currency "bilateral[ism] clearly won't work,"[68] while professor Anne O. Krueger has made a powerful, theoretical and empirical case that "bilateral reciprocity" is not nearly as effective as "multi-party, multi-commodity negotiations."[69] Professor Razeen Sally, when at the London School of Economics and the European Centre for International Political Economy, pleaded for the United States to lead world practice away from preferential trade agreements to recapture the multilateralism that it once emphasized[70]—in other words, to seek the global, "rules-based" approach that Douglas Alexander, when U.K. secretary of state for international development, described as the essence of the multilateral system.[71]

Though such prescriptions are easier to write than to fill, the United States does not lack for avenues by which to effect change. The legacy of past multilateralist approaches has given it supranational institutions that would eagerly work with Washington to promote a more global, rules-based approach. WTO director-general Pascal Lamy has just about begged participating nations to abandon bilateral arrangements and "come back to the table at the political level," by which he means at a level high enough to formulate broad agreements and universal rules to ensure freer trade on a multilateral basis.[72] Any effort to revitalize the latest Doha Round of negotiations on global tariffs could bear multilateral fruit, but only with a powerful commitment from a major power, a role that only the United States can fill.[73] Beyond the WTO, the G8 and the G20 also offer potentially effective avenues on which the United States can lead in this essential direction.[74] Meanwhile the explosion of free trade associations in Asia, though preferential in nature, nonetheless indicates a more general commitment to free trade that American leadership could exploit on a global basis.[75]

Three Special Opportunities

Apart from such general positioning, the United States has an opportunity to use environmental, labor, and global financial issues to enhance its leadership status and advance multilateral solutions. Because intervention in these areas has frequently thwarted free trade and because free financial flows and bilateral arrangements have frequently stumbled over them, they cry out for global agreements and more universal, rules-based solutions. These could better overcome the technical issues bedeviling such efforts and offer each country's domestic leadership political cover. An attempt by Washington to promote reasonable multilateral solutions, therefore, would likely receive a welcome among the many trading nations already frustrated with international failures on these fronts.

There can be little doubt that developed economies have used labor rules to restrain trade.[76] Typically they refuse an open exchange until trading partners adopt working conditions comparable to their own, which are practically impossible for much poorer, emerging economies.[77] American posturing in this regard sounds especially hollow and partisan when Washington makes demands even as U.S. legislation often restricts the right to strike more tightly than in many other countries, and while the United States still refuses to ratify the International Labour Organization's core conventions.[78] Nor do the humanitarian justifications used by America, Europe, or Japan ring entirely true. After all, it does the working man or woman in the emerging economies little good if such exacting standards shut down trade and put him or her out of work. None of this is to say, of course, that working conditions around the globe are not a matter of serious concern or that trading nations have no need to ensure that imports meet minimal safety and health requirements. Leadership in a multilateral setting can at once overcome interests that hamstring each national negotiator and ensure the essential distinction between these issues and trade matters.

Environmental issues are still more complex. On the one side, the developed nations see an urgent global need for more intense environmental controls. On the other, India, China, and other emerging economies see the rules that Japan and the developed West would impose as unfairly hindering their development. As with labor rules, these nations claim they cannot afford the environmental regulations of the developed world, and never will if their trading capacity is blocked by them. Both China and India have confronted G8 meetings, insisting that neither nation can be expected to make carbon emission cuts before each has industrialized. They argue that Japan and the West secured their position of wealth before taking environmental measures, and that they should have the same opportunities.[79] At one such meeting, India's then environmental minister, Jairam Ramesh, pointedly told Secretary of State Hillary Clinton: "There is simply no case for the pressure that we, who have been among the lowest emissions per capita, have to actually reduce emissions." Then, speaking for many in the emerging world, he added: "We look upon you suspiciously because you have not fulfilled what [you] pledged."[80]

Against this record, the weakness of bilateralism should be apparent. Certainly, it shows that there is no room for the unilateralism exhibited by Europe and the United States, when each sought a carbon tax on imports from countries that refused to limit their emissions sufficiently. Indeed it was that American plan that prompted Minister Ramesh's pointed remarks to Secretary Clinton.[81] But these emerging economies might just yield to compromises in multilateral arrangements, not the least because all involved are aware that environmental degradation in one place often spreads, leaving a multilateral approach the only really effective answer. Here, then, is a golden opportunity for America to reassert multilateral over bilateral arrangements. Ironically America's refusal thus far to sign environmental protocols, such as the Kyoto Treaty,[82] makes Washington something of an ideal bridge between strong European and Japanese positions on the one hand and the reluctance of India, China, and other emerging economies on the other.

Financial reform and ownership disputes offer a third area ripe for such multilateral American leadership. It is clear from the crisis of 2008–09 how interlocked global financial markets are putting a strong case for global responses and exposing bilateral arrangements as next to useless. Particularly susceptible is the growing tension about ownership, where only a global approach can break the political, partisan tone that has developed. The United States, for instance, while allowing IBM to sell its personal computer business along with all its technology to the Chinese firm Lenovo, suddenly, and on what appear to have been largely arbitrary criteria, blocked, as mentioned earlier, the bid of the China National Offshore Oil Corporation (CNOOC) to buy Unocal[83] and also balked when Britain's P&O stepped in to manage American ports because Dubai Ports World had a significant ownership stake in the British firm.[84] More recently the Canadian government blocked the U.S.-based bid by Alliant Techsystems to buy the space technology division of MacDonald, Dettwiler, and the Japanese government forbade the United Kingdom's Children's Investment Fund from increasing its stake in the electricity wholesaler J-Power. More countries are establishing screening mechanisms to regulate such buyout transactions, and in the process have blocked international financial flows.[85]

Though none of these or other such denials violate WTO rules, the lack of clear or consistent guidelines nonetheless stymies trade and the efficient use of global financial capital. Prospective buyers waste considerable time and money advancing their deal over a period of months, maybe years, before the authorities, often for undisclosed reasons, render all their previous effort useless. The pattern also has needlessly created bad feeling between governments and corporations,[86] not least because so many of these decisions appear to hinge on the national identity or even the ethnicity of the investor. The United States seems to exhibit less concern over European buyers, for instance, than over Chinese or Middle Eastern buyers. Even long-standing ally Japan has faced more American resistance than have European buyers. The European Union has blocked still more deals than has the United States and has generally shown more resistance to foreign ownership, an attitude exemplified by France's "strategic investment fund," a government-backed asset pool expressly designed to "prevent national industrial groups from falling into [any] foreign hands."[87]

Some nations have tried to use bilateral treaties to avoid such problems. The United States and China have gone down this route.[88] But the bilateral approach has significant shortcomings. Typically such treaties are very narrow in what they cover and therefore still leave truly multinational businesses with little guidance about how to proceed. Rather than try to negotiate an endless maze of specific treaty provisions, the world's multinational businesses doubtless would put their considerable influence behind any nation that led the way toward solutions that were more global and that had clear rules. Only then could they plan. They would no doubt also endorse American leadership for global agreement on such matters as protections for sensitive technologies, intellectual capital, and corporate disclosure standards, including information on the subsidies or low-interest loans that prospective buyers receive from their domestic governments. Though the Organisation for Economic Co-operation and Development has developed a basis for such rules,[89] it has had neither the ability nor the authority to advance the agenda. The United States could press effectively for such solutions, and in so doing remove another source of friction in the international system and to global flows of trade and finance.

The way ahead, if not easy, is nonetheless clear. To maintain its prosperity the world needs to sustain globalization's momentum. Only in that way can it relieve the problems raised by aging demographics in the developed economies and foster further development in the emerging economies. Though each nation's own interests lie along this path, and each has powerful long-term incentives to promote the trend, political strength is essential to overcome the powerful short-term temptations to backslide. If Washington—as the only viable candidate to do so—can rise to the occasion, jettison the partisanship and bilateralism of recent years, and return to the multilateral approach of past decades, the prospects for continued prosperity would improve considerably.

17

Prospects

The pressure, as they say, is on—but, then, it never relents. Even the most placid and predictable of times impose painful adjustments on people, firms, and governments. As should be clear by now, the next 30 years will demand more than the usual amount of pain and adjustment.

Aging demographics in Japan, Europe, and America will create a major threat to growth and prosperity. The inadequacy of purely domestic palliatives and immigration will drive these labor-short developed economies deeper into globalization in order to access the output of the emerging world's eager, youthful workforces, even as they stay at home. As increased globalization offers relief from demographic strains, it will bring ills of its own, sufficient to enlarge an already significant protectionist backlash that, in its turn, threatens to shut down this essential, global route to continued prosperity. Coping with these currents and countercurrents will force still further adjustments on these economies and create an especially urgent need for strong and enlightened leadership, within each country and at a global level.

Much of the adjustment will happen naturally in response to market forces. The relative abundance of cheap labor in the emerging economies will make them a natural destination for buyers from the aging, labor-short developed economies. To trade for the output of this huge workforce, firms in Europe, Japan, and America will leverage their advantages in technology and training so that the global market will settle on a division of economic activity. The emerging economies will produce lower-priced items that require a lot of labor and relatively little equipment, technology, or training—what economists call labor-intensive, low-value-added activities. The developed economies will produce the world's higher-value items, which demand little labor but much training and an abundance of equipment and technology—what economists call "capital-intensive, high-value-added activities."

The tidy answers of pure economies, however, only ever tell part of the story. Because markets, efficient and effective as they are, offer neither equity nor concern for the individual, they almost always spawn dangerous social and political tensions. These have appeared particularly in response to a yawning and expanding income gap between rich and poor and the emergence of destructive boom-bust financial cycles. Failure to address these matters and other undesirable outcomes has already fostered considerable antiglobalization feeling and a growing protectionist sentiment that ignores the benefits of international trade and free financial flows and is ready to fight globalization through political action. In response governments already have adopted more protectionist stances. Such pressures will become even more intense in the future as demographic imperatives create a still greater reliance on globalization.

But for all the genuine harm that globalization has done and can do, protectionism carries still greater dangers. Historically, whenever it has carried the day, protectionism has stifled economic growth and destroyed wealth. Now, in the face of unfolding demographic imperatives, protectionism presents a still greater economic threat, for it would cut the developed world off from the abundant, inexpensive labor of the emerging economies that it so critically needs. An interruption in world trade, by forcing these labor-short economies to produce their own labor-intensive products for their outsized retired populations, would inevitably raise living costs and depress living standards. Emerging economies, too, would suffer, for the absence of trade would steal their main engine of economic growth and development.

Given the enormously high stakes, individuals, firms, and governments will need to find ways to relieve the problems caused by globalization, in order to cope better with the unfolding economic and financial milieu and also to disarm the protectionist threat. The solution will have a number of strands. One will redouble emphasis on technology and innovation to enable the developed economies to maintain their edge in high-value products and reemploy those workers otherwise displaced by globalization. Another will call for significant advances in worker training and education in order to ready workers for this more demanding future and relieve their transitional strains. Still another will produce financial reforms to manage the tidal waves of international financial liquidity that have so contributed to the destructive volatility of the past couple of decades and that would otherwise continue. All these steps will require new, more imaginative government and corporate policies to promote the greatest possible flexibility.

However clear the needed directions and however high the stakes, political responses will remain problematic. On both the domestic and the international level a successful maneuvering between these imperatives and the potential lapses into shortsightedness and protectionism will require talented, principled leadership to focus policies and nations on long-term needs and make clear to domestic populations, as well as other nations, why circumstances call for such actions. Continued prosperity depends on it. If such leaders, domestic and international, are always in short supply, enough have emerged over the course of history to permit hope, even if the present crop in the United States, Europe, and Asia offer little reason for enthusiasm.

Though success seems to require a daunting number of well-placed steps, the weight of probability still favors it. Continued globalization, managed and softened by an effective array of responses and adjustments, is after all in almost everyone's long-term interest. To keep matters on track, the intellectual and business communities need to recognize the fundamental needs of this environment and particularly the demographic reality—especially if history's promise of enlightened leadership fails to emerge. This broad group must explain these needs to the public while having a clear appreciation of the constraints, the needs, and realistic options. In this way they can help guide the worlds of politics and business, and ensure that, despite adverse demographics, future generations will enjoy continued economic growth and increased prosperity.

NOTES

Preface

1 Robert Andrews, ed., *The Columbia World of Quotations* (New York: Columbia University Press, 1996).

1: Growing Old Gracefully

1 The median age of the U.S. population in 1900, for instance, averaged about 23 years; in 1950, it was still a relatively youthful 30 years, compared with the median age of close to 37 years in the most recent census. See Bureau of the Census, www.census.gov.

2 See Idea Finder Web site, www.ideafinder.com.

3 Ibid.

4 See Steven J. Zaloga, *Panther vs. Sherman: Battle of the Bulge 1944* (Oxford: Osprey, 2008). It is further noteworthy for this discussion that the United States during the war produced 40,000 Sherman tanks, compared with only 600 Tiger tanks and 2,100 German tanks altogether.

5 "Foreign News: We Will Bury You," *Time*, November 26, 1956.

6 For a straightforward and brief telling of the story, see "How Sputnik Changed America," *Sunday Morning*, CBS News Web site, www.cbsnews.com.

7 Central Intelligence Agency, *The World Factbook*, www.cia.gov.

8 There is no verification for this story, but the author has encountered

it more than once talking to industrialists and economic historians. If it is not true, it may as well be, for it captures relative circumstances well.

2: The Demographic Imperative

1 See, in particular, David E. Bloom, David Canning, and Gunther Fink, "Population Aging and Economic Growth," working paper 31, *Harvard Initiative for Global Health Program on the Global Demography of Aging* (April 2008), and David E. Bloom, David Canning, Gunther Fink, and Jocelyn E. Finlay, "Does Age Structure Forecast Economic Growth?," working paper 20, *Harvard Initiative for Global Health Program on the Global Demography of Aging* (June 2007).

2 P. G. Peterson, "Gray Down: The Global Aging Crisis," *Foreign Affairs* (January/February 1999).

3 See, for example, Ken Dychtwald, "On the Future," *San Francisco Chronicle,* November 15, 1999.

4 For details on this historic event, see Tony Judt, *Postwar: A History of Europe Since 1945* (New York: Penguin, 2006), pp. 332–35.

5 Bureau of Economic Analysis Web site, www.bea.gov.

6 Bureau of Labor Statistics Web site, www.bls.gov.

7 For comparative productivity figures, see Bureau of Labor Statistics Web site, www.bls.gov.

8 This group has lost wage power in recent years. See ibid.

9 Finis Welsh, "Effects of Cohort Size on Earnings: The Baby Boom Babies' Financial Bust," *Journal of Political Economy* (October 1979).

10 Benjamin F. Jones, "Age and Great Invention," working paper 11359, National Bureau of Economic Research, May 2005.

11 See Herbert Moller, "Youth as a Force in the Modern World," *Comparative Studies in Society and History* (April 1968).

12 David W. Galensor, "A Portrait of the Artist as a Very Young or Very Old Innovator, Creativity at the Extreme of the Life Cycle," working paper 10515, National Bureau of Economic Research, May 2004.

13 Bruce A. Weinberg and David W. Galensor, "Creative Careers: The Life Cycles of Nobel Laureates in Economics," working paper 11799, National Bureau of Economic Research, November 2005.

14 For more detail, see David Chael, "Aging and Demographic Change," *Canadian Public Policy* (August 2000), and Robert Shimer, "The Impact of Young Workers on the Aggregate Labor Market," working paper 7306, National Bureau of Economic Research, August 1999.

15 David W. Galensor, "A Portrait of the Artist as a Very Young or Very Old Innovator, Creativity at the Extreme of the Life Cycle," working paper 10515, National Bureau of Economic Research, May 2004.

16 Taken from, K. Brad Wray, "Is Science Really a Young Man's Game?" *Social Studies of Science* (February 2003).

17 David W. Galensor, "A Portrait of the Artist as a Very Young or Very Old Innovator, Creativity at the Extreme of the Life Cycle," working paper 10515, National Bureau of Economic Research, May 2004.

18 For a complete analysis of these effects, see Robert Shimer, "The Impact of Young Workers on the Aggregate Labor Market," working paper 7306, National Bureau of Economic Research, August 1999, and Geoffrey McNicall, "Growth and Below-Replacement Fertility," *Population and Development Review* 12 (1986).

19 See a thorough analysis in Dick Kruger and Alexander Ludwig, "On the Consequences of Demographic Change for Rates of Return to Capital and the Distribution of Wealth and Welfare," working paper 12453, National Bureau of Economic Research, August 2006; the authors calculate a 0.8 percentage point drop in profitability, which according to Bureau of Economic Analysis data (see Bureau of Economic Analysis, www.bea.gov) and Federal Reserve data (see "Flow of Funds," Federal Reserve System, www.federalreserve.gov) would amount to about a 10 percent reduction in average return on capital during the five years to 2009.

20 Typically, people do their greatest savings between the ages of 40 and 70, after which they cease saving and frequently draw down on their pool of assets. For documentation of savings patterns of different age cohorts on various populations, in both the developed and the emerging economies of the world, see Amlan Roy and Aimi Price, "Demographics, Capital Flows, and Exchange Rates," *Credit Suisse Economic Research*, August 1, 2007; Diana Farrell, Sacha Ghai, and Tim Shavers, "The Demographic Effect: How Aging Will Reduce Global Wealth," *The McKinsey Quarterly* (March 2005); David E. Bloom, David Canning, and Gunther Fink, "Population Aging and Economic Growth," working paper 31, *Harvard Initiative for Global Health Program on the Global Demography of Aging* (April 2008); F. Modigliani, "Life-cycle, Individual Thrifts, and the Wealth of Nations," *American Economic Review* 3 (June 1986); and Matthew Higgins, "Demography, National Savings and International Capital Flows," *International Economic Review* 2 (May 1998).

21 Report of the Trustees of the Social Security and Medicare Trust Funds, 2009, Social Security Administration, www.socialsecurity.gov.

22 See Hans Fehr, Sabine Jokisch, and Laurence Kotlikoff, "The Developed World's Demographic Transition: The Roles of Capital Flows, Immigration,

and Policy," working paper 10096, National Bureau of Economic Research, November 2003.

23 Robert Dekle, "Financing Consumption on Aging Japan: The Roles of Foreign Capital Inflows and Immigration," working paper 10781, National Bureau of Economic Research, September 2004.

24 See National Statistics, Republic of China, http://eng.stat.gov.tw. In Singapore, the economy, after growing at a 5.5 percent annual rate, took off in the mid-1960s and grew at an almost 10 percent annual rate for the next 20 years. For statistics, see Singapore, Government of Singapore, www.singstat.gov. South Korea, after growing sluggishly for decades, took off after 1980, growing at an average annual rate of close to 9 percent until the late 1990s. See Charlie Harvic and Mosayeb Pahlavani, "Sources of Economic Growth in South Korea," proceedings of Korea and the World Economy, a conference held at Korea University, Seoul, Korea, July 7–8, 2006. Thailand surged in the 1980s, so that by the early 1990s its economy, too, was expanding at nearly 10 percent per year. See National Statistic Office, Kingdom of Thailand, http://web.nso.go.th. And similar patterns prevail in all these Asian nations, some surging earlier than others.

25 Nationmaster.com database, www.nationmaster,com.

26 For an illustration of the feeling of the time, see Luke Johnson, "Time to Ride the Asian Tigers," www.telegraph.co.uk, December 10, 2000, or "Improving Latin America's Competitiveness," proceedings of World Economic Forum on Latin America, April 5–6, 2008.

27 For extensive work on these phenomena in general and particularly in Asia, see Edward M. Crenshaw, Ansai Z. Ameen, and Matthew Christenson, "Population Dynamics and Economic Development: Age Specific Population Growth Rates and Economic Growth in Developing Countries, 1965–1990," *American Sociological Review* (December 1999), and David E. Bloom and Jocelyn E. Finlay, "Demographic Change and Economic Growth in Asia," unpublished paper, Harvard School of Public Health, September 2008.

28 For details on the Asian demographic data and the models used to explain growth, see David E. Bloom and Jeffrey G. Williamson, "Demographic Transitions and Economic Miracles in Emerging Asia," *The World Bank Economic Review* (September 1998); and for both the Asian and Irish research, see David E. Bloom and David Canning, "Global Demographic Change: Dimensions and Economic Significance," working paper 10817, National Bureau of Economic Research, September 2004.

29 For a complete analysis of the relationship between savings rates and longevity, see David E. Bloom, David Canning, and Bryan Graham, "Longevity and Life-cycle Savings," *Scandinavian Journal of Economics* (September 2003). For work that uncovered the effect in Taiwan, see A. Deaton and C. Paxson,

"Growth, Demographic Structure, and National Savings in Taiwan," supplement, *Population and Development Review* (2000).

30 For a more detailed analysis, see David E. Bloom, David Canning, and Bryan Graham, "Longevity and Life-cycle Savings," *Scandinavian Journal of Economics* (September 2003).

31 See, for example, Alok Bhargava, Dean T. Jamison, Lawrence J. Lau, and Christopher J. L. Murray, "Modeling the Effects of Health on Economic Growth," *Journal of Health Economics* (May 2001).

32 Department of Economic and Social Affairs, "World Population Prospects: The 2006 Revision," *UN Population Newsletter* (June 2007).

33 See Isaac Ehrlich and Hiroyuki Chuma, "A Model of the Demand for Longevity and the Value of Life Extension," *The Journal of Political Economy* 4 (August 1990); S. Kalemli-Ozcan, "Mortality Decline, Human Capital Investment, and Economic Growth," *Journal of Development Economics* 1 (2000); and Jocelyn Finley, "Endogenous Longevity and Economic Growth," working paper 7, *Harvard Initiative for Global Health Program on the Global Demography of Aging* (July 2006).

34 "Summary of Social Security Amendment of 1983," Social Security Administration, www.socialsecurity.gov.

35 For a sample from Europe, see Didier Blanchet, "Pension Reform in Europe," *Intereconomics* (September 2005), and for further discussion in the United States, see "Reform of Social Security," Social Security Administration, www.socialsecurity.gov.

36 United States General Accounting Office, "Social Security Reform: Implications of Raising the Retirement Age," Report to the Chairman and the Ranking Minority Member, Special Committee on Aging, U.S. Senate, August 1999.

37 See Social Security Administration, www.socialsecurity.gov.

3: More Work, More Efficiently

1 David E. Bloom and David Canning, "Global Demographic Change: Dimensions and Economic Significance," working paper 10817, National Bureau of Economic Research, September 2004.

2 Bureau of Labor Statistics Web site, www.bls.gov.

3 Geoffrey McNicoll, "Economic Growth with Below-Replacement Fertility," *Population and Development Review* 12 (1986).

4 Bureau of Labor Statistics Web site, www.bls.gov.

5 Author's calculations assume that present participation rates of the 65–70 age cohort, approximately 31 percent, would rise to the average participation

rate of the working-age population generally, or about 75 percent. By adding these new workers to the working-age population and subtracting them from the retired population, the dependency ratio changes as indicated under current participation rates reported in Exhibit 4.

6 Author's calculation based on a rise in women's participation from the current 51 percent to 70 percent, a 37 percent increase for about a third of the existing workforce, or about a 12 percent jump in the actual working population.

7 Author's calculation using figures already presented and noted.

8 Research shows a direct link between women's participation in the workforce and child care facilities. See, for example, Sorca M. O'Conner, "Women's Labor Force Participation and Preschool Enrollment: A Cross-National Perspective, 1965–80," *Sociology of Education* (January 1988).

9 Sue Shellenbarger, "First Lady to Speak at White House Workplace Flexibility Forum," *The Wall Street Journal*, March 31, 2010.

10 Ibid.

11 "A Full Life," *The Economist*, September 2, 1999.

12 Department of Economic and Social Affairs, "World Population Prospects: The 2006 Revision," *UN Population Newsletter* (June 2007).

13 For details on Social Security and a number of anecdotes from elsewhere, see "A Full Life," *The Economist*, September 2, 1999.

14 David E. Bloom and David Canning, "Global Demographic Change: Dimensions and Economic Significance," working paper 10817, National Bureau of Economic Research, September 2004.

15 John Thornhill and Scheheherazade Daneshkhu, "EU Told to Transform Social Security Rules," *Financial Times*, March 25, 2008.

16 Department of Economic and Social Affairs, "World Population Prospects: The 2006 Revision," *UN Population Newsletter* (June 2007).

17 For example, see "Hey, Big Spender," *The Economist*, December 1, 2005, and "Now Robots Help Humans Cope with Illness," www.breitbart.com, August 2, 2009.

18 David Cheal, "Aging and Demographic Change," *Canadian Public Policy* (August 2000).

19 For a seminal statement of the wealth of research on this subject, see Robert J. Barro, "Economic Growth in a Cross Section of Countries," *Quarterly Journal of Economics* (May 1991), and also Isaac Ehrlich, "The Mystery of Human Capital as Engine of Growth or Why the U.S. Became the Economic Superpower in the 20th Century," working paper 12868, National Bureau of Economic Research, January 2007.

20 David E. Bloom and David Canning, "Global Demographic Change: Dimensions and Economic Significance," working paper 10817, National Bureau of Economic Research, September 2004.

21 For detailed research on the subject, see M. Abramowitz, "Catching Up, Forging Ahead, and Falling Behind," *Journal of Economic History* 36 (1986); C. Bean and N. Grafts, *Economic Growth in Europe Since 1945* (New York: Cambridge University Press, 1996); and M. O'Mahony, *Productivity in the EU*, HM Treasury, United Kingdom, 2002.

22 Bureau of Economic Analysis Web site, www.bea.gov.

23 Bureau of Labor Statistics Web site, www.bls.gov.

24 For European data, see J. Bradford DeLong, "Post–WWII Western European Exceptionalism: The Dynamic Dimension," University of California at Berkeley Research, December 1997. For Japanese data, see Benjamin Powell, "Japan," *The Concise Encyclopedia of Economics*, Library of Economics Web site, www.econlib.org.

25 Bureau of Economic Analysis Web site, www.bea.gov.

26 These figures are for manufacturing only, where productivity growth tends to outpace the rest of the economy. See Bureau of Labor Statistics Web site, www.bls.gov.

27 Bureau of Economic Analysis Web site, www.bea.gov.

28 Between 1980 and 1990, manufacturing output per hour increased at a 3.3 percent average annual rate, and between 1970 and 1980, it increased at a 2.7 percent average annual rate. Bureau of Labor Statistics Web site, www.bls.gov.

29 Ibid.

30 I. M. Ross, "The Invention of the Transistor," *Proceedings of the IEEE [Institute of Electrical and Electronics Engineers]*, January 1998.

31 For a copy of the Sarbanes-Oxley Act of 2002, H.R. 3763, see FindLaw Web site, www.findlaw.com.

4: Immigration Cuts Two Ways

1 Taken from David E. Bloom and David Canning, "Demographic Challenges, Fiscal Sustainability, and Economic Growth, working paper 8, *Harvard Initiative for Global Health Program on the Global Demography of Aging* (May 2006).

2 David E. Bloom, David Canning, and Jaypee Sevilla, *The Demographic Dividend: A New Perspective on the Economic Consequence of Population Change*, RAND, MR-1274 (Santa Monica, CA, 2002).

3 Diana Farrell, Sacha Ghai, and Tim Shavers, "The Demographic

Deficit: How Aging Will Reduce Global Wealth," *The McKinsey Quarterly* (March 2005).

4 Taken from Erika Kinetz, "As the World Comes of (Older) Age How Economies and Societies Might Adjust to Their Evolving Populations," *The International Herald Tribune*, December 4, 2004. Population figures from CIA *World Factbook*, www.cia.gov.

5 Diana Farrell, Sacha Ghai, and Tim Shavers, "The Demographic Deficit: How Aging Will Reduce Global Wealth," *The McKinsey Quarterly* (March 2005).

6 "Population Challenge and Development Goals," Department of Economic and Social Affairs, United Nations, September 2006.

7 "The Trouble with Migrants," *The Economist*, November 22, 2007.

8 Victor Mallet, "Migrants to Spain Find Welcome Mat Withdrawn," *Financial Times*, September 27–28, 2008.

9 Robert Dekle, "Financing Consumption in an Aging Japan," working paper 10781, National Bureau of Economic Research, September 2004.

10 "Population Challenge and Development Goals," Department of Economic and Social Affairs, United Nations, September 2006. Population figures from CIA *World Factbook*, www.cia.gov.

11 Daniel B. Wood, "Along U.S.-Mexican Border, an Erratic, Patchwork Fence," *The Christian Science Monitor*, April 3, 2008.

12 Jesse McKinley and Malia Wollan, "New Border Fear: Violence by a Rogue Militia," *The New York Times*, June 26, 2009.

13 For just one description of this awkward situation, see Coleen O'Conner, "Is Arizona's Immigration Policy Our New Civil War?," *San Diego News Network*, June 29, 2010, www.sdnn.com.

14 For outlines of the American immigration debate, see BBC News, "U.S. Immigration Debate: Key Players," BBC News Web site, http://news.bbc.co.uk and "In Focus: The Immigration Debate," *Institute for Policy Studies and Interhemisphere Resource Center* 2:31 (March 1997).

15 "Senate Slashes Guest Worker Program," *USA Today*, May 23, 2007.

16 "Obama's Immigration Straddle," editorial, *The Christian Science Monitor*, June 7, 2009.

17 For a reasonable summary of the Senate's agony on this subject, see Sara Murray, "Senate Plan Sets High Bar on Border Security," *The Wall Street Journal*, April 10, 2013.

18 Lawrence Harrison, "What Will America Stand for in 2050?," *The Christian Science Monitor*, May 31, 2009.

19 Quoted in Michael Powell, "U.S. Immigration Debate Is a Road Well Traveled," *The Washington Post*, May 8, 2006.

20 Geoffrey McNicoll, "Economic Growth with Below-Replacement Fertility," *Population and Development Review* 12 (1986).

21 Stephanie Giry, "France and Its Muslims," *Foreign Affairs* (September/October 2006).

22 Doug Sanders, "Why Our Thinking About Immigration Remains Borderline," *Globe and Mail*, November 3, 2007.

23 Matthew Clark, "Germany's Angela Merkel: Multiculturalism Has 'Utterly Failed,'" *The Christian Science Monitor*, October 17, 2010.

24 Paul Cullen, "Minister's Warning on Immigration Rates," *The Irish Times*, October 3, 2007.

25 Nicholas Cecil, "Most Britons Want Jobless Immigrants to Be Asked to Leave," *The Evening Standard*, March 26, 2009.

26 "The Trouble with Migrants," *The Economist*, November 22, 2007.

27 Victor Mallet, "Migrants to Spain Find Welcome Mat Withdrawn," *Financial Times*, September 27–28, 2008.

28 "The Trouble with Migrants," *The Economist*, November 22, 2007.

29 For a summary of the feeling, see Stephen Castle, "Thousands Protest Ahead of 'Polish Plumber' Vote," *The Independent*, February 15, 2006.

30 "The Trouble with Migrants," *The Economist*, November 22, 2007.

31 All quoted in Fareema Alam, "Beyond the Veil," *Newsweek* (international edition), November 27, 2006.

32 "The Trouble with Migrants," *The Economist*, November 22, 2007.

33 "The Integration Dilemma," *The Economist*, July 21, 2007.

34 "Germany Closing Up with New, Toughened Immigration Rules," *The Nation* (Thailand), May 24, 2008.

35 "The Trouble with Migrants," *The Economist*, November 22, 2007.

36 Anna Momigliano, "'Xenophobic Climate' Fueling Policies, Violence in Italy," *The Christian Science Monitor*, October 1, 2008.

37 Barbie Nadeau, "The World Condemns Rome, but Europe Is the Problem," *Newsweek* (international edition), June 9, 2008.

38 Charles Farelle, "Sarkozy Blasts EU as Flap over Gypsies Grows," *The European Wall Street Journal*, September 17, 2010.

39 Lisa Abend and Anna Momigliano, "Spain, Italy: Two Tactics to Tackling Illegal Immigration," *The Christian Science Monitor*, August 7, 2008.

40 Allen Hall, "EU Open Border Deal Threatens a 'Wave of Migration and Crime,'" *Daily Mail*, November 20, 2007.

41 Barbie Nadeau, "The World Condemns Rome, but Europe Is the Problem," *Newsweek* (international edition), June 9, 2008.

42 James Blitz, "Berlusconi's Immigration Policy Rings Alarm Bells," *Financial Times*, April 11, 2000, and Barbie Nadeau, "The World Condemns Rome, but Europe Is the Problem," *Newsweek* (international edition), June 9, 2008.

43 Quoted from *Die Welt* Web site by BBC Worldwide Monitoring, "EU-Wide Study Says Majority of Turks in Germany Complain About Discrimination," April 23, 2009.

44 All references from the *Die Welt* Web site quoted by the BBC Worldwide Monitoring, "Paper Reports on Anti-Muslims Mobilizing in Germany," BBC, August 12, 2007.

45 Gary Younge, "To Believe in a European Utopia Before Muslims Arrived Is Delusional," *The Guardian*, December 10, 2007.

46 Stephanie Giry, "France and Its Muslims," *Foreign Affairs* (September/October 2006).

47 *Die Welt* Web site by BBC Worldwide Monitoring, "EU-Wide Study Says Majority of Turks in Germany Complain About Discrimination," April 23, 2009.

48 Hueseyin Uzerli, "Turks in Germany," Letter to the Editor, *The International Herald Tribune*, July 18, 2007.

49 DPP News Agency report by BBC Worldwide Monitoring, "Four Turkish Associations Pull Out of German Integration Summit," BBC, July 11, 2007.

50 Matthew Clark, "Germany's Angela Merkel: Multiculturalism Has 'Utterly Failed,'" *The Christian Science Monitor*, October 17, 2010.

51 All references from Paul Belien, "Emigration Nation: Europeans' Flight from Europe," *The Washington Times*, June 6, 2007.

52 Ibid.

53 Miriam Jordan, "Ladder to American Success," *The Wall Street Journal*, February 7, 2013.

54 Needless to say, the research on such issues fails to offer a summary metric or even group of metrics that makes consistent comparisons across countries at the same time. Canadian research indicates that immigrants earn about 80 percent of comparable native wages within four years of arrival. (See Elizabeth McIssac, "Immigrants in Canadian Cities: Census 2001—What Do the Data Tell Us?," *Policy Options* [May 2003].) American research shows that immigrants on average close the wage gap with comparable native workers within 10 years of arrival and, on average, by the second generation turn an initial 20 percent wage disadvantage to comparable native workers into a 3

percent premium. For more detail, see Robert J. LaLonde and Robert H. Topel, "Immigrants and the American Labor Market: Quality, Assimilation, and Distributional Effects," *American Economic Review* (May 1991), and David Card, John DiNardo, and Eugena Estes, "The More Things Change: Immigrants and the Children of Immigrants in the 1940s, the 1970s, and the 1990s," in George J. Borjas, ed., *Issues in the Economics of Immigration* (Chicago: University of Chicago Press, 2000). In contrast to these pictures from North America, Swedish, British, and German research found a persistent income gap between immigrants and comparable native workers. See James Albrecht, Anders Bjorklund, and Susan Vroman, "Is There a Glass Ceiling in Sweden?," *Journal of Labor Economics* 1 (2003); Kevin J. Denny, Colm P. Harmon, and Maurice J. Roach, "The Distribution of Discrimination in Immigrant Earnings—Evidence from Britain, 1974–93," unpublished paper, Department of Economics, University College Dublin; and Gunter Lang, "Native-Immigrant Wage Differentials in Germany: Assimilation, Discrimination, or Human Capital?," unpublished paper, Faculty of Economics, University of Augsburg. Further, admittedly spotty material shows considerably more intermarriage between immigrants and natives, especially by the second generation, in the United States and Canada than in Europe, except perhaps France. See, for example, David Card, John DiNardo, and Eugena Estes, "The More Things Change: Immigrants and the Children of Immigrants in the 1940s, the 1970s, and the 1990s," in George J. Borjas, ed., *Issues in the Economics of Immigration* (Chicago: University of Chicago Press, 2000), and Stephanie Giry, "France and Its Muslims," *Foreign Affairs* (September/October 2006).

55 Jacob L. Vigdor, "Measuring Immigrant Assimilation in Post-Recession America," Civic Report Number 76, Manhattan Institute for Policy Research, March 2013.

56 Jennifer Harper, "Immigration, Loss of Culture Worry Nations Around World," *The Washington Times*, October 5, 2007.

57 "German Study on Immigration Finds Turks Poorly Integrated in Germany," *Spiegel* online (English), November 26, 2008.

58 Ibid.

59 Stephanie Giry, "France and Its Muslims," *Foreign Affairs* (September/October 2006).

60 Sarah Neville, "Fear over School Ban of Muslim Headgear," *Herald.ie*, June 10, 2008.

61 Stephanie Giry, "France and Its Muslims," *Foreign Affairs* (September/October 2006).

62 Many of the U.S. programs vary by state. For a sample of several, see the National Immigration Law Center Web site, www.nilc.org.

63 For a detailed review of Canadian programs, including the role of the

ISAP, see "Canadian Immigrant Programs," Workpermit.com, www.workpermit.com/immigration-video.htm?v=Canada-immigrant-program.

64 *Die Welt* Web site by BBC Worldwide Monitoring, "German Chancellor Says Foreigners Apply for Naturalization," BBC, May 13, 2009.

65 Author's own experience and Douglas Saunders, "Why Our Thinking About Immigration Remains Borderline," *Globe and Mail*, November 3, 2007.

66 Department of Economic and Social Affairs, "World Population Prospects: The 2006 Revision," *UN Population Newsletter* (June 2007).

67 William Underhill, "A Sharp Departure," *Newsweek* (international edition), March 24, 2008.

5: A Global Means to Relief

1 For just a small sample of the historical research in this area, see Paul Bairoch, "Free Trade and European Economic Development in the 19th Century," *European Economic Review* 3 (1972); William J. Collins, Kevin H. O'Rourke, and Jeffrey G. Williamson, "War, Trade and Factor Mobility Substitutes in History," in R. Faini, J. DeMelo, and K. F. Zimmermann, eds., *Migration: The Controversies and the Evidence* (New York: Cambridge University Press, 1999); Barry R. Chiswick and Timothy J. Hutton, "International Migration and the Integration of Labor Markets," in M. D. Bordo, A. M. Taylor, and J. G. Williamson, eds., *Globalization in Historical Perspective* (Chicago: University of Chicago Press, 2002); Kevin H. O'Rourke, "Tariffs and Growth in the Late 19th Century," *Economic Journal* 110 (2000); and Daniel Trefler, "International Factor Price Differences: Leontief Was Right!," *Journal of Political Economy* 6 (1993).

2 For a good overview of Britain's industrial revolution, its causes and support mechanisms, see Robert C. Allen, *The British Industrial Revolution in Global Perspective* (Cambridge: Cambridge University Press, 2009), especially pp. 57–79 and 106–131.

3 For a broader view, including Germany's nineteenth-century strides, see Peter N. Stearnes, *The Industrial Revolution in World History* (Boulder, CO: Westview, 1998), especially pp. 50–53 and 134–138.

4 For a good summary of the beginning of the American industrial experience, see Maury Klein, *The Genesis of Industrial America, 1870–1920* (New York: Cambridge University Press, 2007), especially pp. 5–16 and 105–30.

5 See Chapter 2, "The Demographic Imperative." The calculation starts with the recognition that total imports as tracked in the national income and product accounts have risen as a percent of overall gross domestic product from 10.5 percent in 1980 to 17.6 percent more recently. For underlying data, see Bureau of Economic Analysis Web site, www.bea.gov.

6 See Chapter 2, "The Demographic Imperative." The calculation assumes that the drop in labor supply relative to the retired population indicated in Exhibit 6 of that chapter will require a proportionate jump in imports to meet the consumption demands of the retired population next to the reduced relative supply of the domestic workforce. Thus, the American figures show a drop in the relative size of the workforce from 5.2 of working age per person over 65 presently to 3.0 by 2030, for a 42.3 percent relative drop in the availability of domestic labor. The Japanese figures show a drop in this ratio from 2.9 at present to 1.8 by 2030, a change of 37.9 percent; and so on for other economies as shown in Exhibit 6.

7 Calculations for each economy extend the annual rate of increase in the proportion of imports for the past 30 years, and add to it the calculations described in the previous note in order to determine the overall share of imports by 2030. For sources on trend growth for the United States, see Bureau of Economic Analysis Web site, www.bea.gov. The source for Japan is Statistics Bureau Web site, Ministry of Internal Affairs and Communications, www.stat.go.jp/english. For the United Kingdom, see the Office for National Statistics Online, www.statistics.gov.uk. For continental Europe, see OECD Statistical Extracts Web site, http://stats.oecd.org.

8 The historical trend, for instance, could in part reflect the already developing shortfall in the relative amount of domestic labor. Neither do the calculations take into account the changing foreign exchange values of currencies during this time, nor do any of them try to adjust for accelerations in productivity or changing rates of labor participation in any of these countries.

9 Total imports as tracked in the national income and product accounts have risen as a percent of overall GDP from 10.5 percent in 1980 to 17.6 percent more recently. For underlying data, see Bureau of Economic Analysis Web site, www.bea.gov.

10 The expansion of imports' share of the economy from 10.5 percent in 1980 to 18 percent presently amounts to an average annual jump of 0.25 percentage point a year. A rise over the next 20 years to 30 percent, for demographic reasons alone, amounts to an annual rise of 0.6 percentage point. Combined, the trends would amount to an increase of 0.85 percent a year.

11 Alan M. Taylor, "Globalization, Trade, and Development: Some Lessons from History," working paper 9326, National Bureau of Economic Research, November 2002.

12 U.S. China Business Council Web site, www.uschina.org. See also Dong He and Wen Lang Zhang, "How Dependent Is the Chinese Economy on Exports and in What Sense Has Its Growth Been Export Led?," working paper 14, Hong Kong Monetary Authority, October 2008.

13 Reserve Bank of India Web site, www.rbi.org.in.

14 Data on many of these countries are limited. For what are available, see the databases of the International Monetary Fund, www.imf.org, and the World Bank, www.worldbank.org. Brazil actually has seen its total production outstrip exports, but it depends heavily on minerals sold to the rest of the world. For what statistics exist on Brazil, see the government's official Instituto Brasileiro de Geografia e Estatística Web site, www.ibge.gov.br.

15 CIA *World Factbook*, www.cia.gov.

16 Quoted in Alan Tonelson, "Secretary Snow's Beijing Cave-in Leaves America's China Policy Critics No Choice but to Fight White House," *American Economic Alert*, October 27, 2005.

17 Michael P. Dooley, David Folkerts-Landau, and Peter Garber, "Direct Investment, Rising Wages and the Absorption of Excess Labor in the Periphery," working paper 10626, National Bureau of Economic Research, July 2004.

18 Wang Yaguang and Xie Yunting, "Labor Shortfall Felt in Coastal China as Orders Pile Up," Xinhua News Service, August 27, 2009.

19 Bureau of Labor Statistics, www.bls.gov.

20 Li Cui, Chang Shu, and Xiaojing Su, "How Much Do Exports Matter for China's Growth?," *China Economic Issues,* Hong Kong Monetary Authority, March 2009.

21 Quoted in "China's Excessive Dependence on Export Development Models Needs to Adjust, Unsustainable," Source China Trade Knowledge Web site, www.sourcejuice.com.

22 D. He and W. Zhang, "How Dependent Is the Chinese Economy on Exports and in What Sense Has Its Growth Been Export Led?," working paper 14, Hong Kong Monetary Authority, October 2008.

23 Li Cui, Chang Shu, and Xiaojing Su, "How Much Do Exports Matter for China's Growth?," *China Economic Issues,* Hong Kong Monetary Authority, March 2009.

24 For the two sides of this statistical debate, see Robert C. Feenstra and Chang Hong, "China's Exports and Employment," working paper 13552, National Bureau of Economic Research, October 2007, and Michael P. Dooley, David Folkerts-Landau, and Peter Garber, "Direct Investment, Rising Real Wages, and the Absorption of Excess Labor in the Periphery," working paper 10626, National Bureau of Economic Research, July 2004.

25 Research done at the University of California, Santa Cruz, determined that each $1,000 of Chinese exports supported 0.242 person years of employment. Since China's overall exports averaged the equivalent of $1.4 trillion in 2008, the ratio points to 330 million full-time jobs or about one-third of the

workforce. For Chinese export figures, see U.S.-China Business Council Web site, www.uschina.org. For background on the calculated ratio, see Xikang Chen, Leonard Cheng, K. C. Fung, Lawrence J. Lau, Yun Wing Sung, C. Yang, K. Zhu. J. Pei, and Z. Tang, "Domestic Value Added and Employment Generated by Chinese Exports: A Quantitative Estimation," paper 15663, Munich Personal Re PEc Archive, June 2009.

26 Robert C. Feenstra and Chang Hung, "China's Exports and Employment," working paper 13552, National Bureau of Economic Research, October 2007.

27 "China Economic Growth Accelerates," BBC News Web site, October 22, 2009.

28 "India's Job Losses Could Reach 10 Million by March," *Area Development Online*, www.areadevelopment.com, January 7, 2009.

29 Renaud Lambert, "Brazil: More Dependent than Ever," *Le Monde* (English edition), June 5, 2009.

30 "Asia GDP Forecast," *IMF Regional Economic Outlook*, International Monetary Fund, May 2009.

31 "China Economic Growth Accelerates," BBC News Web site, October 22, 2009.

32 Tom Mitchell, "Daunting Departure," *Financial Times*, January 8, 2009.

33 "Impact of Global Meltdown on India's Garment Exports," Fibre 2 Fashion Web site, www.fibre2fashion.com.

34 "India's Job Losses Could Reach 10 Million by March," *Area Development Online*, www.areadevelopment.com, January 7, 2009.

35 See, for example, Raymond Colitt, "Brazil Unveils $5.1 Billion Investment Plan to Defuse Growing Unrest," *Financial Times*, April 1, 2004; Kirk Semple, "Turmoil in Latin America Threatens Decades of Reform, Economic Woes, Political Unrest Raise Anxieties," *The Boston Globe*, August 18, 2002; and Geraldo Samos, "Brazil's Self-Image Bruised by Unrest," *The Wall Street Journal*, May 18, 2006. Also see "Asia GDP Forecast," *IMF Regional Economic Outlook*, International Monetary Fund, May 2009.

36 Krittivas Mukherjee, "Economic Apartheid Breeds Unrest," *The Vancouver Sun*, October 15, 2008.

37 See, for example, Raymond Colitt, "Brazil Unveils $5.1 Billion Investment Plan to Defuse Growing Unrest," *Financial Times*, April 1, 2004; Kirk Semple, "Turmoil in Latin America Threatens Decades of Reform, Economic Woes, Political Unrest Raise Anxieties," *The Boston Globe*, August 18, 2002; and Geraldo Samos, "Brazil's Self-Image Bruised by Unrest," *The Wall Street Journal*, May 18, 2006.

38 "Asia GDP Forecast," *IMF Regional Economic Outlook*, International Monetary Fund, May 2009.

39 Keith Bradsher, "China's Unemployment Swells as Exports Falter," *The New York Times*, February 6, 2009.

40 Tom Mitchell, "Daunting Departure," *Financial Times*, January 8, 2009.

41 BBC Monitoring Asia Pacific, July 11, 2009.

42 Philip Stephens, "Western Awe and Domestic Anxiety: A Tale of Two Chinas," *Financial Times*, July 10, 2009.

43 Tom Lasseter, "Despite Continued Economic Growth, China Fears Labor Unrest," McClatchy-Tribune News Service, September 12, 2009.

44 Bill Schiller, "Economic Crisis Tops Woes of China Congress," *Toronto Star*, March 6, 2009.

45 "Premier Vows to Promote Employment, Exports," China Daily.com, March 5, 2009.

46 Zhou Xin, "China Must Boost Exports as West Retreats: Minister," Reuters Wire, April 2, 2009.

47 After allowing a 20-plus percent appreciation of the yuan against the dollar after 2005, the People's Bank of China abruptly froze the value of the yuan in late 2008 and held it at that level until exports began to improve in 2010. See Bloomberg Financial Service, www.bloomberg.com.

48 Tom Mitchell, "Daunting Departure," *Financial Times*, January 8, 2009.

49 Updated by applying China's nominal growth rate to the figure originally quoted in Martin Wolf, "The Dragon's Turning China into the World's Workshop," *Financial Times*, November 26, 2003.

50 Malcolm Moore, "How Much Higher Can Factory Wages Go?," *China Economic Review*, March 11, 2010.

51 "Bears in a China Shop," *The Economist*, January 14, 2010.

52 Andrew Batson, "China Bets Highways Will Drive Its Growth," *The Wall Street Journal*, November 11, 2008.

53 "Inequality Check in Asia," *Wall Street Journal (Europe)*, August 21, 2007.

54 All data from the CIA *World Factbook*, www.cia.gov.

55 Nationmaster.com Web site, from Rapid Intelligence, New South Wales, Australia, www.nationmaster.com.

56 Quoted in Ashish Arora and Alfonso Gambardella, "The Globalization of the Software Industry: Perspective and Opportunities for Developed

and Developing Countries," working paper 10538, National Bureau of Economic Research, June 2004.

57 "Be Careful What You Wish For," *The Economist*, August 4, 2007.

58 For the most recent review of this well-known history, see Niall Ferguson, *The Ascent of Money* (New York: Penguin, 2008).

59 Author's calculations from data drawn from the Bloomberg Financial Database, www.bloomberg.com.

60 Committee on the Global Financial System, "Institutional Investors, Global Savings and Asset Allocation," Bank for International Settlements, February 2007.

61 U.S. Census Bureau, "Statistical Abstract of the United States," Commerce Department, 2009, p. 783.

62 Eurostat Web site, http//epp.eurostat.ec.europa.eu.

63 "The 3rd Surging Wave of Japanese Investment in China," *People's Daily* online, http://english.peopledaily.com, December 22, 2007.

64 "Overtaking," *The Economist*, December 7, 2009.

65 For detail on the development impact of such financial flows, see Eswar Prasad, Kenneth Rogoff, Shang-Jin Wei, and M. Ayhan Kose, "Financial Globalization, Growth and Volatility in Developing Countries," working paper 10942, National Bureau of Economic Research, December 2004.

66 For a thorough discussion of these complex interactions, see Peter Henry, "Stock Market Liberalization, Economic Reform, and Emerging Market Equity Prices," *Journal of Finance* (April 2000), and Renee Stulz, "International Portfolio Flows and Security Markets," *International Capital Flows, National Bureau of Economic Research Report Series* (Chicago: University of Chicago Press, 1999), pp. 257–93.

67 For examples, see Eswar Prasad, Kenneth Rogoff, Shang-Jin Wei, and M. Ayhan Kose, "Financial Globalization, Growth, and Volatility in Developing Countries," working paper 10942, National Bureau of Economic Research, December 2004.

68 Specifically, "bridges to nowhere" refers to the Gravina Island Bridge in Alaska, which was to use a $398 million earmark in the 2005 federal budget to replace a ferry to an island with only 50 inhabitants. It was purely a favor to a powerful Alaska politician. It has come to mean any politically motivated outlay that has no cultural, commercial, or military value. For a reference and an entertaining explanation, see Rebecca Clarren, "A Bridge to Nowhere," Salon.com, www.salon.com, August 9, 2005.

69 For research on these important channels of influence and the benefits they bring emerging economies, see Gerard Caprio and Patrick Honohan, "Restoring Banking Stability: Beyond Supervised Capital Requirements," *Journal*

of Economic Perspectives, Fall 1999, and Ross Levine, "Foreign Bonds, Financial Development, and Economic Growth," *International Financial Markets: Harmonization Versus Competition*, American Enterprise Institute paper (Washington, D.C., 1996), pp. 224–54.

70 For a thorough assessment of these critical advantages, see Eduardo Borenstein, Jose DeGregorio, and Jong-Wha Lee, "How Does Foreign Direct Investment Affect Growth?," *Journal of International Economics* (June 1998).

71 For examples and analysis, see Hiroshi Sato, "Diversification into Non-Japanese Deals Becoming Key to Profits, Survival," *The Nikkei Weekly*, April 15, 1989.

72 Eswar Prasad, Kenneth Rogoff, Shang-Jin Wei, and M. Ayhan Kosc, "Financial Globalization, Growth and Volatility in Developing Countries," working paper 10942, National Bureau of Economic Research, December 2004.

73 For a complete exposition of these data, drawn from the World Bank's World Development Indicators, see Eswar Prasad, Kenneth Rogoff, Shang-Jin Wei, and M. Ayhan Kose, "Financial Globalization, Growth, and Volatility in Developing Countries," working paper 10942, National Bureau of Economic Research, December 2004.

6: Forcing Change in Industrial Structures

1 Bureau of Labor Statistics, "International Case Provision of Hourly Compensation Costs in Manufacturing," January 25, 2008.

2 Author's 2003 conversation with a General Electric engineer (name now forgotten), recently back from Brazil, describing his experience there and earlier in China and verified in subsequent conversations with product managers, businesspeople, and engineers with experience in emerging economies.

3 Author's own observation during a visit outside Shanghai in the late 1990s.

4 Story told to the author by a colleague, Zane Brown, on his return from joint venture negotiation in China.

5 This general picture is drawn from reports on problems at the export factories in the coastal city of Wenzhou, but it is indicative of more broad-based problems throughout the manufacturing bases on the Pearl River and Yangtze River deltas. See Wang Yaguang and Xie Yunting, "Labor Shortfall Felt in Coastal China as Orders Pick Up," Xinhua News Service, August 27, 2009.

6 Jamil Anderlini, "Siemens Boards Chinese Rail Bid," *Financial Times*, March 17, 2010.

7 Wang Yaguang and Xie Yunting, "Labor Shortfall Felt in Costal China as Orders Pile Up," Xinhua New Service, August 27, 2009.

8 All comparisons in Kunal Sen, "International Trade and Manufacturing Employment Outcomes in India," research paper 2008/87, United Nations University, World Institute for Development Economics Research (UNU-WIDER), October 2008.

9 CIA *World Factbook*, www.cia.gov.

10 "Performance," Development Commissioner (MSME) Ministry of Micro, Small and Medium Enterprises, Government of India, September 25, 2009.

11 Ibid.

12 Ibid.

13 "Indian Apparel and Textile Industry," Indian Exports and Business Trends Zone Web site, www.india-exports.com.

14 "Steps to Boost Handicraft Exports," *The Hindu Business Line*, March 20, 2006.

15 Taken from Glenda Mallon and John Whalley, "China's Past Accession WTO Stance," working paper 10649, National Bureau of Economic Research, August 2004.

16 Kunal Sen, "International Trade and Manufacturing Employment Outcomes in India," research paper 2008/87, United Nations University, World Institute for Development Economics Research (UNU-WIDER), October 2008.

17 Figure on textile employment from China's Ministry of Commerce, taken from "Ministry: No Surge Expected in China's Textile Exports," *People's Daily* (English edition), January 22, 2009. Overall Chinese labor force from CIA *World Factbook*, www.cia.gov.

18 Xikang Chen, Leonard Cheng, K. C. Fung, Lawrence J. Lau, Yun-Wing Sung, C. Yang, K. Zhu, J. Pei, and Z. Tang, "Domestic Value Added and Employment Generated by Chinese Exports: A Quantitative Estimation," Munich Personal; RePEc Archive (MPRA), December 2008.

19 Lee Brangstetter and Nicholas Lardy, "China's Embrace of Globalization," working paper 12373, National Bureau of Economic Research, July 2006.

20 Kunal Sen, "International Trade and Manufacturing Employment Outcomes in India," research paper 2008/87, United Nations University, World Institute for Development Economics Research (UNU-WIDER), October 2008.

21 CIA *World Factbook*, www.cia.gov.

22 Quoted in Lee Branstetter and Nicholas Lardy, "China's Embrace of

Globalization," working paper 12373, National Bureau of Economic Research, July 2006.

23 Taken from "Service Exports in Developing Asia," *The Hindu Business Line*, September 8, 2009.

24 CIA *World Factbook*, www.cia.gov.

25 "Press Release," Department of Commerce, Government of India, September 29, 2005.

26 "India's Small IT Firms to Shift Focus from U.S. to New Markets," *Thaindian News*, October 20, 2008.

27 S. Athreye, "The Indian Software Industry," in A. Arora and A. Gambardella, eds., *The Rise and Growth of the Software Industry in Some Emerging Economies* (New York: Oxford University Press, 2005).

28 For commentary on India's pharmaceutical area, see "Pharmaceutical Companies Venture into Export Markets," *India News* online, www.news.indiamotr.com, September 25, 2009.

29 For commentary on Brazil's pharmaceutical area, see "Brazil Pharmaceuticals and Healthcare Report," *irbo*, Online Business Intelligence for the Bio Pharma Industry, www.piribo.com, third quarter 2008.

30 CIA *World Factbook*, www.cia.gov.

31 For a summary of the analysis, see John Engler, "American Industry Can Still Stay Ahead of China," *Financial Times*, August 18, 2008. For up-to-date value-added data on the United States and China both, see Bureau of Economic Analysis, National Income and Product Accounts, www.bea.gov.

32 Ashish Arora and Alfonso Gambardella, "The Globalization of the Software Industry: Perspective and Opportunities for Developed and Developing Countries," working paper 10538, National Bureau of Economic Research, June 2004.

33 CIA *World Factbook*, www.cia.gov.

34 S. Athreye, "The Indian Software Industry," in A. Arora and A. Gambardella, eds., *The Rise and Growth of the Software Industry in Some Emerging Economies* (New York: Oxford University Press, 2005).

35 Commonwealth of Massachusetts South America Office, "Brazil Aerospace Industry," Massachusetts Office of International Trade and Industry (MOITI) Report, June 2007.

36 Author's updates of figures from Mary Amiti and Shang-Jin Wei, "Fear of Service Outsourcing: Is It Justified?," working paper 10808, National Bureau of Economic Research, September 2004.

37 For greater insight into Ricardo's theory, see David Ricardo, *On the*

Principles of Political Economy and Taxation (London: G. Bell and Sons, 1819), particularly Chapter VII, pp. 113–19.

38 For more modern treatments and statistical support, see R. Dornbusch, A. S. Fischer, and P. A. Samuelson, "Comparative Advantage, Trade, and Payments in a Ricardian Model with a Continuum of Goods," *The American Economic Review* 67:5 (1977); P. Sameulson, "A Ricardo-Sraffa Paradigm Comparing Gains from Trade in Inputs and Finished Goods," *Journal of Economic Literature* 39:4 (2001); and Ronald W. Jones, "Heckscher-Ohlin Trade Flows: A Reappraisal," *Trade and Development Review* 1:1 (2008).

39 Some hypothetical figures might make this matter clearer. Say even though China at this distant date were better at everything than America, its labor advantages might make it four times as effective at labor-intensive activities and only half again as effective as America in the sophisticated area. Say further that America, with its labor shortage, was twice as effective at high-value, capital-intensive activity as it was at low-value, labor-intensive activity. The relative production ratios for the two countries, then, would look like this:

	Low-Value- Added	High-Value-Added
America	1	2
China	4	3

Such a circumstance would enable China to produce 33 percent more from a focus on labor-intensive than on sophisticated, capital-intensive activities, four being one-third larger than three. Since America, though less effective than China at all things, is still in this illustration twice as effective in itself at capital-intensive than at labor-intensive activities, it would produce twice the value if it were to concentrate entirely on the former. Clearly, both countries would be better off if they made these concentrations and traded to get the kinds of outputs they choose not to produce for themselves.

40 Readers who enjoy economic theory will note that Ricardo did not reference factor endowments—relative amounts of labor, physical capital, available land, etc.—when developing his theories of comparative advantage and trade. These were emphasized in theories under the title by Heckscher-Ohlin. For a complete statement, see Bertil Ohlin, *Interregional and International Trade* (Cambridge: Harvard University Press, 1933). Though statistical research has not universally verified Heckscher-Ohlin, the present, applied case seems to fit well and allows a combination of the two theories with Heckscher-Ohlin, in this one instance, a special case of Ricardo.

7: Still More Exaggerated Change

1 Internetnews.com, December 2, 2004, www.internetnews.com.

2 Ibid.

3 Kunio Saijo, "Ability to Innovate Holds the Key to Future," *The Nikkei Weekly*, February 28, 2008.

4 Jathon Sapsford, "Industrial Evolution: Japan's Economy Gains Steam from Manufacturing Heartland," *The Wall Street Journal*, October 11, 2005.

5 Peter Marsh, "Westinghouse Buy Sets Foundation for Profitability," *Financial Times*, June 10, 1999.

6 Peter Marsh, "Lackluster Performance a Thing of the Past," *Financial Times*, October 25, 2000.

7 Marc Chandler, *Making Sense of the Dollar* (New York: Bloomberg, 2009).

8 "Korea Investment and Securities Signs $157 Million Strategic Outsourcing Agreement with IBM," IPR News Wire, October 13, 2009.

9 Kunio Saijo, "Ability to Innovate Holds the Key to Future," *The Nikkei Weekly*, February 28, 2008.

10 Jathon Sapsford, "Industrial Evolution: Japan's Economy Gains Steam from Manufacturing Heartland," *The Wall Street Journal*, October 11, 2005.

11 Ashish Arora and Alfonso Gambardella, "The Globalization of the Software Industry: Perspective and Opportunities for Developed and Developing Countries," working paper 10538, National Bureau of Economic Research, June 2004.

12 Christopher Swann, "Diversity Needed to Balance Economy," *Financial Times*, March 25, 2002.

13 Sarah Murray, "A Specialist in Emerging Markets: Company Profile: Globeleq," *Financial Times*, September 14, 2005.

14 Chris Prystay, "Beauty China's Success Using Outsourcing Attracts Notice," *The Asian Wall Street Journal*, January 19, 2005.

15 Stephanie E. Curcuru, Toman Dvorak, and Francis E. Warnock, "The Stability of Large External Imbalances: The Role of Return Differentials," National Bureau of Economic Research, May 2007.

16 Calculated by applying this 5-percentage-point differential to data on foreign holdings of U.S. Treasury debt on the Federal Reserve Board Web site, www.federalreserve.gov.

17 See definitions and procure data on the overall U.S. foreign trade deficit on the Bureau of the Census Web site, www.census.gov.

18 All statistics and comparisons from Anil Kumar, "Globalizing Texas: Exports and High-Tech Jobs," Review of the Federal Reserve Bank of Dallas, September/October 2007.

19 All insights and measures from Edward L. Glaeser, "Reinventing Boston: 1640–2003," working paper 10166, National Bureau of Economic Research, December 2003.

20 "Research Spending 'Must Increase' to Help Catch U.S.," EIU ViewsWire, February 5, 2009.

21 "In Praise of Services," *Sunday Business*, September 17, 2006.

22 Peter Wise, "Search for Its Place in the New Europe," *Financial Times*, October 20, 2004.

23 Chapter 8, "A Tide of Resistance," will delve more deeply into how the country has used research and technology to raise worker productivity and cope with foreign competition in the past.

24 Calculation from aggregates reported in "Battelle-*R&D Magazine* 2009 Funding Forecast," December 18, 2008, Battelle Memorial Institute Web site, www.battelle.org.

25 Ann Huff Stevens, "The More Things Change, the More They Stay the Same: Trends in Long-Term Employment in the United States, 1969–2002," working paper 11878, National Bureau of Economic Research, December 2005.

26 Job security in this case is measured by average job tenure. See ibid. and Robert Z. Lawrence, "Does a Kick in the Pants Get You Going or Does it Just Hurt?," in Robert C. Feenstra, ed., *The Impact of International Trade on Wages* (Chicago: University of Chicago Press, 2000).

27 Calculations made from a comparison of 2007 and 2000 data drawn from Occupational Employment Survey, Bureau of Labor Statistics Web site, www.bls.gov.

28 Ibid.

29 For a detailed, if highly abstract, discussion of these effects, see Jicmin Guo and Much Planting, "Using Input-Output Analysis to Measure U.S. Economic Structural Change over a 24-Year Period," paper presented at the 13th International Conference on Input-Output Techniques, Macerate, Italy, August 21–28, 2000.

30 Hans G. Mueller, "The Steel Industry," *The Annals of the American Academy* 460 (March 1982).

31 Bruce Western, "A Comparative Study of Working-Class Disorganization," *American Sociological Review* 60 (1995).

32 Melanie Trottman and Kris Maher, "Organized Labor Loses Members," *The Wall Street Journal*, January 24, 2013.

33 At present, teachers and civil service employees make up some 27 percent of AFL-CIO membership, a sharp jump from 1979, at the peak in

union membership, when civil servants and teachers amounted to only 15 percent of total membership.

34 For examples of such alliances, see Hans G. Mueller, "The Steel Industry," *The Annals of the American Academy* 460 (March 1982); Michael Wallerstein, "Unemployment, Collective Bargaining, and the Demand for Protection," *The American Journal of Political Science* 31 (1987); National Weekly Edition, *The Washington Post*, July 2, 1984; Ronald P. Dora, "Adjustment in Process: A Lancashire Town," in Jagdish N. Bhagwati, ed., *Import Competition and Response* (Chicago: University of Chicago Press, 1982); and Stephen P. Magee, "Three Single Tests of the Staples-Samuelson Theorem," in Peter Oppenheimer, ed., *Issues in International Economics* (Stocksfield, U.K.: Oriel, 1980).

35 For just a small sample of such discussions, see John R. Logan and Reid M. Golden, "Suburbs and Satellite: Two Decades of Change," *American Sociological Review* 51 (1986); Daron Acemoglu, Simon Johnson, and James A. Robinson, "Reversal of Fortune: Geography and Institution in the Making of the Modern World Income Distribution," *Quarterly Journal of Economics* 117:4 (2002); George Akerlof and Rachel E. Kronton, "Identity and the Economics of Organization," *Journal of Economic Perspectives* 19:1 (2005); Richard D. Alba, *Ethics Identify: The Transformation of White America* (New Haven: Yale University Press, 1990); T. N. Clark and S. M. Lipsat, "Are Social Classes Dying?," *International Sociology*, 1993; N. D. DeGroof, P. Nicuwbeerta, and A. Heath, "Mobility and Political Preference: Individual and Contexted Effects," *American Journal of Sociology* 100 (1995); M. Hout, C. Brooks, and J. Manza, *The Democratic Class Struggle in the United States, 1948–1992*; Harvey Marshall, "White Movement to the Suburbs: A Comparison of Explanations," *American Sociological Review* 44 (1979); and John R. Logan and Ried M. Golden, "Suburbs and Satellite: Two Decades of Change," *American Sociological Review* 51 (1986).

36 See especially John R. Logan and Reid M. Golden, "Suburbs and Satellite: Two Decades of Change," *American Sociological Review* 51 (1986).

8: A Tide of Resistance

1 For a typical statement, see Lindley H. Clark, Jr., "Peace and Free Trade Should Go Together," *The Wall Street Journal*, November 29, 1990.

2 Michael Orresker, "Poll Finds U.S. Expects Peace Dividend," *The New York Times*, January 25, 1990.

3 For a good example of such sentiments, see David Warsh, "Successful GATT Talks Are Good for Democracy," *The Boston Globe*, December 19, 1993.

4 David Gergen, "The Good News of 1990," *U.S. News & World Report*, January 7, 1991.

5 "Brave New World," editorial, *Financial Times*, January 1, 1999.

6 Waichi Sekiguchi, "New Decade Brings New World Role for Japan;

Global Economy Replacing Force of Arms as Framework for Peace," *Japan Economic Journal* (December 30, 1989).

7 For example, see William Raspberry, "NAFTA Debate Is, in the End, About Class," *The Plain Dealer* (Cleveland), November 21, 1993, and Elizabeth Furse and Peter De Fazio, "Environment and Labor Unprotected Under NAFTA," *The Oregonian*, November 25, 1993.

8 Thomas Oliphant, "The Great Myths Surrounding the NAFTA Vote," *The Boston Globe*, November 21, 1993.

9 For a detailed picture of such positive enthusiasm, see "Views of a Changing World, 1994," Pew Research Center, 1994, available on the Pew Research Center Web site, www.pewglobal.org.

10 See, for example, Amy Dunkin and Suzanne Woolley, "Going Global? Here's How," *Business Week*, July 2, 1990.

11 President George H. W. Bush, "Address Before a Joint Session of the Congress on the State of the Union," January 31, 1990, and George H. W. Bush, "Address Before a Joint Session of the Congress on the State of the Union," January 28, 1992, both in John T. Woolley and Gerhard Peters, the American Presidency Project [online], University of California at Santa Barbara, http://www.presidency.ucsb.edu.

12 See President William J. Clinton, "Address Before a Joint Session of the Congress on the State of the Union," February 17, 1996, and William J. Clinton, "Address Before a Joint Session of the Congress on the State of the Union," February 4, 1997, both in John T. Woolley and Gerhard Peters, the American Presidency Project [online], University of California at Santa Barbara, http://www.presidency.ucsb.edu.

13 See Bureau of Economic Analysis, National Income and Product Accounts, www.bea.gov.

14 See President George H. W. Bush, "Address Before a Joint Session of the Congress on the State of the Union," January 31, 1990, and George H. W. Bush, "Address Before a Joint Session of the Congress on the State of the Union," January 28, 1992, both in John T. Woolley and Gerhard Peters, the American Presidency Project [online], University of California at Santa Barbara, http://www.presidency.ucsb.edu., and President William J. Clinton, "Address Before a Joint Session of the Congress on the State of the Union," February 17, 1996, and William J. Clinton, "Address Before a Joint Session of the Congress on the State of the Union," February 4, 1997, both in John T. Woolley and Gerhard Peters, the American Presidency Project [online], University of California at Santa Barbara, http://www.presidency.ucsb.edu.

15 Data from the International Monetary Fund, World Economic Outlook Database, www.imf.org. These comparisons used the IMF calculations of World GDP plus its groupings for these categories: Emerging

Economies, Africa, Commonwealth of Independent States, and Developing Economies.

16 Francis Fukuyama, *The End of History and the Last Man* (New York: Free Press, 1992), p. xiii.

17 Ibid.

18 Ibid., p. xiv.

19 Ibid., p. xii.

20 World Trade Organization, "What Is the World Trade Organization?," World Trade Organization Web site, www.wto.org/english, July 2008.

21 Peter Sutherland, "Spirit of New Trade Order—Making the Uruguay Round Effective," *Financial Times*, June 7, 1994.

22 *The Daily Yomiuri*, editorial, December 4, 1994.

23 "GATT Long Last," editorial, *The Boston Globe*, November 29, 1994.

24 "Triumph and Tragedy," *The Straits Times*, December 31, 1994.

25 Robert T. Matsui, "Interdependence Is Here," *The Washington Times*, November 29, 1994.

26 For a detailed picture of the declining popular support, compare Pew Research Center, "Pew Global Attitudes Project," Pew Research Center, Washington, D.C., 2000, with Pew Research Center, "Views of a Changing World 2003," Pew Research Center, Washington, D.C., 2003, both available on the Pew Research Center Web site www.pewglobal.org.

27 "Battle Lines," *The Economist*, December 24, 1994/January 6, 1995.

28 For descriptions of these, see Michael Hardt and Antonio Negri, "What the Protesters in Genoa Want," *The New York Times*, July 20, 2001, and Arthur Santana and Manny Fernandez, "Police Await 100,000 Protesters," *The Washington Post*, August 18, 2001.

29 For a review of the elements involved in the protests and the suicide, see Patrick Moser, "South Korean Militants Mourn Suicide Death at Cancun Protest," Agence France Presse, September 12, 2003.

30 Robert Gavin, "Job Security a Worry in Changing Economy," *The Boston Globe*, July 26, 2004.

31 Joanna Slater, "Focus on Outsourcing," *The Wall Street Journal*, May 5, 2004.

32 "Norwegian Farmers Complete 2,200 Kilometer WTO Protest," Agence France Presse, July 26, 2005.

33 "More Pain than Gain," *The Economist*, September 14, 2006.

34 See Bob Davis, "IMF Fuels Critics of Globalization," *The Wall Street Journal*, October 16, 2007.

35 Alan S. Blinder, "Americans Are Losing Their Faith in Globalization," *The New York Times*, January 7, 2008.

36 See, for example, John Plender, "The Pitfalls of Financial Globalization Grow Clearer," *Financial Times*, November 20, 2007, and Dani Rodrik and Arvind Subramanian, "Why We Need to Curb Global Flows of Capital," *Financial Times*, February 26, 2008.

37 Leonie A. Marks, Nicholas Kalaitandonakes, and Srinivasa Konduru, "Images of Globalization in the Mass Media," *Journal Compilation* (Oxford: Blackwell, 2006).

38 Andrew Kohut, "Assessing Globalization: Benefits and Drawbacks of Trade and Integration," Pew Research Center, Washington, D.C., June 24, 2008.

39 Jagdish N. Bhagwadi, "Globalization in Your Face: A New Book Humanizes Global Capitalism," *Foreign Affairs* (July/August 2000).

40 See "More Pain than Gain," *The Economist*, September 14, 2006.

41 Calculation by Capital Economics, www.capitaleconomics.com.

42 Bureau of Labor Statistics, "International Comparisons of Hourly Compensation Costs on Manufacturing, 2006," January 25, 2008.

43 For import figures, see Bureau of the Census Web site, www.census.gov. For GDP figures, see Bureau of Economic Analysis Web site, www.bea.gov. Percent calculation takes dollar value of imports in each period divided by the GDP for that same period.

44 See official Web sites for European Union statistics, Eurostat, Brussels, Belgium, www.http://epp.eurostat.ec.europa.eu; Japan, Statistics Bureau, Ministry of Internal Affairs and Communications, www.stat.go.jp; and the United Kingdom, U.K. Statistics Authority, www.statisticsauthority.gov.uk.

45 See International Monetary Fund Web site, www.imf.org.

46 Bureau of Labor Statistics Web site, www.bls.gov, 2008.

47 See Hans-Warner Sinn, "The Welfare State and the Forces of Globalization," working paper 12946, National Bureau of Economic Research, 2007.

48 Raymond J. Mataloni, Jr., "A Note on Patterns of Production and Employment by U.S. Multinational Companies," *Survey of Current Businesses*, Bureau of Economic Analysis, March 2004.

49 For a thorough review of this specific issue, see Raymond J. Mataloni, Jr., "A Note on Patterns of Production and Employment by U.S. Multinationals Companies," *Survey of Current Business*, Bureau of Economic Analysis, March 2004.

50 Business spending on technology has increased at an annualized growth rate of 16.6 percent from only a 12.0 percent rate during the previous decade. For a complete review of these data, see Bureau of Economic Analysis

database, www.bea.gov. These calculations were made from the BEA designation of business spending on "information processing equipment, and software."

51 Ann E. Harrison and Margaret S. McMillan, "Outsourcing Jobs? Multinationals and U.S. Employment," working paper 12372, National Bureau of Economic Research, 2006.

52 For a good summary of the range of studies, see Lori G. Kletzer, "Trade and Job Losses in U.S. Manufacturing, 1979–1994," in *The Import of International Trade on Wages* (Chicago: University of Chicago Press, 2000), pp. 358 and 362, and Ann E. Harrison and Margaret S. McMillan, "Outsourcing Jobs? Multinationals and U.S. Employment," working paper 12372, National Bureau of Economic Research, 2006

53 See "More Pain than Gain," *The Economist*, September 14, 2006.

54 Robert Gavin, "Job Security a Worry in Changing Economy," *The Boston Globe*, July 26, 2004.

55 Patrik Jonsson, "A Beleaguered Mill Town Struggles Toward Reinvention," *The Christian Science Monitor*, November 3, 2004.

56 See, for another example, Fran Daniel, "Bassett-Walker Will Lose 3 Sewing Plants; It Plans to Increase Overseas Production," *Winston-Salem Journal*, January 16, 1998.

57 Amy Martinez, "North Carolina Workers Suffer in Global Economy," *Knight Rider Tribune Business News*, May 31, 2004.

58 Tim McKeel, "Spittin' Image," *Lancaster New Era*, April 26, 2004.

59 See, for example, "Clinton Hammers Obama on NAFTA Before Crucial Primaries," www.cnnpolitics.com, March 4, 2008.

60 James Kanter, "EU Plans Fund for Retraining Workers: Half Billion Euros Linked to Jobs Lost to Globalization," *International Herald Tribune*, March 1, 2006.

61 Alessandra Galloni, Cecilie Rohwedder, and Teri Agins, "Foreign Luxuries: Breaking a Taboo," *The Wall Street Journal*, September 27, 2005.

62 Data from the International Monetary Fund, World Economic Outlook Database, International Monetary Fund, www.imf.org, except Japan, which comes from the Organisation for Economic Co-Operation and Development database, www.stats.oecd.org.

63 Data from the International Monetary Fund, World Economic Outlook Database, International Monetary Fund, www.imf.org. Also, for a good overall comparison of the relative size of economies, see Martin Wolf, "Challenge Ahead for the World's Divided Economy," *Financial Times*, January 9, 2008.

64 Peter Marsh, "China Reverting to Form as the World's Workshop," *Financial Times*, August 11, 2008.

65 Forecasts in Paul Gruenwald, "Asia Forecast to Keep Up Strong Growth," *IMF Survey Magazine*, October 19, 2007.

66 Taken from Peter Marsh, "China Reverting to Form as the World's Workshop," *Financial Times*, August 11, 2008.

67 For just a few examples, see David Serchuk, "China and Commodities: A Discussion," *Forbes*, June 4, 2009; "China Is the Key to the Commodities Market," *MoneyWeek*, March 2, 2007; Charles Wallace, "Slackening Copper Demand in China Hurts Commodities," *Daily Finance*, March 4, 2011; and Jeffrey Currie, "China's Forgotten Power in Commodities Markets," *Financial News*, November 22, 2010.

68 For just a few examples of China's aggressiveness in this regard, see "China to Cooperate with Iran on Oil," *UPI Arabia*, December 27, 2004; "Tehran's Triumph," *The Asian Wall Street Journal*, December 3, 2004; Wu Lei and Qinyu Shen, "Will China Go to War over Oil?," *Far Eastern Economic Review*, April 2006; and "Has Iran Won?," *The Economist*, January 31, 2008.

69 Hany Besada, Yang Wang, and John Wally, "China's Growing Economic Activity in Africa," working paper 14024, National Bureau of Economic Research, May 2008.

70 For just a sample of references to this issue, see Drew Thompson, "Darfur Complications: Disaccord on Sudan Could Poison China-U.S. Ties" *International Herald Tribune*, November 18, 2004; "China's Quest for Resources, No Strings," *The Economist*, March 13, 2008; and Mark Lange, "The Only Way to Alter China's Hand in Darfur," *The Christian Science Monitor*, April 30, 2008.

71 Eduardo Lora, "Should Latin America Fear China?," working paper 531, Inter-American Development Bank, 2005. For a sample of other references to China's rising profile in Latin America, see "China and Latin America," *The Economist*, December 29, 2004; Xuan-Trang Ho, "China's Burgeoning Role in Latin America—a Threat to the U.S.?," *Political Affairs*, February 24, 2005; Stephen Johnson, "Balancing China's Growing Influence in Latin America," the Heritage Foundation, October 24, 2005; and "China's Claim in Latin America: So Far, a Partner Not a Threat," Council on Hemispheric Affairs, July 25, 2008.

72 See James T. Haltmaier, Shaghil Ahmad, Brahima Coulibaly, Ross Knippenberg, Sylvain Leduc, Mario Marazzi, and Beth Ann Wilson, "Role of China in Asia: Engine, Conduit, or Steamroller?," International Finance Discussion Paper Number 94, Board of Governors of the Federal Reserve System, 2007.

73 See, for example, James Kyrge, "World Is Dancing to a Chinese Tune," *Financial Times*, December 7, 2004.

74 See, for example, John McBeth, "Exercising Sovereignty," *Far Eastern Economic Review*, September 19, 1996; S. Vatikiokis et al., "Drawn to the Fray," *Far Eastern Economic Review*, April 3, 1997; Tony Walker and Jeremy Great, "China Denies Exploring for Oil in Vietnamese Waters," *Financial Times*,

March 18, 1997; and Robert Marguard, "Japan-China Tensions Rise over Tiny Islands," *The Christian Science Monitor*, February 11, 2005.

75 For a small sample of commentary on this issue, see John J. Tkacik, Jr., "A Chinese Military Superpower?," the Heritage Foundation, March 8, 2007; Jill Drew, "China's Military Budget Reported at $59 Billion," *The Washington Post*, March 5, 2008; Office of the Secretary of Defense, "Military Power of the People's Republic of China 2007," *Annual Report to Congress*, Washington, D.C., 2007.

76 For just a few references on the near war and India's more aggressive diplomatic and military posture, see "Kashmir Dreaming," *The Economist*, July 6, 2006; "India-Pakistan Trust Deficit Persists, More Realism on Kashmir," *The Hindustan Times*, December 26, 2006; and Ghulam Hasnain and Nicholas Rufford, "Pakistan Raises Kashmir Nuclear Stakes," *Sunday Times*, December 30, 2001.

77 David Dilling, "China and India Knock on Club's Door," *Financial Times*, July 7, 2008.

78 For a thorough, sober statement that also outlines these popular fears, see Wayne M. Morrison and Marc Labonte, "China's Holdings of U.S. Securities: Implications for the U.S. Economy," CRS Report for Congress, January 9, 2008.

79 For a discussion of the skit, see James Joyner, "SNL Obama China Skit," *Outside the Beltway*, November 23, 2009.

80 China would do its own finances harm, much less its export strategy of keeping the yuan cheap to the dollar, if it sold its holdings of U.S. Treasury bonds or even slowed its rate of acquisition.

81 Andrew England, "Abu Dhabi Fund to Name U.S. Targets," *Financial Times*, August 6, 2008.

82 See David R. Francis, "Will Sovereign Wealth Funds Rule the World?," *The Christian Science Monitor*, November 26, 2007.

83 All these statistics come from "Spreading the (Sovereign) Wealth," *The Lord Abbett Review*, Summer 2008, which gathered them from an array of official sources, noted there.

84 See "Asset-Backed Insecurity," *The Economist*, January 19, 2008.

85 Quoted in Jason Singer, Henry Sender, Jason Dean, and Marcus Walker, "Governments Get Bolder in Buying Equity Stakes," *The Wall Street Journal*, July 24, 2007.

86 Jason Singer, Henry Sender, Jason Dean, and Marcus Walker, "Governments Get Bolder in Buying Equity Stakes," *The Wall Street Journal*, July 24, 2007.

9: More Intense Pressures

1 See Bureau of Economic Analysis Web site, www.bea.gov.

2 See "Selected Measures of Household Income Dispersion," Bureau of the Census Web site, www.census.gov.

3 See John Thornhill, "Income Inequality Seen as the Great Divide," *Financial Times*, May 19, 2008.

4 See Arthur C. Brooks, "The Left's 'Inequality' Obsession," *The Absurd Report*, July 19, 2007.

5 For a good summary of the immense IRS data, see Greg Ip, "Income Inequality Gap Widens," *The Wall Street Journal*, October 13, 2007.

6 See "More Pain than Gain," *The Economist*, September 14, 2006.

7 Michiyo Nakamoto, "Poverty Widens the Crack in Japan's Facade," *Financial Times*, July 10, 2008.

8 John Thornhill, "Income Inequality Seen as the Great Divide," *Financial Times*, May 14, 2008.

9 For a thorough discussion of all these effects, see Alan Reynolds, "The Truth About the Top 1%," *The Wall Street Journal*, October 25, 2007, and Thomas Sowell, "Income Confusion," *Real Clear Politics*, November 20, 2007.

10 For a good summary of this study, see "Movin' On Up," editorial, *The Wall Street Journal*, November 13, 2007.

11 Lori G. Kletzer, "Trade and Job Loss in U.S. Manufacturing, 1979–1994," in Robert C. Feenstra, ed., *The Impact of International Trade on Wages* (Chicago: University of Chicago Press, 2000).

12 Tim McKeel, "Spitting Image," *Lancaster New Era*, April 26, 2004.

13 For just one example, see "More Pain than Gain," *The Economist*, September 14, 2006.

14 For illustrations of this effect, see Bob Davis, "IMF Fuels Critics of Globalization," *The Wall Street Journal*, October 16, 2007.

15 Robert C. Feenstra and Gordon Hanson, "Globalization, Outsourcing and Wage Inequality," working paper 75424, National Bureau of Economic Research, 1996.

16 John Thornhill, "Income Inequality Seen as the Great Divide," *Financial Times*, May 19, 2008.

17 Quoted in Bob Davis, "IMF Fuels Critics of Globalization," *The Wall Street Journal*, October 16, 2007.

18 Data on global investment flows are less readily available than for

trade, but U.S. data can help provide an estimate. According to Karen H. Johnson, "Gross or Net International Financial Flows," working paper, Council on Foreign Relations, July 2009, investment flows into and out of the United States amount to some $4.0 trillion, about equal to the country's trade flows. Applying that same relative correspondence to global trade flows implies some $20 trillion in global investment flows, added to trade flows, roughly $40 trillion a year. Since the United States has a stronger home bias in investing than other countries, this global figure probably underestimates reality.

19 Bureau of Economic Analysis Web site, www.bea.gov.

20 Figures updated by the author from Michael J. Fleming, "Measuring Treasury Market Liquidity," *Economic Policy Review*, Federal Reserve Bank of New York, September 2003.

21 World Economic Outlook database, International Monetary Fund, www.imf.org.

22 Census Bureau Web site, www.census.gov.

23 Bloomberg Financial Database, www.bloomberg,com.

24 Calculated by the author comparing yuan-dollar variation with comparable moves in euro-dollar, sterling-dollar, rupiah-dollar, yen-dollar, and real-dollar rates for the last five years. All data were drawn from the Bloomberg Financial Database, www.bloomberg.com.

25 Bloomberg Financial Database, www.bloomberg,com.

26 World Economic Outlook database, International Monetary Fund, www.imf.org. For a thorough analysis of the net foreign deficits of the major developed economies as a group, see Richard H. Clarida, "G-7 Current Account Imbalances: Sustainability and Adjustment," working paper 12194, National Bureau of Economic Research, April 2006.

27 International Reserves and Foreign Currency Liquidity, International Monetary Fund Web site, www.imf.org.

28 For a thorough exposition of these positions, see "China's Exchange Rate Regime and Its Effect and the U.S. Economy," Testimony by John B. Taylor, undersecretary of the treasury for international affairs, before the House Subcommittee on Domestic and International Monetary Policy, Trade, and Technology, October 1, 2003, and Joshua Aizenman and Reuven Glick, "Sterilization, Monetary Policy, and Global Financial Integration," working paper 13902, National Bureau of Economic Research, March 2008.

29 For a detailed description of this process and the reasoning behind it, see Joshua Aizenman and Reuven Glick, "Sterilization, Monetary Policy, and Global Financial Integration," working paper 13902, National Bureau of Economic Research, March 2008.

30 In particular, see Ben S. Bernanke, "Global Savings Glut and the U.S.

Current Account Deficit," speech given for the Homer Jones Lecture, St. Louis, Missouri, April 14, 2005.

31 Treasury Bulletin, Treasury Department, www.fms.treas.gov.

32 Author's calculation from data on the Bloomberg Financial Database, www.bloomberg,com.

33 Between 1991 and 1997, South Korea averaged real growth of 7.1 percent a year, far above the U.S. annual average of 3.5 percent. Indonesia's economy also grew in real terms by 7.1 percent a year. Taiwan's annual growth was 6.3 percent a year, Thailand's 6.5 percent, Malaysia's 8.5 percent, and Singapore's 8.6 percent. All data were derived from the International Monetary Fund Web site, www.imf.org.

34 South Korea, for instance, saw its foreign balance shift from a deficit equal nearly to 3 percent of that country's GDP in 1991 to a surplus equivalent to 11.7 percent of GDP by 1998. Indonesia during that time went from a deficit on its foreign balance equal to 3.3 percent of its GDP to a 4.3 percent surplus. (All data were derived from the International Monetary Fund Web site, www.imf.org.) Singapore's foreign account surplus increased by 20 percent a year during this time. (See Statistics Singapore, Government of Singapore, www.singstat.gov.sg.) Taiwan's balance of payments improved by almost 40 percent between 1991 and 1996 but then deteriorated in 1997 and 1998 with the crisis. (See Central Bank of the Republic of China Web site, www.cbc.gov.tw.) Thailand's current account went from a 193 billion baht deficit in 1991 to a 592 billion baht surplus in 1998. (See Bank of Thailand website, www.bot.or.th.) Malaysia's current account went from a deficit of 11.6 billion ringgits in 1991 to a surplus of 34.7 billion by 1998. (See Malaysia Department of Statistics website, www.statistics.gov.ny.)

35 Central Bank of the Republic of China (Taiwan) Web site, www.cbc.gov.tw.

36 Bank of Thailand Web site, www.bot.or.th.

37 See U.S. Treasury Web site, www.ustreas.gov.

38 The nominal or dollar economy as measured by the GDP. See Bureau of Economic Analysis Web site, www.bea.gov.

39 In this case, basic money is defined as the monetary base—bank reserves plus currency in circulation—as tracked by the Federal Reserve Board. (For that data and statistics on total borrowing, see Federal Reserve Board Web site, www.federalreserve.gov.) Strict scholarship might dispute that the economy's nominal growth rate determines the pace at which liquidity should expand, but the difference here is so vast that any dispute would center on how excessive liquidity growth was rather than whether it was excessive.

40 Between 1991 and 1998, the prices of all American asset classes rose, and accordingly all interest rates fell. Prices on long Treasury notes rose

sufficiently to depress yields by 2.6 percentage points, further than corporate bond yields, which dropped by 2.2 percentage points. See Federal Reserve Board Web site, www.federalreserve.gov.

41 Federal Reserve Board Web site, www.federalreserve.gov.

42 Bloomberg Financial Database, www.bloomberg.com.

43 Over that same time, exports to the United States from Hong Kong grew at only a 2.0 percent annual rate; those from Malaysia grew at an 8.8 percent annual rate; Thailand, at a 6.9 percent rate; South Korea, at a 5.7 percent rate; and Singapore, at a 9.3 percent annual rate. The closest to China was Indonesia, where exports to America expanded at a 12.0 percent annual rate, still significantly slower than China. For all data, see Bureau of the Census Web site, Commerce Department, Washington, D.C., www.census.gov.

44 Bloomberg Financial Database, www.bloomberg.com.

45 See "East Asian Economies: The Lost (Half) Decade," *The Economist*, July 4, 2002.

46 Ibid.

47 Ibid.

48 Between 1990 and 1998, the Thai baht fluctuated in a range of 2 percent around the U.S. dollar, but for the eight years after 1998, the range of fluctuation expanded to almost 30 percent. For these other currencies, the comparable percentages are 12 and 20 for the Taiwanese dollar, 30 and 80 for the South Korean won, and 10 and 85 for the Indonesian rupiah. The Singapore dollar floated throughout this time, while controls after the crisis held the Malaysian ringgit at a more or less fixed rate between 1999 and 2005. All calculations made by the author from data on the Bloomberg Financial Database, www.bloomberg.com.

49 "1997's Asian Economic Legacy," editorial, *The Daily Yomiuri*, July 8, 2002.

50 America's trade deficit expanded by more than 7 percent with Taiwan, from $15.0 billion in 1998 to $16.1 billion in 2000; by more than 66 percent with South Korea, from $7.5 to $12.5 billion; by almost 20 percent with Thailand, from $8.2 to $9.8 billion; by 46 percent with Malaysia, from $10.0 to $14.6 billion; and by almost 43 percent with Indonesia, from $7.0 to $10.0 billion. All data from Bureau of the Census Web site, www.census.gov.

51 Federal Reserve Board Web site, www.federalreserve.gov.

52 See remarks by Chairman Alan Greenspan at the Annual Dinner and Francis Boyer Lecture of the American Enterprise Institute for Public Policy Research, December 5, 1996, Federal Reserve Board Web site, www.federal reserve.gov.

53 Measures of money available in the economy come from the monetary base, which includes bank reserves plus currency circulation. For data, see Federal Reserve Board Web site, www.federalreserve.gov. Measures of the overall economy come from the nominal gross domestic product. For data, see Bureau of Economic Analysis Web site, www.bea.gov.

54 See Alpha financial Web site, www.seekingalpha.com.

55 Rebecca Buckman and Aaron Lucchetti, "Cooling It: Wall Street Firms Try to Keep Internet Mania from Ending Badly," *The Wall Street Journal*, February 24, 1999.

56 Consumer prices rose at a 2.7 percent annual rate that year compared to only 1.6 percent in 1998. See Bureau of Labor Statistics Web site, www.bls.gov.

57 Federal Reserve Board Web site, www.federalreserve.gov.

58 Again using the monetary base, from Federal Reserve Board Web site, www.federalreserve.gov.

59 Bloomberg Financial Database, www.bloomberg,com.

60 Bureau of the Census Web site, www.census.gov.

61 State Administration of Foreign Exchange, People's Bank of China data, from the Chinability website, www.chinability.com.

62 For money and lending figures, see Federal Reserve Board Web site, www.federalreserve.gov. For nominal economic growth figures, see Bureau of Economic Analysis Web site, www.bea.gov.

63 For just a sample of the opinion on the relative safety of real estate as preferable to the uncertainties of technology investing, see Kary Wukowski, "The Calpers Machine—Banking and Finance Special Report," *Los Angeles Business Journal*, May 10, 2004, which explains the strategy adopted by the nation's largest pension plan; Raymond Fazzi, "REITs Strut Their Teflon Stuff," *Financial Advisor Magazine*, April 2006; "Real Estate Investing—an Alternative to Traditional Stock Market Investment," MyFinanceOnline.info, March 13, 2006; proceedings of Shaping the Future, Milken Institute Global Conference, April 23–25, 2007, especially the session with Steven Green, Larry Mizel, Herbert Simon, and Robert Toll, "Real Estate: What Does the Future Hold?"; and Sara Clemence, "Real Estate vs. Stocks," www.forbes.com, 2000.

64 Steven Malanga, "Obsessive Housing Disorder," *City Journal*, Spring 2009.

65 Ibid.

66 National Association of Realtors Web site, www.realtor.org.

67 During this time, median household incomes in the United States rose

by 5.0 percent a year, far less than housing prices and squeezing out buyers by just this difference. For income figures, see Bureau of Economic Analysis Web site, www.bea.gov.

68 For a good description of the entire bubble and particularly this late, precarious phase, see Ryan Barnes, "The Fuel That Fed the Subprime Meltdown," www.investopedia.com (accessed March 18, 2010). For a more formal review of the problems, see "House Prices and Subprime Mortgage Delinquencies," Economic Letter of the Federal Reserve Bank of San Francisco, June 8, 2007.

69 Federal Reserve Board Web site, www.federalreserve.gov.

70 National Association of Realtors Web site, www.realtor.org.

71 Federal Reserve Board Web site, www.federalreserve.gov.

72 Ibid.

10: A Record of Relative Success

1 See Bureau of Labor Statistics Web site, www.bls.gov. In 1950, the American manufacturing worker earned $8.10 an hour, compared with $1.00 an hour in West Germany, $1.50 in France, $1.70 in Italy, $1.30 in the Netherlands, $2.10 in Sweden, and $2.90 in the United Kingdom.

2 For anecdotes of European and American prices on popular consumer goods at the time, see the People History Web site, www.thepeoplehistory.com.

3 For all these data, see Bureau of Economic Analysis Web site, www.bea.gov.

4 For a succinct description of this founding, see Guy de Carmoy, "The European Alternatives: The Community Energy Policy: Oil," *Government and Opposition*, April 27, 2007.

5 See Bureau of Economic Analysis Web site, www.bea.gov.

6 Melvin J. Lasky, "The Volkswagen: A Success Story," *The New York Times*, October 2, 1955.

7 Richard Rutter, "Imports of Cars Turning Upward," *The New York Times*, January 26, 1964.

8 Edward T. O'Toole, "Success of Foreign-Car Sales in U.S. Cited in Trade Dispute," *The New York Times*, June 5, 1964.

9 See President John F. Kennedy, "Address Before a Joint Session of the Congress on the State of the Union," January 30, 1961, and President John F. Kennedy, "Address Before a Joint Session of the Congress on the State of the Union," January 14, 1963, both in John T. Woolley and Gerhard Peters, the American Presidency Project [online], University of California at Santa Bar-

bara, http://www.presidency.ucsb.edu. For later quotes, see "The Nation," *The New York Times,* March 11, 1962.

10 Quoted in Bruce Bartlett, "The (Out)Source of All Confusion," *National Review* online, March 29, 2004.

11 James T. Rowe, Jr., "May Trade Deficit Shrinks as Imports of Steel Decline," *The Washington Post,* June 28, 1978.

12 See "Meany Asks Carter to Create More Jobs," *Los Angeles Times,* December 8, 1977.

13 See President Jimmy Carter, "Address Before a Joint Session of the Congress on the State of the Union," January 16, 1981, in John T. Woolley and Gerhard Peters, the American Presidency Project [online], University of California at Santa Barbara, http://www.presidency.ucsb.edu.

14 See Bureau of Labor Statistics Web site, www.bls.gov.

15 See Bureau of Economic Analysis Web site, www.bea.gov.

16 For all these comparisons, see Bureau of Labor Statistics Web site, www.bls.gov.

17 Author's calculation from data drawn from the Bureau of Economic Analysis Web site, www.bea.gov.

18 See World Economic Outlook Database, International Monetary Fund Web site, www.imf.org.

19 Norman S. Fideke, "The Automobile Industry," *Annals of the American Academy of Political and Social Science* 460 (March 1982).

20 Worldwatch Institute Web site, International Organization of Motor Vehicle Manufacturers, Paris, France, www.oica.net.

21 Bryan T. Johnson, "The U.S.-Japan Semi-Conductor Agreement: Keeping Up the Managed Trade Agenda," the Heritage Foundation, January 24, 1991.

22 Discussed in: Doyle McManus, "U.S. in 2nd Industrial Revolution," *Los Angeles Times,* June 28, 1983.

23 Theodore H. White, "The Danger from Japan," *The New York Times,* July 28, 1985.

24 James Fallows, "Containing Japan," *The Atlantic,* May 1989.

25 William J. Holstein, *The Japanese Power Game* (New York: Charles Scribner's Sons, 1990).

26 Pat Choate, *Agents of Influence* (New York: Alfred A. Knopf, 1990).

27 Quoted in Richard B. McKenzie, *The American Job Machine* (New York: Universe Books, 1988), pp. 90–91.

28 Ibid., p. 46.

29 Noted in Clyde Haberman, "Japanese Protest Curbs on Toshiba," *The New York Times*, April 2, 1988, and Jill Smolowe, "Special Report: Does Japan Play Fair?," *Time*, June 5, 1989.

30 President George H. W. Bush, "Address Before a Joint Session of the Congress on the State of the Union," January 31, 1990, in John T. Woolley and Gerhard Peters, the American Presidency Project [online], University of California at Santa Barbara, http://www.presidency.ucsb.edu.

31 Michael Wines, "Bush in Japan," *The New York Times*, April 2, 1988.

32 Bureau of Labor Statistics Web site, www.bls.gov.

33 Office of Aerospace and Automotive Industries, "Report on U.S. Automotive Employment Trends," U.S. Department of Commerce, March 30, 2005.

34 Bureau of the Census Web site, www.census.gov.

35 Bureau of Economic Analysis Web site, www.bea,gov.

36 Chapter 9, "More Intense Pressures," examines this distressing development in some detail.

37 For all these data, see Bureau of the Census Web site, www.census.gov.

38 Data comparison calculated from price deflators in the National Income and Product Accounts, Bureau of Economic Analysis Web site, www.bea.gov.

39 Data comparisons calculated from price deflators in the National Income and Product Accounts, Bureau of Economic Analysis Web site, www.bea.gov.

40 Taken from Kenneth F. Scheve and Matthew J. Slaughter, "A New Deal for Globalization," *Foreign Affairs* (July/August 2007).

41 For a complete description of these pivotal events, see Hans G. Mueller, "The Steel Industry," *The Annals of the American Academy of Political and Social Science* 460 (March 1982).

42 Mike Allen and Jonathan Weisman, "Steel Tariffs Appear to Have Backfired on Bush," *The Washington Post*, September 19, 2003.

43 Peter Whoriskey and Anne Komblut, "U.S. to Impose Tariff on Tires from China," *The Washington Post*, September 12, 2009.

44 Quoted in Peter Fritsch, "Chinese Tire-Import Spat Puts Obama in Trade-Policy Pickle," *The Wall Street Journal*, August 28, 2009.

45 Robert Olsen, "Tire Trade Tiff Rolls On," www.forbes.com, September 9, 2009.

46 Joonhyung Lee, "Who Benefited from U.S. Tariffs on Chinese Tires?," Munich RePEc Archive 2011.

47 For a detailed industry-by-industry analysis of the link between foreign competition and technological application, see Robert Z. Lawrence, "Does a Kick in the Pants Get You Going or Does It Just Hurt?," in Robert C. Feenstra, ed., *The Impact of International Trade on Wages* (Chicago: University of Chicago Press, 2000).

48 Author's calculation using data from these sources: For research and development outlays, see Bureau of Economic Analysis/National Science Foundation, "2007 Research and Development Satellite Account," September 28, 2007. For price data to gauge real R&D spending, see GDP price deflators, Bureau of Economic Analysis Web site, www.bea.gov. For capital spending figures, see Bureau of Economic Analysis Web site, www.bea,gov. For the employment data, see Bureau of Labor Statistics Web site, www.bls.gov.

49 Bureau of Labor Statistics Web site, www.bls.gov.

50 For a thorough study of how research and development spending lost effectiveness in the 1970s, see Zvi Griliches, "R & D and the Productivity Slowdown," National Bureau of Economic Research, working paper 434, January 1980.

51 Bureau of Economic Analysis Web site, www.bea.gov. To make the inflation adjustments, inflation measures come from GDP deflators on the Bureau of Economic Analysis Web site, www.bea.gov.

52 In order to make the author's calculation of equipment per worker, the outstanding value of equipment and software owned by American business comes from Federal Reserve Web site, www.federalreserve.gov, and the employment data come from the Bureau of Labor Statistics Web site, www.bls .gov.

53 Bureau of Labor Statistics Web site, www.bls.gov.

54 Author's calculation from data on the Bureau of Economic Analysis Web site, www.bea.gov.

55 Bureau of Economic Analysis Web site, www.bea.gov.

56 U.S. data from Bureau of Economic Analysis web site, www.bea.gov. For Germany, Japan, and China, see World Bank Web site, http://www.world bank.org.

57 For data on the early decades, see Bureau of Economic Analysis Web site, www.bea.gov. For data on the period since 1960, see Bureau of Labor Statistics Web site, www.bls.gov.

58 For data prior to 1959, see Mitra Toossi, "A Century of Change: The U.S. Labor Force, 1950–2050," *Monthly Labor Review* (May 2002). For more recent data, see Bureau of Labor Statistics web site, www.bls.gov.

59 All these data from Bureau of Labor Statistics Web site, www.bls.gov.

60 See Lori G. Kletzer, "Trade and Job Losses in U.S. Manufacturing,

1979–1994," in Robert C. Feenstra, ed., *The Impact of International Trade on Wages* (Chicago: University of Chicago Press, 2000), and Ana L. Revenga, "Exporting Jobs? The Impact of Import Competition on Employment and Wages in U.S. Manufacturing," *Quarterly Journal of Economics* 1 (1992).

61 Taken from Lori G. Kletzer, "Trade and Job Losses in U.S. Manufacturing, 1979–1994," in Robert C. Feenstra, ed., *The Impact of International Trade on Wages* (Chicago: University of Chicago Press, 2000), and Ana L. Revenga, "Exporting Jobs? The Impact of Import Competition on Employment and Wages in U.S. Manufacturing," *Quarterly Journal of Economics* 1 (1992).

62 For a thorough discussion of the interaction between technology and the challenge of trade, see Robert Z. Lawrence, "Does a Kick in the Pants Get You Going or Does It Just Hurt?," in Robert C. Feenstra, ed., *The Impact of International Trade on Wages* (Chicago: University of Chicago Press, 2000).

63 Bureau of Economic Analysis Web site, www.bea.gov.

64 Bureau of Labor Statistics Web site, www.bls.gov.

65 Data for these calculations come from Bureau of Labor Statistics Web site, www.bls.gov. The first comparison measures the jobs actually lost in manufacturing against those actually gained in technology, which for these purposes combine the employment figures for the information and professional and business services categories of the Bureau of Labor Statistics. The second comparison measures the actual growth of technology jobs as a portion of the difference between manufacturing employment now and what it might have been had manufacturing jobs grown after 1980 at the 1.0 percent annual growth rate they averaged during the previous 30 years. The third comparison uses the actual job loss in manufacturing and contrasts it with the jobs growth in technology above and beyond the jobs creation that would have occurred if the industry had failed to show its remarkable growth and employment in the area had grown only at the average national rate between 1980 and the present. The last comparison uses the same manufacturing job shortfall as in the second comparison and contrasts it with the jobs growth in technology above and beyond the jobs creation that would have occurred if the industry had simply expanded its employment at the national rate.

66 Data drawn from Bureau of Labor Statistics Web site, www.bls.gov, and Ronald S. Jarmin, Shawn D. Klimek, and Javier Miranda, "The Role of Retail Chains: National, Regional, and Industry Result," occasional paper, Bureau of the Census, December 14, 2007.

67 These comparisons are calculated in a manner analogous to that used in the technology comparisons and described in note 65.

68 FedEx Web site, www.fedex.com.

69 For the jobs creation in this area, see Bureau of Labor Statistics Web site, www.bls.gov. The worker absorption ability is calculated as in note 65.

70 Data from the Survey of Current Business, Bureau of Economic Analysis Web site, www.bea.gov. Comparisons calculated in a manner analogous to that described in note [#65?:]511.

71 Much of this information comes from the author's personal business dealings with Edward Jones financial advisors and their clients across the country. See also the Edward Jones Web site, www.edwardjones.com.

72 For raw data, see Bureau of Labor Statistics Web site, www.bls.gov. The author's calculation compares the total jobs created in the financial sector less the jobs that would have existed had old structures prevailed and employment in the area had grown at the national rate.

73 Calculated in a manner analogous to that used in other industry comparisons and described in note 65.

11: Dangerous Political Responses

1 For a good review of the interaction between politics and organized labor on trade, see Claude Barfield, "The Fast Track Trade War," *The American*, May 7, 2008.

2 Quoted in Bruce Bartlett, "The (Out)Source of All Confusion," *National Review* online, March 29, 2004.

3 "16 Nations Offer to Speed Tariff Cut on U.S. Exports," *The New York Times*, May 2, 1968.

4 For example, see William Raspberry, "NAFTA Debate Is, in the End, About Class," *The Plain Dealer* (Cleveland), November 21, 1993, and Elizabeth Furse and Peter De Fazio, "Environment and Labor Unprotected Under NAFTA," *The Oregonian*, November 25, 1993.

5 Commission on Presidential Debates, transcript of October 19, 1992, debate, www.debates.org.

6 President William J. Clinton, "Address Before a Joint Session of the Congress on the State of the Union," January 27, 1998, in John T. Woolley and Gerhard Peters, the American Presidency Project [online], University of California at Santa Barbara, http://www.presidency.ucsb.edu.

7 Negotiated by President George H. W. Bush in the late 1980s, the agreement was certified and signed by President Bill Clinton in the 1990s. See Office of the United States Trade Representative Web site, www.ustr.gov.

8 See, for example, "Clinton Hammers Obama on NAFTA Before Crucial Primaries," www.cnnpolitics.com, March 4, 2008.

9 Josh Gerstein, "During Debate, Democrats Talk of NAFTA Withdrawal," *The New York Sun*, February 27, 2008.

10 Matthew Benjamin, "Candidate Returns to Protectionism," Bloomberg News, August 30, 2008.

11 John Harwood, "Republicans Skeptical on Free Trade," *The Wall Street Journal*, October 4, 2007.

12 James Politi and Edward Luce, "Democrats Tougher Anti-Trade Rhetoric," *Financial Times*, May 7, 2008.

13 Nicholas D. Kristof, "The New Scapegoat for U.S. Presidential Candidates," *The International Herald Tribune*, July 26, 2007.

14 Andrew Ward and Daniel Dombey, "Candidates Rebuked for Attacks on Nafta," *Financial Times*, February 28, 2007.

15 James Politi and Edward Luce, "Democrats Tougher Anti-Trade Rhetoric," *Financial Times*, May 7, 2008.

16 John Harwood, "Republicans Skeptical on Free Trade," *The Wall Street Journal*, October 4, 2007.

17 Kenneth F. Scheve and Matthew J. Slaughter, "A New Deal for Globalization," *Foreign Affairs* (July/August 2007).

18 John Thornhill, "Trading Stories," *Financial Times*, October 2, 2008.

19 Lionel Barber and Tony Barber, "Barroso Protectionism Alert," *Financial Times*, March 3, 2008.

20 Joshua Chaffin, "WTO Saw Increase in Barriers to Trade," *Financial Times*, July 2, 2009.

21 John W. Miller, "Nations Rush to Set Trade Barriers," *The Asian Wall Street Journal*, February 9, 2009.

22 David Pilling, Christian Oliver, and Song Jung-a, "South Korea Seeks to Halt Drift to Protectionism," *Financial Times*, March 30, 2009.

23 Duane Layton and Tiffany Smith, "Ditching Doha," *The International Economy* (Spring 2009).

24 David Pilling, Christian Oliver, and Song Jung-a, "South Korea Seeks to Halt Drift to Protectionism," *Financial Times*, March 30, 2009.

25 Holly Yeager, "Senators Drop Call for Chinese Tariffs After Paulson Meeting," *Financial Times*, September 29, 2006.

26 John W. Miller, "EU Tariff Sought on Chinese Steel Imports," *The Wall Street Journal*, October 29, 2007.

27 "China Probes Unfair Trade in U.S. Chicken and Auto Products," Bloomberg News, September 13, 2009.

28 See Doug Palmer, "Panel Urges U.S. to Label China Currency Manipulator," Reuters Web site, www.reuters.com, November 17, 2010.

29 John W. Miller, "EU Tariff Sought on Chinese Steel Imports," *The Wall Street Journal*, October 29, 2007.

30 Alan Beattie, "Brussels Extends Import Tax on Shoes," *Financial Times*, September 29, 2008.

31 Nikki Tait, "EU States Call for China Tariffs," *Financial Times*, February 26, 2008.

32 John W. Miller, "EU Signals Tougher Standards on Tariffs," *The Wall Street Journal*, February 13, 2007.

33 Stephen King, "Roquefort Cheese Dispute May Be First Whiff of a Return to Financial Nationalism," *The Independent*, February 2, 2009.

34 "China Probes Unfair Trade in U.S. Chicken and Auto Products," Bloomberg News, September 13, 2009.

35 "The Next Great Wall," *The Economist*, March 12, 2009.

36 "World Tariff Wars," editorial, *The Wall Street Journal*, April 9, 2010.

37 Jamil Anderlini, "Asian Economies Feeling the Pull of Protectionism," *Financial Times*, June 24, 2009.

38 Dave Graham, "Germany Takes Swipe at French Car Deal Pre-G7," Reuters Web site, reuters.com, February 11, 2009.

39 Carl Mortished, "Give Us the Subsidies Our European Rivals Are Getting," *The Times* (London), January 27, 2009.

40 John W. Miller, "U.S. Sues EU over Tariffs on Electronics," *The Wall Street Journal*, May 29, 2008.

41 Francesco Guerrera, "Monti Backs Down over R&D Subsidies," *Financial Times*, April 22, 2002.

42 Sarah O'Connor, "Tug-of-War over Buy American," *Financial Times*, June 24, 2009.

43 "If China Sharply Revalued the Yuan," *The Economist*, May 17, 2007.

44 "The Next Great Wall," *The Economist*, March 12, 2009.

45 For a comprehensive review, see W. Gu and Shigemi Yabuuchi, "Local Content Requirements and Urban Unemployment," *International Review of Economies & Finance* 4 (2003).

46 Andrew Bounds, "EU Subsidy Plan for Poor Farmers," *Financial Times*, May 21, 2008.

47 Edward Alden, Jonathan Wheatly, and Frances Williams, "Cotton Ruling Could Affect Farm Subsidies," *Financial Times*, April 28, 2004.

48 "World Tariff Wars," editorial, *The Wall Street Journal*, April 9, 2010.

49 Dole Jewett, "UAW Against China," *Automotive News*, March 22, 2004.

50 Christopher Conkey, "LaHood Pitches Mexican Truck Plan to Skeptical Lawmakers," *The Wall Street Journal*, March 25, 2009.

51 Hugh Williamson, "Germany Calls for Higher Health Standards for Food Exports to EU," *Financial Times*, May 12, 2008.

52 Andrew Bounds, "EU Eyes Stricter Standards for Biofuel Imports," *Financial Times*, April 28, 2008.

53 Peggy Hollinger, "Sarkozy Calls for Carbon Taxes on Imports," *Financial Times*, September 10, 2009.

54 Tony Barber, "EU Ministers Wary of Carbon Tariffs," *Financial Times*, February 13, 2008.

55 Mia Shanley and Ilona Wissenbach, "Germany Calls Carbon Tariffs 'Eco-Imperialism,'" Reuters Web site, www.reuters.com, July 24, 2009.

56 "Obama's Trade Deflection," editorial, *The Wall Street Journal*, February 6, 2009.

57 Sarah O'Connor, "Tug-of-War over Buy American," *Financial Times*, June 24, 2009.

58 Stephen King, "Roquefort Cheese Dispute May Be First Whiff of a Return to Financial Nationalism," *The Independent*, February 2, 2009.

59 Jamil Anderlini, "Asian Economies Feeling the Pull of Protectionism," *Financial Times*, June 24, 2009; and "The Next Great Wall," *The Economist*, March 12, 2009.

60 Analyst report from Michael A. Schneider, Robert W. Baird & Co., October 5, 2008.

61 "The Next Great Wall," *The Economist*, March 12, 2009.

62 Amol Sharma, "India to Western Tech Firms: To Sell It Here, Build It Here," *The Wall Street Journal*, January 8, 2013.

63 Stephen King, "Roquefort Cheese Dispute May Be First Whiff of a Return to Financial Nationalism," *The Independent*, February 2, 2009.

64 Alan Beattie, "Left in the Cold," *Financial Times*, April 25, 2008.

65 Bertrand Benoit, "Berlin Foreign Inventors Bill Clears Hurdle," *Financial Times*, August 21, 2008.

66 Deborah Solomon, "Foreign Investors Face New Hurdles Across the Globe," *The Wall Street Journal*, July 6, 2007.

67 Michiyo Nakamoto, "One Way Street," *Financial Times*, March 3, 2008.

68 Both the Italian and the Spanish references from "Don't Take the High Road," *The Economist*, August 7, 2006.

69 Kenneth F. Scheve and Matthew J. Slaughter, "A New Deal for Globalization," *Foreign Affairs* (July/August 2007).

70 Andrew Browne and Lingling Wei, "China Fund Chief Raps U.S.," *The Wall Street Journal*, April 8, 2013.

71 Aline van Duyn and Gillian Tett, "Bankers Warn of Protectionism Risk," *Financial Times*, July 24, 2009.

72 Alan Beattie, "Left in the Cold," *Financial Times*, April 25, 2008.

73 Editors, "Bernanke's Seoul Brothers," *The Wall Street Journal*, November 28, 2012.

74 Francisco Guerrera, "Currency War Has Started," *The Wall Street Journal*, February 5, 2013.

75 Peggy Hollinger, "Lamy in Warning over Bush Bail-Outs," *Financial Times*, July 6, 2009.

76 See Chapter 8, "A Tide of Resistance," for a thorough discussion of the public's souring attitude toward globalization.

77 See Chapter 10, "A Record of Relative Success," for a thorough discussion of the gains from trade and international financial flows.

78 See Chapter 5, "A Global Means to Relief," for a thorough discussion of the relief offered by trade and international financial flows.

79 Peggy Hollinger, "Lamy in Warning over Bank Bail-Outs," *Financial Times*, July 6, 2009.

80 Michael Steen, "Weidmann Warns of Currency War Risk," *Financial Times*, January 21, 2013.

81 Douglas A. Irwin, "Trade Restrictiveness and Deadweight Losses from U.S. Tariffs," working paper 13450, National Bureau of Economic Research, September 2007.

82 For a thorough overview of the Corn Laws, see "Corn Laws," *Encyclopaedia Britannica*, www.britannica.com/EBchecked/topic/137814/Corn-Law#.

83 For a description of France's strict protectionism, especially compared with Britain, see John Vincent Nye, "The Myth of Free-Trade Britain and Fortress France," in Jean-Pierre Dormois and Pedro Lains, eds., *Classical Trade Protectionism* (Oxford: Routledge, 2006).

84 John Vincent Nye, "The Myth of Free-Trade Britain and Fortress France," in Jean-Pierre Dormois and Pedro Lains, eds., *Classical Trade Protectionism* (Oxford: Routledge, 2006).

85 First used in an anonymous pamphlet that circulated from Roubaix, France, during the 1830s. Quoted in Henri Astier, "Winds of Change in the Cornfield," *Times Literary Supplement*, March 19, 2010.

86 Detailed statistical estimates in John Nye, "Corn Laws, Free Trade, and Protectionism," in Steven N. Durluaf and Lawrence E. Blume, eds., *The New Palgrave Dictionary of Economics*, 2nd ed. (London: Macmillan, 2008).

87 "Smoot-Hawley Tariff Act," *Encyclopaedia Britannica* Web site, www.eb.com.

88 To bracket this debate, see on the side of less effect, Barry Eichengreen, "The Political Economy of the Smoot-Hawley Tariffs," in Roger L. Ranson, ed., *Research in Economic History*, vol. 12 (Oxford: JAI Press, 1989), and on the side of greater effect, see Alan Meltzer, "Monetary and Other Explanations of the Start of the Great Depression," *Journal of Monetary Economics* (November 1976). For a detailed weighing of the evidence, see Douglas A. Irwin, "The Smoot-Hawley Tariff: A Quantitative Assessment," working paper 5509, National Bureau of Economic Research, March 1996.

89 Quoted in Douglas A. Irwin, "The Smoot-Hawley Tariff: A Quantitative Assessment," working paper 5509, National Bureau of Economic Research, March 1996.

90 "Dow 1929 Bear Market Rally Compared to 2009 Rally," www.distressedvolatility.com, August 9, 2009.

91 Figures taken from Chen Deming, "Protectionism Doesn't Pay," *The Asian Wall Street Journal*, February 20, 2009.

92 Figures taken from Hans F. Sennholz, "The Great Depression," *The Freeman*, October 1969.

93 William Hynes, David S. Jocks, and Kevin H. O'Rourke, "Commodity Market Disintegration in the Interwar Period," working paper 14767, National Bureau of Economic Research, March 2009.

94 Alan Beattie, "EU Trade Chief Hits Out at Democrat Hopefuls," *Financial Times*, May 8, 2008.

95 "Mexico Retaliates," editorial, *The Wall Street Journal*, March 19, 2009.

96 Sarah O'Connor, "U.S. Companies Suffer Repercussions from Buy American Initiatives," *Financial Times*, May 26, 2009.

97 Geoff Dyer, Jamil Anderlini, and James Politi, "China Pressures U.S. Groups in Protectionism Dispute," *Financial Times*, March 17, 2010.

98 Keith Bradsher, "Chinese Moves to Retaliate Against U.S. Tire Tariff," *The New York Times*, September 14, 2009.

99 Stephanie Kirchfgaessner, "China Hits Out at U.S. 'Protectionism,'" *Financial Times*, June 6, 2008.

100 Jamil Anderlini and Alan Beattie, "Beijing Attacks Europe's Anti-Dumping Duties," *Financial Times*, September 10, 2008.

101 David Pilling, "Will China's Coke Moment Spark Retaliation?," *Financial Times*, March 26, 2009.

102 See Chapter 10, "A Record of Relative Success," for a more elaborate discussion of the gains from trade and international financial flows.

12: Helping the Economy and People Cope

1 See the discussion in Chapter 10, "A Record of Relative Success." For specific examples and an impressive analysis of the process, see John Aubrey Douglass, "The Cold War, Technology, and the American University," Research and Occasional Paper Services: CSH8.2.99, University of California at Berkeley, July 1999.

2 Quoted in Walter Adams and Joel B. Dinlam, "Big Steel, Invention and Innovation," *The Quarterly Journal of Economics* (May 1966).

3 See Martin Feldstein, "Why Is Productivity Growing Faster?," *Journal of Policy Making* 25 (2003). For a particularly detailed if remarkably abstract study, see Rolf Sternberg and Olaf Arndt, "What Determines the Innovative Behavior of European Firms?," *Economic Geography* (October 2001). Touching on this aspect of innovation as well as others, see David T. Coe and Elhanan Helpman, "International R&D Spillovers," *European Economic Review* 39 (1995); Gustavo Crespi, Chiara Criscuolo, Jonathan E. Haskel, and Matthew Slaughter, "Productivity Growth, Knowledge Flows, and Spillovers," working paper 13959, National Bureau of Economic Research, April 2008; and David T. Coe, Elhanan Helpman, and Alexander W. Hoffmaister, "International R&D Spillovers and Institutions," working paper 14069, National Bureau of Economic Research, June 2008.

4 Rolf Sternberg and Olaf Arndt, "What Determines the Innovative Behavior of European Firms?," *Economic Geography* (October 2001).

5 See David T. Coe, Elhanan Helpman, and Alexander W. Hoffmasiter, "International R&D Spillovers and Institutions," working paper 14069, National Bureau of Economic Research, June 2008.

6 Joseph H. Golec and John A. Vernon, "European Pharmaceutical Price Regulation, Firm Profitability, and R&D Spending," working paper 12676, National Bureau of Economic Research, November 2006.

7 For three particularly detailed and well-documented examples of this work, see David T. Coe and Elhanan Helpman, "International R&D Spillovers," *European Economic Review* 39 (1995); Gustavo Crespi, Chiara Criscuolo, Jonathan E. Haskel, and Matthew Slaughter, "Productivity Growth, Knowledge Flows, and Spillovers," working paper 13959, National Bureau of Economic Research, April 2008; and David T. Coe, Elhanan Helpman, and Alexander

W. Hoffmaister, "International R&D Spillovers and Institutions," working paper 14069, National Bureau of Economic Research, June 2008.

8 "Global Trends 2015: A Dialogue About the Future with Nongovernmental Experts," National Intelligence Council, December 2005.

9 For a particularly good example of these difficulties, see Maria Elena Bontempi and Jacques Mairesse, "Intangible Capital and Productivity: An Exploration on a Panel of Italian Manufacturing Firms," working paper 14108, National Bureau of Economic Research, June 2008.

10 Benjamin F. Jones, "The Knowledge Trap: Human Capital and Development Reconsidered," working paper 14138, National Bureau of Economic Research, June 2008.

11 "History of Cable Television," National Cable and Telecommunications Web site, www.neta.com.

12 See Chapter 10, "A Record of Relative Success," for more detail.

13 For a remarkable catalogue of such innovations, see "NASA Spinoffs," the Ultimate Space Place Web site, www.thespaceplace.com. Also see Leah Krauss, "To the Moon," Space History Web site, www.spacehistory.tripod.com, and Steven J. Dick, "Societal Impact of the Space Age," www.nasa.gov.

14 For examples, see Tom Farley, "Mobile Telephone History," *Telektronikk*, March 4, 2005; Roy Dholakia and Bari Harlam, "Telecommunication, and Economic Development," *Telecommunications Policy* (August 1994); John K. Mayo, Gary R. Heald, and Steven J. Klees, "Commercial Satellite Telecommunications and National Development," *Telecommunications Policy* (January/February 1992); and Sameer Kumar, "Mobile Communications: Global Trends in the 21st Century," *International Journal of Mobile Communications* 2:1 (2004).

15 For examples, see Maria Collier, "Air Force Funds Fibre Laser Research, Considers Applications," Air Force Material Command, January 4, 2008; Jeannette L. Fraser, "Laser Applications: Implications for Vocational Education," Educational Resources Information Center, Ohio State University, 1985; Loretta Hidalgo Whitsider, "Microfibre Composit Actuator Named NASA Government Invention of the Year," *Wired Science*, December 27, 2007; Peter Morgan, "The Uses of Carbon Fibres," *Carbon Fibres and Their Composites* (New York: CRC Press, 2005), Chapter 23; and Audria Mockus, Roy T. Fielding, and James Herbsleb, "A Case Study of Open Source Software Development: The Apache Server," *Proceedings of the 22nd International Conference on Software Engineering*, June 4–11, 2000.

16 For a detailed narrative and analysis of these changes, see Richard N. Langlois and W. Edward Steinmueller, "Strategy and Circumstance: The Response of American Firms to Japanese Competition on Semiconductors, 1980–1995," *Strategic Management Journal* (October/November 2000).

17 For examples and analyses, see "Lean Guru Masaaki Imai: Arrogance, Complacency Cause of Auto Crisis," *Canadian Manufacturing*, May 8, 2009; Paul Krugman, "No JOLTS to Complacency," *The New York Times*, March 16, 2011; and John McElroy, "Good Times Feed Complacency in Detroit," *Wards-Auto World*, May 1, 2009.

18 For examples over long stretches of time, see Walter Adams and Joel B. Dirlam, "Big Steel, Invention, and Innovation," *The Quarterly Journal of Economics* (May 1966), and Mark Turnbull, "The Innovation Economy," *The Christian Science Monitor*, February 21, 2010.

19 Bertrand Benoit, "State Steadies Course of German Industry," *Financial Times*, December 29, 2008.

20 For two very different but naturally supporting studies, see Kazuyuki Motohashi, "Growing R&D Collaborations of Japanese Financial Policy Implications for Reforming the National Innovation System," *Asia Pacific Business Review*, July 2008, and Richard Florida and Martin Kenney, "The Globalization of Japanese R&D," *Economic Geography* (October 1994).

21 Tor Eriksson and Niels Westergaard-Nielsen, "International Productivity Differences in a Pharmaceutical Firm," *International Differences in the Business Practice and Productivity of Firms* (Chicago: University of Chicago Press, forthcoming), Chapter 6.

22 For a thorough development of this dividing line and examples of how this more subtle aspect of innovation occurs, see Ludwig von Mises, *Human Action*, 4th ed. rev. (San Francisco: Fox & Wilkes, 1963), particularly pp. 303–20, and Henry K. H. Woo, *The Unseen Dimensions of Wealth* (Fremont, CA: Victoria Press, 1984), particularly pp. 75–130.

23 See Chapter 10, "A Record of Relative Success," for more detail.

24 For a complete review of all these differences and their relative effects, see Giuseppe Bertolo, Francine D. Blau, and Lawrence M. Kahn, "Comparative Analysis of Labor Market Outcomes; Lesson for the U.S. from International Long-Run Evidence," working paper 8526, National Bureau of Economic Research, October 2001.

25 For basic research on this question, see Udo Staber and Jorg Sydow, "Organizational Adaptive Capacity: A Structural Perspective," *Journal of Management Enquiry* (October 2001).

26 For a careful, if somewhat dated, analysis, see Horst Siebert, "Labor Market Rigidities: At the Root of Unemployment in Europe," *Journal of Economic Perspectives* (Summer 1997).

27 See Marianne Bertrand and Francis Kramarz, "Does Entry Regulation Hinder Job Creation? Evidence from the French Retail Industry," working paper 8211, National Bureau of Economic Research, April 2001.

28 See Chapter 10, "A Record of Relative Success," for more detail.

29 See Marianne Bertrand and Francis Kramarz, "Does Entry Regulation Hinder Job Creation? Evidence from the French Retail Industry," working paper 8211, National Bureau of Economic Research, April 2001.

30 Robert J. Gordon, "Why Was Europe Left at the Station When America's Productivity Locomotive Departed?," working paper 10661, National Bureau of Economic Research, August 2004.

31 For just a few examples, see "AFL-CIO Urges Pension Fund Aid to Sick Industries," *Los Angeles Times*, August 22, 1980; "AFL-CIO Chief Denounces Reagan Wall Street Policy," *Los Angeles Times*, July 13, 1981; Carl Mostished, "Give Us the Subsidies Our European Rivals Are Getting," *The Times* (London), January 27, 2009; or the more carefully researched Bruce A. Blonigan, Benjamin H. Lieberman, and Wesley W. Wilson, "Trade Policy and Market Power," working paper 13671, National Bureau of Economic Research, December 2007.

32 Author's calculation from data in the Statistical Extracts Web site, Organisation for Economic Co-operation and Development, www.oecd.org.

33 Mihir A. Desai and James R. Hines, Jr., "Market Reactions to Exports Subsidies," working paper 10233, National Bureau of Economic Research, January 2004.

34 Ibid.

35 Original research in Mariah L. Tupy, "Who Pays for Farm Subsidies?," *The Washington Times*, November 25, 2005. Author's calculations update them to 2010.

36 Mariah L. Tupy, "Who Pays for Farm Subsidies?," *The Washington Times*, November 25, 2005. Author's calculations update them to 2010.

37 For an especially concise and comprehensive exposition of this effect, see Lawrence H. Summers, "Unemployment," *The Concise Encyclopedia of Economics* (The Library of Economics and Liberty), www.econlib.org.

38 Ibid.

39 Employment and Training Administration, Trade Adjustment Assistance write-up, Labor Department, www.doleta.gov.

40 For examples of the more strident arguments in this regard, see "Why Globalization Is in Trouble," *Financial Times*, September 8, 2006; "A Pair of Deadbeats," *The Economist*, September 18, 2003; or "Fear Faces the Future," *The Economist*, March 30, 2006.

41 "Europe's Urgent Need for Reform," editorial, *Financial Times*, January 2, 2008.

42 Torben M. Anderson, Nicole Bosch, Anja Decaln, and Rob Euwals, "The Danish Flexicurity Model in the Great Recession," Vox Research, www.voxeu.org, April 8, 2011.

43 Hans-Werner Sinn, "The Welfare State and the Forces of Globalization," working paper 12946, National Bureau of Economic Research, March 2007.

44 Bruce Chelimsky Fallick, "The Industrial Mobility of Displaced Workers," *Journal of Labor Economics* (April 1993).

45 See Chapter 6, "Forcing Change in Industrial Structures," and Chapter 7, "Still More Exaggerated Change," for more detail.

46 See Milton Ezrati, *Kawari: How Japan's Economic and Cultural Transformation Will Alter the Balance of Power Among Nations* (New York: Perseus, 2000), pp. 53–54.

47 "Still Work to Be Done," *The Economist*, November 29, 2007.

48 For a detailed analysis of these developments, see John Tschetter, "Producer Services Industries: Why Are They Growing So Rapidly?," *Monthly Labor Review* (December 1987), and Angela Clinton, "Flexible Labor: Restarting the American Workforce," *Monthly Labor Review* (August 1997).

49 James R. Hagerty, "Industry Puts Heat on Schools to Teach Skills Employers Need," *The Wall Street Journal*, June 6, 2011.

50 For a detailed accounting, see Boyan Jovanovic and Peter L. Rousseau, "Specific Capital and Technological Variety," working paper 13998, National Bureau of Economic Research, May 2008.

51 See U.S. Patent and Trademark Office Web site, www.uspto.gov.

52 Taken from Boyan Jovanovic and Peter J. Rousseau, "Specific Capital and Technological Variety," working paper 13998, National Bureau of Economic Research, May 2008.

53 For a good review of the American effort, see George Psacharopoulus, "Vocational Education and Training Today: Challenges and Responses," *Journal of Vocational Education and Training* 49:3 (1997).

54 See Robert W. Glover, "The German Apprenticeship System: Lessons for Austin, Texas," *Annals of the American Academy of Political and Social Science* (March 1996); Philip Whyte, "Why Free Markets Have Little to Do with Irregularity," *Financial Times*, June 2, 2008; and Leon Muszynski and David A. Wolfe, "New Technology and Training: Lessons from Abroad," *Canadian Public Policy* (September 1989).

55 Leon Muszynski and David A. Wolfe, "New Technology and Training: Lessons from Abroad," *Canadian Public Policy* (September 1989).

56 Norihiko Shirouzu, "Curriculum in Vitro: Vocational Schools in Japan Are Increasingly Irrelevant," *The Asian Wall Street Journal*, December 20, 1994.

57 See, for example, Jonathan R. Veum, "Sources of Training and Their Impact on Wages," *Industrial and Labor Relations Review* (July 1995).

58 See, for example, Richard B. Freeman, "Troubled Workers in the Labor Market," working paper 816, National Bureau of Economic Research, December 1981; Peter T. Kilborn, "When Plant Shuts Down, Retraining Laid-Off Workers Is Toughest Job Yet," *The New York Times*, April 23, 1990; Ross Koppel and Alice Hoffman, "Dislocation Policies in the USA: What Should We Be Doing?," *Annals of the American Academy of Political and Social Science* (March 1996); and David Muhlhausen and Paul Kersey, "In the Dark on Job Training: Federal Job Training Programs Have a Record of Failure," the Heritage Foundation, July 6, 2004.

59 William Harms, "Unemployed Reroute Careers to Make a Working Comeback," *Chicago Tribune*, June 3, 1983, and Dale Russakoff, "Brawn Forged into Brain," *The Washington Post*, April 12, 1987.

60 Philip Whyte, "Why Free Markets Have Little to Do with Inequality," *Financial Times*, June 2, 2008.

61 Leon Muszynski and David A. Wolfe, "New Technology and Training: Lesson from Abroad," *Canadian Public Policy* (September 1989).

62 Norihiko Shirouzu, "Curriculum in Vitro: Vocational Schools in Japan Are Increasingly Irrelevant," *The Asian Wall Street Journal*, December 20, 1994.

63 Steven Greenhouse, "Start a New Career at 50? In Syracuse, Life After Layoffs," *The New York Times*, January 20, 2005.

64 Eric Schmitt, "Price of Freedom and Budget Cuts: Retraining on L.I.," *The New York Times*, April 20, 1990.

65 Caroline E. Mayer, "GE Job Retraining Gives New Hope to Laid-Off Workers," *The Washington Post*, February 16, 1986.

66 Robert Lerman, "A Better Way to Get Educated," www.urban.org, August 3, 2009.

67 William E. Schmidt, "Out of Work Michiganders No Longer Out of Luck," *The New York Times*, March 31, 1988.

68 David Leadbeater and Peter Suschnigg, "Training as the Principal Focus of Adjustment Policy: A Critical View from Northern Ontario," *Canadian Public Policy* (March 1997).

69 "The People Puzzle," *The Economist*, December 30, 2008.

70 Sonia L. Nazario, "Education (a Special Report)," *The Wall Street Journal*, February 9, 1990.

71 "The People Puzzle," *The Economist*, December 30, 2008.

72 James J. Heckmann and Jeffrey A. Smith, "The Determinants of Participation in a Social Program: Evidence from a Prototypical Job Training Program," working paper 9818, National Bureau of Economic Research, July 2003.

73 For examples of this research, see Mary Ellen Benedict and Peter Vandertant, "Reemployment Differences Among Dislocated Workers," *American Journal of Economics and Sociology*, January 1997; James J. Heckman and Jeffrey A. Smith, "The Determinants of Participation in a Social Program: Evidence from a Prototypical Job Training Program," working paper 9818, National Bureau of Economic Research, July 2003; and Giuseppe Moscarini and Francis G. Vella, "Occupational Mobility and the Business Cycle," working paper 13819, National Bureau of Economic Research, February 2008.

74 Jonathan R. Veum, "Sources of Training and Their Impact on Wages," *Industrial and Labor Relations Review* (July 1995).

75 Ibid.

76 Gordon Thompson, "Unfilled Prophecy: The Evolution of Corporate Colleges," *The Journal of Higher Education* (May/June 2000).

77 Ibid.

78 Melissa Korn, "Firms, Schools Team Up on Training Programs," *The Wall Street Journal*, November 7, 2007.

79 Fred R. Bleakley, "Ready to Work: To Bolster Economies, Some States Rely More on Two-Year Colleges," *The Wall Street Journal*, November 26, 1996.

80 David Leadbeater and Peter Suschnigg, "Training as a Principal Focus of Adjustment Policy: A Critical View from Northern Ontario," *Canadian Public Policy* (March 1997).

81 Kevin J. Dougherty, "The Uneven Distribution of Employee Training by Community Colleges: Description and Explanation," *Annals of the American Academy of Political and Social Science* (March 2003).

82 For just a few samples, see "Europe's Urgent Need for Reform," editorial, *Financial Times*, January 2, 2008; Christine Brinck, "Germany's Long Climb Back," *The American Interest* (Summer 2009); "Secrets of Success," *The Economist*, September 8, 2005; and James W. Guthrie and Lawrence C. Pierce, "The International Economy and National Education Reform: A Comparison of Education Reforms in the United States and Great Britain," *Oxford Review of Education* 2 (1990).

83 John Aubrey Douglass, "The Cold War, Technology, and the American University," Research and Occasional Paper Services: CSHE.2.99, University of California at Berkeley, July 1999.

84 Quoted in Steve Lohr, "Do We Overrate Basic Research?," *The New York Times*, November 30, 2008.

85 "Global Trends 2015: A Dialogue About the Future with Nongovernmental Experts," National Intelligence Council, December 2005.

86 Itamar Rabinovich, "The American Advantage," *The American Interest* (Summer 2009).

87 James W. Guthrie and Lawrence C. Pierce, "The International Economy and National Education Reform: A Comparison of Education Reforms in the United States and Great Britain," *Oxford Review of Education* 2 (1990).

88 James J. Heckman, "Policies to Foster Human Capital," working paper 7288, National Bureau of Economic Research, August 1999.

89 For examples and comparisons, see Chapter 10, "A Record of Relative Success," for more detail.

90 Robert J. Gordon, "Why Was Europe Left at the Station When America's Productivity Locomotive Departed?," working paper 10661, National Bureau of Economic Research, August 2004.

91 See Itamar Rabinovich, "The American Advantage," *The American Interest* (Summer 2009), and U.S. Department of Education, Institute of Educational Sciences, National Center for Education Statistics, *Digest of Educational Statistics*, 2009–2010, www.nces.ed.gov.

92 "Secrets of Success," *The Economist*, September 8, 2005.

13: Helping Finance Cope

1 For a full explanation, see Chapter 9, "More Intense Pressures."

2 David R. Sands, "U.S. Hits China on Currency Policy," *The Washington Times*, May 26, 1993.

3 For a thorough discussion, see Chapter 9, "More Intense Pressures."

4 "Zhu Stands by Yuan Vow," *South China Morning Post*, June 28, 1998.

5 Bloomberg Financial Database, www.bloomberg.com.

6 Mark Lander, "Clinton in China," *The New York Times*, June 27, 1998.

7 Bloomberg Financial Database, www.bloomberg.com.

8 "After the Friday Massacre," *The Economist*, December 14, 2002.

9 "China Exchange Rate Regime and Its Effects on the U.S. Economy," testimony by John B. Taylor, undersecretary of the treasury for international affairs before the Subcommittee on Domestic and International Monetary Policy, Trade, and Technology, House Committee on Financial Services, October 1, 2003.

10 Bloomberg Financial Database, www.bloomberg.com.

11 "Time to Let Go, Time to Let Go," *The Economist,* May 21, 2005.

12 Paul Blustein, "Senators Told China Will Loosen Policy on Currency," *The Washington Post,* July 1, 2005.

13 Morris Goldstein, "Paulson's First Challenge," *The Industrial Economy* (Summer 2006).

14 Alan Tonelson, "Secretary Snow's Beijing Cave-in Leaves American China Policy Critics No Choice but to Fight White House," *American Economic Alert View,* October 27, 2005.

15 Bloomberg Financial Database, www.bloomberg.com.

16 David Lague, "Rejects Europe's Call for Currency Rise Faster," *The New York Times,* November 28, 2007.

17 For detail on this exchange, see "Treasury's Paulson Wants Faster China Yuan Rise," Reuters Web site www.reuters.com, October 23, 2007, or Li Yanping and Dune Lawrence, "China's Yuan Is 'Spanner in the Works' at Paulson Talks," Bloomberg News, December 3, 2008.

18 See description of Chinese export needs in Chapter 5, "A Global Means to Relief," and Bloomberg Financial Database, www.bloomberg.com.

19 "China and America, War of Words," *The Economist,* January 24, 2009.

20 "Obama Says He Will Raise the Yuan Issue with China," *The New York Times,* November 11, 2009.

21 "Time for a Beijing Bargain," *The Economist,* May 30, 2009.

22 Author's calculation from data on Bloomberg Financial Database, www.bloomberg.com.

23 David Lague, "Rejects Europe's Call for Currency to Rise Faster," *The New York Times,* November 28, 2007.

24 "China and U.S. Trade: Lost in Translation," *The Economist,* May 17, 2007.

25 See Allan Chernoff, Sr., "Madoff Whistleblower Blasts SEC," Cnnmoney.com, February 4, 2009, and H. David Katz, inspector general, SEC, "Investigation of Failure of the SEC to Uncover Bernard Madoff's Ponzi Scheme," SEC Report of Investigation, Case No. OIG-509, United States Securities and Exchange Commission Office of Inspector General, August 31, 2009.

26 For an excellent summary of Madoff's former stature, see Julie Creswell and Landon Thomas, Jr., "The Talented Mr. Madoff," *The New York Times,* January 25, 2009.

27 For more detail on the regulations and their initial reception, see Julia

Black and Stephane Jacobzone, "Tools for Regulatory Quality and Financial Sector Regulation," OECD Working Papers on Public Governance, No. 16 (Paris: OECD Publishing, 2009), and Guy Sorman, "Wild Randomness," *City Journal* (Summer 2009).

28 Julia Black and Stephane Jacobzone, "Tools for Regulatory Quality and Financial Sector Regulation," OECD Working Papers on Public Governance, No. 16 (Paris: OECD Publishing, 2009).

29 Guy Sorman, "Wild Randomness," *City Journal* (Summer 2009).

30 See Chapter 9, "More Intense Pressures," for more detail.

31 "Bubble and Squeak," *The Economist*, September 28, 2002.

32 See, for example, Steven Radelet and Jeffrey D. Sachs, "The East Asian Financial Crisis: Diagnosis, Remedies, Prospects," Brookings Papers on Economic Activity, No. 1 (1998); Rosa Maria Lastra, "Central Banks as Lenders of Last Resort," *Journal of Financial Regulation and Compliance* 3 (1999); and Petro Alba, Amar Bhattacharya, Stijn Claessens, Swati Ghosh, and Leonardo Hernandez, "Volatility and Contagion in a Financially Integrated World," Policy Working Paper 2008, World Bank, November 1998.

33 See, for example, Dale A. Krane, "The State of American Federalism, 2001–2202: Resilience in Response to Crisis," *Publius* 4 (2002); Mark Doms, "The Boom and Bust in Information Technology Investment," *Economic Review*, Federal Reserve Bank of San Francisco, 2004; and Reena Aggarwal, "Regulatory Infrastructure Covering Financial Markets," Brookings-Wharton Papers on Financial Services (2001).

34 See "Summary of the Provisions of the Sarbanes-Oxley Act of 2002," Center for Audit Quality Web site, American Institute of Certified Public Accountants, thecaq.aicpa.org.

35 For just a sample of the opinion that real estate presented a haven after the uncertainties of technology investing, see Kary Wukowski, "The Calpers Machine—Banking and Finance Special Report," *Los Angeles Business Journal*, May 10, 2004, which explains the strategy adopted by the nation's largest pension plan; Raymond Fazzi, "REITs Strut Their Teflon Stuff," *Financial Advisor Magazine*, April 2006; "Real Estate Investing—an Alternative to Traditional Stock Market Investment," *MyFinanceOnline.info*, March 13, 2006; proceedings of the conference Shaping the Future, Milken Institute, April 23–25, 2007, especially the session with Steven Green, Larry Mizel, Herbert Simon, and Robert Toll, "Real Estate: What Does the Future Hold?"; and Sara Clemence, "Real Estate vs. Stocks," www.forbes.com, 2006.

36 "Bubble and Squeak," *The Economist*, September 28, 2002.

37 See William S. Anderson, *Essays on Roman Satire* (Princeton: Princeton University Press, 1982).

38 "Financial Regulatory Reform, a New Foundation: Rebuilding Financial Supervision and Regulation," Treasury Department, March 2009, p. 25.

39 Ibid., p. 29.

40 Nicole Gelinas, "Too Big to Fail Must Die," *City Journal* (Summer 2009).

41 For a complete discussion, see Kevin Dowd, "Moral Hazard and the Financial Crisis," *Cato Journal* 1 (2009), and James Surowiecki, "Moral Hazard and the Crisis," *The New Yorker*, January 14, 2010.

42 For a thorough discussion of all these rules, see the reading materials of the CFA Institute, www.cfainstitute.org, and the licensing rules and reading materials for the various designations and licenses from the Web site of the financial self-regulatory agency, the Financial Industry Regulatory Authority (FINRA), www.finra.org.

43 Quoted in Tim Fernholz, "Reining In, and Reigning over Wall Street," *Newsweek*, December 7, 2009.

44 See the review of past crisis in Chapter 9, "More Intense Pressures," for more detail.

45 For a summary of the concept, see Jang-Yung Lee, "Sterilizing Capital Inflows," Economic Series No. 7, International Monetary Fund, March 1997. For a more complete view of the extensive literature and empirical work, see Joshua Aizenman and Reuven Glick, "Sterilization, Monetary Policy, and Global Financial Integration," working paper 13902, National Bureau of Economic Research, March 2008.

46 Jang-Yung Lee, "Implications of a Surge in Capital Inflows: Available Tools and Consequences for the Conduct of Monetary Policy," working paper 96/53, International Monetary Fund, May 1996.

47 For unemployment and inflation figures, see Bureau of Labor Statistics Web site, www.bls.gov. For growth statistics, see Bureau of Economic Analysis Web site, www.bea.gov.

48 For gauges of this excess, see Chapter 9, "More Intense Pressures."

49 John M. Berry, "Greenspan Warns of Inflation Threat," *The Washington Post*, July 23, 1999.

50 Testimony of Chairman Alan Greenspan Before the Committee on Banking, Housing and Urban Affairs, United States Senate, February 16, 2005.

51 Larry Elliott, "European Central Bank Sticks to Its Anti-Inflation Guns," *The Guardian*, May 3, 2001.

52 For a recent reference to this singular focus, see Simon Kennedy and Jana Randow, "ECB Officials Reject IMF-Proposed Inflation Targets," *Business*

Week, February 25, 2010. (The IMF had proposed more latitude on allowable inflation.)

53 See, for instance, the Bank of England Web site, www.bankofengland.co.uk.

14: Reform in Emerging Economies: China

1 All data in Gene Sperling, "The Role of International Development in a Changing World," Council on Foreign Relations press briefing, July 13, 2007. According to the United Nations, extreme poverty is defined as living on less than a dollar a day.

2 See Patrick Allen, "U.S. to Lose Second Place in World Trade to India: Citi," CNBC Web site, www.cnbc.com, and for data, see CIA *World Factbook*, www.cia.gov.

3 CIA *World Factbook*, www.cia.gov.

4 World Bank Web site, www.worldbank.org.

5 All figures drawn from the CIA *World Factbook*, www.cia.gov.

6 Author's calculation based on a nominal 5.0 percent real growth in global trade and a 9.0 percent real growth target for China, far less than its historical 10–12 percent average annual rate. China's historical growth rate was drawn from the CIA *World Factbook*, www.cia.gov. China's trade figures are taken from U.S.-China Business Council Web site, www.uschina.org. Global trade figures are taken from World Trade Organization Web site, www.wto.org.

7 See Chapter 10, "A Record of Relative Success," for more detail.

8 Taken from Malcolm Moore, "How Much Higher Can Factory Wages Go?," *China Economic Review*, March 11, 2010.

9 See Bureau of Labor Statistics Web site, www.bls.gov.

10 Andrew Batson and Bob Davis, "China Starts Looking Beyond Its Era of Breakneck Growth," *The Wall Street Journal*, July 15, 2010.

11 "Is China's Labor Market at a Turning Point?," *The Economist*, June 12, 2010.

12 Taken from Andrew Batson and Bob Davis, "China Starts Looking Beyond Its Era of Breakneck Growth," *The Wall Street Journal*, July 15, 2010.

13 Mei Fong and Sky Canaves, "Factories on China's South Coast Love Their Edge," *The Wall Street Journal*, February 22, 2008.

14 Tom Mitchell, "Shoe Industry Under Pressure Avoids Rising Costs," *Financial Times*, February 26, 2008.

15 Sui-Lee Wee, "China Risks Getting Old Before It Gets Rich," Reuters Newswire, April 27, 2011.

16 "Is China's Labour Market at a Turning Point?," *The Economist*, June 12, 2010.

17 For these demographic comparisons and the likely retarding effect on overall rates of economic expansion, see Chapter 2, "The Demographic Imperative." For detailed analysis of China's demographic circumstances and their effect on the economy, see Rod Tyers and Jane Golley, "China's Growth to 2030: The Roles of Demographic Change and Investment Premia," unpublished paper, College of Business and Economics, Australian National University May 2006, and Jane Golley and Rod Tyers, "China's Growth to 2030: Demographic Change and the Labor Supply Constraint," unpublished paper, College of Business and Economics, Australian National University, June 2006.

18 "Is China's Labour Market at a Turning Point?," *The Economist*, June 12, 2010.

19 Patti Waldmeir, "Shanghai Calls on Chosen Couples to Exceed China's 'One Child' Limit," *Financial Times*, July 25–26, 2009.

20 Jane Golley and Rod Tyers, "China's Growth to 2030: Demographic Change and the Labor Supply Constraint," unpublished paper, College of Business and Economics, Australian National University, June 2006.

21 See Chapter 3, "More Work, More Efficiently," for more detail.

22 Katherine Hille, "China Faces Pressure to Alter One-Child Policy," *Financial Times*, April 28, 2011.

23 See Chapter 6, "Forcing Change in Industrial Structures," for more detail.

24 Alwyn Young, "The Razor's Edge: Distortion and Incremental Reform in the People's Republic of China," *Quarterly Journal of Economics* 4 (2000).

25 Taken from Arthur Waldron, "Message from Dr. K," *The Weekly Standard*, June 13, 2011.

26 For a more through description of how China suffered during this time, see Chapter 5, "A Global Means to Relief."

27 "What Chinese Stimulus Package Means," *The New York Times*, November 23, 2008.

28 In the year after China's program went into effect, its economy had returned to its trend growth rate of over 10 percent. A year after America's program, the American economy, though growing at an average annual rate of real GDP growth of 2.9 percent, was still below the 3–3.5 percent a year growth that is considered its long-term trend. For Chinese growth figures, see Chinese

Statistical Yearbook 2010, National Bureau of Statistics of China, Beijing, www.stats.gov.cn. For American data, see Bureau of Economic Analysis Web site, www.bea.gov.

29 Stephen S. Roach, "China 2025," Council on Foreign Relations Web site, www.cfr.org, October 19, 2009.

30 "Trouble down the Track," *The Economist*, January 14, 2010.

31 Andrew Batson, "China's Policymakers Meet to Discuss Plight of Farmers as Rural Residents Hope for Clearer Rules on Land Rights," *The Wall Street Journal*, October 10, 2008.

32 Li Cui and Murtaza Syed, "The Shifting Structure of China's Trade and Production," working paper, International Monetary Fund, September 2007.

33 Bob Davis and Chuin-Wei Yap, "China Seeks to Lift Domestic Demand," *The Wall Street Journal*, December 17, 2012.

34 Bob Davis and Tom Orlik, "Beijing Seen Speeding Its Reform Approach," *The Wall Street Journal*, February 7, 2013.

35 Chinese Statistical Yearbook 2010, National Bureau of Statistics of China, Beijing, www.stats.gov.cn.

36 Stephen S. Roach, "China 2025," Council on Foreign Relations Web site, www.cfr.org, October 19, 2009.

37 Taken from Richard Dobbs, Andrew Grant, and Jonathan Woetzel, "Unleashing the Chinese Consumer," *Newsweek International*, September 5, 2009.

38 For the Japanese figures, see Japanese Government Cabinet Office Web site, www.esri.cao.go.jp, and also David Pilling, "Asia Export Policy Goes Beyond Sell-By Date," *Financial Times*, May 27, 2009. For the American data, see National Income and Product Assets, Bureau of Economic Analysis Web site, www.bea.gov.

39 For a detailed analysis in context, see Gokhan Akinei and James Crittle, "Special Economic Zones," the World Bank, April 2008.

40 For a review of the Japanese model, see Milton Ezrati, *Kawari: How Japan's Economic and Cultural Transformation Will Alter the Balance of Power Among Nations* (New York: Perseus, 2000), pp. 28–34. For a detailed description of these practices, see Stephen S. Roach, "China 2025," Council on Foreign Relation Web site, www.cfr.org, October 19, 2009; Li Cui and Murtaza Syed, "Shifting the Structure of China's Trade and Production," working paper, International Monetary Fund, September 2007; Criton M. Zoakos, "Germany and China Chart Course to Global Economic Conflict," *Leto Market Insight*, March 10, 2009; and Lee Branstetter and Nicholas Lardy, "China's Embrace of Globalization," working paper 12373, National Bureau of Economic Research, July 2006.

41 Dani Rodrik, "What's So Special About China's Exports?," working paper 11947, National Bureau of Economic Research, January 2006.

42 Guonan Ma and Wang Yi, "China's High Savings Rate: Myth and Reality," working paper 312, Bank for International Settlements, June 2010.

43 For the American figures, see Bureau of Economic Analysis Web site, www.bea.gov. For the Japanese figures, see Ministry of Internal Affairs and Communications, Japanese Statistics Bureau Web site, www.stat.go.jp.

44 Michael Wines, "China Fortifies State Businesses to Fuel Growth," *The New York Times*, August 29, 2010. For a good overall review of insurance in China or the lack of it, see "China Insurance Industry," *China Knowledge* Web site, www.chinaknowledge.com; Tony Allison, "Risks and Rewards in China's Insurance Market," *Asia Times*, February 16, 2001; and Sam Radwan, "China's Insurance Market: Lessons from Taiwan," *Bloomberg Newsweek*, June 15, 2010. For a discussion of consumer finance, see Shen Bingxi and Yan Lijuan, "Development of Consumer Credit in China," working paper 46, Bank for International Settlements, 2008; "China Prepares for Consumer Finance Companies," *The Wall Street Journal*, May 13, 2009; and "China Issues First Consumer Finance Loan," *Beijing Review*, March 3, 2010.

45 For elaboration on these points, see Stephen S. Roach, "China 2025," Council on Foreign Relations Web site, www.cfr.org, October 19, 2009.

46 All data and comparisons in Yao Li, John Walley, Shurming Zhang, and Xiliang Zhao, "The Higher Educational Transformation of China and Its Global Implications," working paper 13849, National Bureau of Economic Research, March 2008.

47 See Minxin Pei, "How Beijing Can Boost Its Human Capital," *Financial Times*, January 9, 2009, and Peter Ford, "Tiananmen's Legacy of Boldness," *The Christian Science Monitor*, June 7, 2009.

48 For more detail, see Chapter 5, "A Global Means to Relief."

49 Taken from "Beijing Battling Protest Fires on All Fronts," *The Australian*, June 12, 2011.

50 See Minxin Pei, "Vighur Riots Show the Need for a Rethink in Beijing," *Financial Times*, January 9, 2009, and Peter Ford, "Tiananmen's Legacy of Boldness," *The Christian Science Monitor*, June 7, 2009.

51 See Chapter 9, "More Intense Pressures," for more detail.

52 Ibid.

53 For details on these points, see Chapter 8, "A Tide of Resistance," and Chapter 13, "Helping Finance Cope."

54 For commentary on nations in these regions, see Ben Simpfendorfer, "Chinese Exports Could Crush Fragile Markets," *Financial Times*, June 30,

2009. For IMF commentary and quotes, see Sarah O'Connor, "Beijing Can Launch New Stimulus Says IMF," *Financial Times*, July 23, 2009.

55 See Chapter 9, "More Intense Pressures," for more detail.

56 Ibid.

57 Steve Levine, "China's Yuan: The Next Reserve Currency?," *Bloomberg Businessweek*, May 26, 2009.

58 For a readable but detailed analysis of why reserve currencies become overvalued, see Markus Yaeger, "Yuan as a Reserve Currency," *Deutsche Bank Review*, July 16, 2010. For a more extended treatment, see Richard Dobbs, David Skilling, Wayne Hu, Susan Lund, James Manyika, and Charles Roxbugh, "An Exorbitant Privilege? Implications of Reserve Currencies for Competitiveness," McKinsey Global Institute, December 2009.

59 Michael Wines, "China Fortifies State Businesses to Fuel Growth," *The New York Times*, August 29, 2010.

15: Adjustment in Other Emerging Economies and the Curse of Oil

1 See Chapter 14, "Reform in Emerging Economies: China," for more detail.

2 Philip Stephens, "Western Awe and Domestic Anxiety: A Tale of Two Chinas," *Financial Times*, July 10, 2009.

3 Andrew B. Bernard, Raymond Robertson, and Peter K. Schott, "Is Mexico a Lumpy Country?," working paper 10898, National Bureau of Economic Research, November 2004.

4 See Adrian Wood, "Openness and Wage Inequality in Developing Countries: The Latin American Challenge to East Asian Conventional Wisdom," *World Bank Economic Review* (January 1997), and Andrew B. Bernard, Raymond Robertson, and Peter K. Schott, "Is Mexico a Lumpy Country?," working paper 10898, National Bureau of Economic Research, November 2004.

5 For the logic of this argument and, as an illustration for all countries, calculations regarding China, see Chapter 14, "Reform in Emerging Economies: China."

6 CIA *World Factbook*, www.cia.gov.

7 See Chapter 2, "The Demographic Imperative," for more detail.

8 For a review of per capita incomes and poverty rates, see Chapter 14, "Reform in Emerging Economies: China."

9 For a description of the Indian economy, see Chapter 5, "A Global Means to Relief."

10 All figures in Steve Sjuggerud, "India's Economy—Why Go with India over China," Investment University Web site, www.investmentu.com, May 6, 2005.

11 Ibid.

12 China Statistical Yearbook 2010, National Bureau of Statistics of China, Beijing, www.stats.gov.cn. For those with an arithmetic bent, the figures would seem to sum to greater than 100 percent. They do, and in the final analysis they are brought back into balance by China's huge imports of machinery and raw materials to support the export machine and which count on a negative in national accounting.

13 Indian Ministry of Statistics Web site, http://mospi.nic.in.

14 For Indian statistics, see Handbook of Statistics, Reserve Bank of India Web site, www.rbi.org. For Chinese statistics, see the U.S.-China Business Council Web site, www.uschina.org.

15 For a succinct description of this classic development model, see John Kay, "Why India Cannot Take Growth for Granted," *Financial Times*, January 9, 2008.

16 See the description of the Indian economy in Chapter 5, "A Global Means to Relief."

17 Jackie Range, "India Bank Offices Grow Costly," *The Wall Street Journal*, February 11, 2008.

18 For descriptions of how this circumstance affected India, see Barry Bosworth and Susan M. Collins, "Accounting for Growth: Comparing China and India," working paper 12943, National Bureau of Economic Research, February 2007, and Dani Rodrik and Arvind Subramanian, "From 'Hindu Growth' to Productivity Surge: The Mystery of the Indian Growth Transition," *IMF Staff Papers* 52:2 (2005). For descriptions of Latin American counterparts, see Andrew B. Bernard, Raymond Robertson, and Peter K. Schott, "Is Mexico a Lumpy Country?," working paper 10898, National Bureau of Economic Research, November 2004, and Sebastian Edwards, "Trade and Industrial Policy in Latin America," working paper 4772, National Bureau of Economic Research, June 1994.

19 For particularly poignant references to the permit Raj, see Public Broadcasting System, "Commanding Heights," July 1, 2001, interview with Jairam Ramesh, former secretary of India's Congress Party, Economic Affairs Department, and PBS, February 6, 2001, interview with Palaniappan Chidambaram, India's finance minister between 1996 and 1998, both available on the PBS Web site, www.pbs.org/wgbh.

20 See Chapter 6, "Forcing Change in Industrial Structures," for more detail.

21 For a description of India's currency policy, see Chapter 9, "More Intense Pressures."

22 Author's calculation from data provided by Bloomberg Financial News, www.bloomberg.com.

23 Joe Leahy, "India's Report Card Fails to Make the Grade," *Financial Times,* June 19, 2008.

24 Diana Furchtgott-Roth, "India's in the News for All the Wrong Reasons," *Real Clear Markets,* February 5, 2013.

25 Ibid.

26 Public Broadcasting System, "Commanding Heights," July 1, 2001, interview with Jairam Ramesh, former secretary of India's Congress Party, Economic Affairs Department, available on the PBS Web site, www.pbs.org/wgbh.

27 See the discussion of Indian literacy levels in Chapter 6, "Forcing Change in Industrial Structures." Quote from Public Broadcasting System (PBS), "Commanding Heights," July 1, 2001, interview with Jairam Ramesh, former secretary of India's Congress Party, Economic Affairs Department, available on the PBS Web site, www.pbs.org/wgbh.

28 For a concise review of this policy approach, see Daniel A. Yergin and Joseph Stanislaw, *The Commanding Heights* (New York: Simon & Schuster, 2002), especially pp. 232–44.

29 Author's calculation from data provided by Bloomberg Financial News, www.bloomberg.com.

30 Author's calculation from data provided by World Economic Outlook Database, International Monetary Fund, www.imf.org.

31 "G20 Statistical Update: Saudi Arabia," prepared by the International Labor Office for the G20 meetings in Washington, D.C., April 20–21, 2010.

32 Observations made by the author and any number of associates and colleagues during a long period of providing investment services in Saudi Arabia and the Persian Gulf.

33 Quoted in Simon Kerr, "Output Slides in Gulf in Spite of Oil Boom," *Financial Times,* June 12, 2008.

34 Bloomberg Financial Database, www.bloomberg.com.

35 All figures in Simon Kerr, "Output Slides in Gulf in Spite of Oil Boom," *Financial Times,* June 12, 2008.

36 For two older but still relevant and helpful studies on these questions, see M. Yousef Tarik, "Development, Growth and Policy Reform in the Middle East and North Africa," *Journal of Economic Perspectives* 91:96 (2004), and Kuran

Timur, "Why the Middle East Is Economically Underdeveloped: Historical Mechanisms of Institutional Stagnation," *Journal of Economic Perspectives* 71:71 (2004).

37 For just one of many items, see Amena Bakr, "Dubai World Document Reveals Price of Failure," Reuters Newswire, July 22, 2010.

38 "Dubai Kiss Row Shows That the Emirate Can No Longer Have Its Cake and Eat It," *The Telegraph*, March 15, 2010.

39 CIA *World Factbook*, www.cia.gov.

40 For a quick statement of the problems with this approach, see Alessandra Stanley, "Yeltsin Vows to Clean Up Privatization in Russia," *The New York Times*, August 16, 1997.

41 For a detailed analysis, see Marshall I. Goldman, "Putin and the Oligarchs," *Foreign Affairs* (November/December 2004).

42 Criton M. Zoakos, "The Geopolitical Tremors of 2009," *Leto Market Insight*, December 23, 2008.

43 "The Wizards of Oil," editorial, *Wall Street Journal*, December 30, 2008.

44 Author's calculation. For the petroleum estimate, see *Commentary*, October 2008. For the GDP estimates, see CIA *World Factbook*, www.cia.gov.

45 Patrick Jenkins, "Moscow to Shift Wealth Fund's Investment Focus," *Financial Times*, April 28, 2008.

46 Arthur Merman, "Putin and the Polite Pundits," *Commentary*, October 2008.

47 Author's calculation from data provided by the U.S. Department of Energy Web site, www.cia.gov.

48 Russian data in Criton M. Zoakos, "The Geopolitical Tremors of 2009," *Leto Market Insight*, December 23, 2008. U.S. industrial production data taken from Federal Reserve Board Web site, www.federalreserve.gov.

49 CIA *World Factbook*, www.cia.gov.

50 Judith Miller, "Will Iraq Fall Victim to the Oil Curse?," *The Wall Street Journal*, August 9, 2010.

51 Rachael Douglas, "Russian Candidate Medvedev: In Tune with Putin's Rooseveltian Thrust," *Executive Intelligence Review*, December 21, 2007.

52 Bloomberg Financial Database, www.bloomberg.com.

53 U.S. Department of Energy Web site, www.energy.gov.

54 Ibid.

55 Bloomberg Financial Database, www.bloomberg.com.

56 Paul Abelsky, "Medvedev Promotes Ruble to Lessen Dollar Dominance," *Bloomberg Businessweek*, June 10, 2010.

57 Niusha Boghrati, "Iran's Oil Bourse: A Threat to the U.S. Economy?," worldpress.org, April 11, 2006.

58 Key World Energy Statistics 2010, International Energy Agency, Paris, France.

59 Taken from Iran Primer 2010, United States Institute of Peace, www.iranprimer.usip.org.

60 The combined gross domestic product of the nations of the eurozone exceeds that of the United States, as does the size of their combined financial markets. Author's calculation taken from data in CIA *World Factbook*, www.cia.gov.

16: Leadership

1 Robert E. Baldwin, "The New Protectionism: A Response to Shifts in National Economic Power," working paper 1823, National Bureau of Economic Research, January 1996.

2 Ibid.

3 Charles P. Kindleberger, "U.S. Foreign Economic Policy, 1776–1976," *Foreign Affairs* (January 1977).

4 Kendall W. Stiles, "The Ambivalent Hegemon: Explaining the 'Lost Decade' in Multilateral Trade Talks, 1948–1958," *Review of International Political Economy* (Winter 1995).

5 Quoted in Charles P. Kindleberger, "U.S. Foreign Economic Policy, 1776–1976," *Foreign Affairs* (January 1977).

6 Quoted in Kendall W. Stiles, "The Ambivalent Hegemon: Explaining the 'Lost Decade' in Multilateral Trade Talks, 1948–1958," *Review of International Political Economy* (Winter 1995).

7 Ibid.

8 Anne O. Krueger, "Prospects for Liberalizing the International Trading Systems," working paper 2409, National Bureau of Economic Research, October 1987.

9 For a good, quick review of these events, see Roger Lowenstein, "The Nixon Shock," *Bloomberg Businessweek*, August 4, 2011.

10 See Treaty of Rome, March 25, 1957, http://ec.europe.eu.

11 Criton M. Zoakos, "Competing Variants of Economic Statements," *Leto Market Insight*, July 10, 2007.

12 Thomas W. Zeiler, "Kennedy, Oil Imports, and the Fair Trade Doctrine," *The Business History Review* (Summer 1990).

13 Taken from Angus Maddison, "The World Economy: A Millennial Perspective," Organisation for Economic Co-operation and Development, Paris, 2001.

14 Barry Eichergreen and Marc Flandreau, "The Rise and Fall of the Dollar, or When Did the Dollar Replace Sterling as the Leading International Currency?," working paper 14154, National Bureau of Economic Research, July 2008.

15 Bruce Stoke, "U.S. Economic Hegemony Ebbs," *National Journal*, January 26, 2008.

16 Diana Farrell, Christian S. Folster, and Susan Lund, "Long-Term Trends in Global Capital Markets," *The McKinsey Quarterly* (February 2008).

17 Census Bureau Web site, www.census.gov.

18 By 2011, the federal budget deficit equaled some $1.6 trillion, a whopping 11.0 percent of America's entire GDP. See Budget of the United States, Office of Management and Budget, Washington, D.C., www.whitehouse.gov.

19 Treasury Department Web site, www.treasury.gov.

20 See, for example, Enoch Yiu, "Euro, Not the Yuan, Seen as Likely Challenger to Dollar's Global Role," *South China Morning Post*, May 23, 2009; "A Global Euro?," *The Economist*, July 28, 2001; or "Becoming Global by Stealth?," *The Economist*, July 2, 2001. See also Menzie Chinn and Jeffrey Frankel, "Will the Euro Eventually Surpass the Dollar as Leading International Reserve Currency?," working paper 11510, National Bureau of Economic Research, July 2005, or the more thorough reprise of the question in Menzie D. Chinn and Jeffrey A. Frankel, "The Euro May over the Next 15 Years Surpass the Dollar as Leading International Currency," working paper 13909, National Bureau of Economic Research, April 2008.

21 See the discussion of Chinese currency policy in Chapter 9, "More Intense Pressures."

22 "Demonstrably Durable," *The Economist*, December 30, 2008.

23 The French voted down the EU constitution on May 29, 2005, by a 55 percent margin. For a description of the voters' opinions and the issues surrounding the vote, see "French Say Firm 'No' to EU Treaty," BBC News Web site, http://news.bbc.co.uk, May 30, 2005. Irish voters rejected the Lisbon Treaty in June 2008. For a description of that vote and the issues surrounding it, as well as the subsequent passage under intense political pressure, see Bruno Waterfield, "Ireland Gives 'Convincing' Yes Vote to Lisbon Treaty," *The Telegraph*, October 3, 2009.

24 Tony Barber, "Dublin to Be Offered Protocol to Same Accord," *Financial Times*, June 17, 2008.

25 Ben Hall, "Tax Harmonization on Ice After Irish Poll," *Financial Times*, June 19, 2008.

26 Ben Hall, "Sarkozy Warns of Europe's Identity Crisis," *Financial Times*, November 14, 2007.

27 Leif Pagrotsky, "A Declining Europe Must Focus on the Nitty-Gritty," *Financial Times*, August 15, 2008.

28 Much has been written on this subject. For a good summary, see "The Lesson of History," *The Economist*, July 12, 2007, and Charles Wyplosz, "What Dream Will Europe Dream Now?," *Financial Times*, June 10, 2008.

29 "Demonstrably Durable," *The Economist*, December 30, 2008.

30 Václav Klaus, "Europe's Big Test: Why the Euro Will Not Help," *Financial Times*, June 12, 2008.

31 Tony Barber, "Lack of Unity Makes Zone 'Political Dwarf,'" *Financial Times*, May 8, 2008.

32 Quoted in Kishore Mahbubani, "Europe Is a Geopolitical Dwarf," *Financial Times*, May 22, 2008.

33 Gideon Rachman, "Irrelevance, Europe's Logical Choice," *Financial Times*, May 19, 2008.

34 Frank Aherns and Anthony Faiola, "Greece Edges Closer to Defaulting on Its Debt," *The Washington Post*, April 29, 2010.

35 Tristana Moore, "Germany Comes to Greece's Rescue," *Time*, April 29, 2010.

36 Ibid.

37 See the May 20, 2010, congressional testimony of Federal Reserve governor Daniel K. Tarullo, "International Response to European Debt Problems," Federal Reserve Board Web site, www.federalreserve.gov.

38 See, for example, "Common Currency Woes," www.spiegel.de, January 25, 2010.

39 In a thorough search by the author of articles in financial and general media, he could turn up no item in which China, India, Japan, or any nation outside Europe apart from the United States was even mentioned, except in passing.

40 See, for example, Willy Lam, "Beijing Won't Rein In Reckless Neighbor," *Asia Times*, December 9, 2010.

41 For example, see James Lamont and Amy Kazmin, "Fear of Influence," *Financial Times*, July 13, 2009.

42 See, for instance, Joshua Kurlantzick, "Avoiding a Tempest on the South China Sea," Council on Foreign Relations Web site, www.cfr.org, September 2, 2010.

43 For a thorough analysis, see Robert Sutter and Chin-Ho Huang, "ASEAN and Asian Regional Diplomacy," *Comparative Connections, E-Journal,* www.csis.org, January 9, 2010.

44 See, for example, Willy Lam, "Beijing Won't Rein In Reckless Neighbor," *Asia Times,* December 9, 2010; James Lamont and Amy Kazmin, "Fear of Influence," *Financial Times,* July 13, 2009; Joshua Kurlantzick, "Avoiding a Tempest on the South China Sea," Council on Foreign Relations Web site, www.cfr.org, September 2, 2010. For a more thorough analysis, see Robert Sutter and Chin-Ho Huang, "ASEAN and Asian Regional Diplomacy," *Comparative Connections, E-Journal,* www.csis.org, January 9, 2010.

45 See Chapter 2, "The Demographic Imperative," for more detail.

46 For a good, popular discussion of this question, see Ambrose Evans-Pritchard, "HSBX Bids Farewell to Dollar Supremacy," *The Telegraph,* September 20, 2009. For a good, popular discussion of these points, see Robert Hormats and Jim O'Neill, "A New World Faces the Next Leader," *Financial Times,* June 27, 2008.

47 For just one example, see Rebecca Christie, "Geithner Says Strong Dollar Is in National Interest," Bloomberg News Service, January 22, 2009.

48 "Medvedev Calls for New Reserve Currencies," Yahoo! News, June 16, 2008.

49 Oliver Biggadike and Chris Fournice, "Dollar Declines as Nations Mull Reserve Currency Alternatives," Bloomberg News Service, June 2, 2009.

50 George Parker, Guy Dinmore, Krishna Guha, and Justine Lau, "China in New Dig at Dollar," *Financial Times,* July 10, 2009.

51 Geoff Dyer, "Beijing Glimpses Opportunities in Greenback's Decline," October 19, 2009.

52 Mark Deen and Simon Kennedy, "Russia, India Question Dollar Reliance Before Summit," Bloomberg News Service, July 6, 2009.

53 Robert Fisk, "The Demise of the Dollar," *The Independent,* October 6, 2009.

54 Simon Rabiontvitch and Wayne Cole, "Oil States Say No Talks on Replacing Dollar," www.uk.biz.yahoo.com, October 6, 2009.

55 "World Bank Says Don't Take Dollar's Place for Granted," Yahoo! News, September 27, 2009.

56 "World Bank Chief Says China's Yuan Can Be Alternative Currency in 15 Years," Xinhua News Agency, November 11, 2009.

57 For a recent IMF statement, see Harry Dunphy, "Hand of IMF Proposals New Reserve Currency," Associated Press newswire, February 26, 2010. For the U.N. statement, see "UN Calls for New Reserve Currency," Breitbart News Service, www.breitbart.com, October 6, 2009.

58 Barry Eichengreen, "Sterling's Past, Dollar's Future: Historical Perspectives on Reserve Currency Competition," working paper 11336, National Bureau of Economic Research, May 2005.

59 See Chapter 13, "Helping Finance Cope," for more detail.

60 See Chapter 9, "More Intense Pressures," for more detail.

61 Here are just two examples. In 2005, the United States threatened a 27.5 percent tariff on all Chinese goods entering the country. For a description of that move, see Edward Alden and Christopher Swann, "U.S. Set to Get Tough over Renmimbi," *Financial Times*, April 8, 2005. Again in 2010, the U.S. House of Representatives voted to label China a "currency manipulator," a description, should the legislation pass into law, that could make it much easier for the United States to place targeted tariffs on Chinese goods. For a description, see "Panel Urges U.S. to Label China Currency Manipulator," Reuters Newswire, November 17, 2010.

62 For a thorough description of such a destructive environment, see the discussion in Chapter 11, "Dangerous Political Responses."

63 Thomas Wright, "America Must Find a New China Strategy," *Financial Times*, August 9, 2010.

64 For a thorough investigation of all those options, see Bob Davis, "Short List of Options for the U.S. on Yuan," *The Wall Street Journal*, October 8, 2010.

65 For a description of this proposal by Daniel Gros, of the Center for European Policy Studies in Brussels, see Martin Wolf, "How to Fight the Currency with a Stubborn China," *Financial Times*, October 6, 2010.

66 Jagdish Bhagwati, *Termites in the Trading System: How Preferential Trading Agreements Undermine Free Trade* (New York: Oxford University Press, 2008).

67 Jagdish Bhagwati, "The Selfish Hegemon Must Offer a New Deal on Trade," *Financial Times*, August 20, 2008.

68 Roya Wolverson, Interviewer, "Is China a Currency Manipulator?," Council on Foreign Relations Web site, www.cfr.org, April 15, 2010.

69 Anne O. Krueger, "Prospects for Liberalizing the International Trading System," working paper 2409, National Bureau of Economic Research, October 1987.

70 Clive Crook, "Obama Has to Lead the Way on Trade," *Financial Times*, December 22, 2008.

71 Release from Council on Foreign Relations from Britain, July 13, 2007.

72 Quoted in William Rhodes, "Rich Nations Must Act on Free Trade," *Financial Times*, July 8, 2009.

73 For a discussion of the politics behind such an effort, see "So Near and Yet So Far," *The Economist*, July 31, 2008.

74 For a discussion of some of the alignments in these areas, see "U.S. to Push for New Economic World Order at G-20," Reuters Newswire, September 21, 2009.

75 For more on this promise, see Kishore Mahbubani and William Weld, "Asia Keeps the West's Betrayed Faith," *Financial Times*, July 22, 2009.

76 See Chapter 11, "Dangerous Political Responses."

77 For just a few reports on such accusations and on analysis of their specifics, see Martin Wolf, "How to Preserve the Open Economy at a Time of Stress," *Financial Times*, May 21, 2008, and Alan Beattie, "U.S. Vows to Fight Use of Import Barriers," *Financial Times*, July 17, 2009.

78 See Jagdish Bhagwati, "The Selfish Hegemon Must Offer a New Deal on Trade," *Financial Times*, August 20, 2008.

79 For a reference to these long-standing policies, see David Pilling, "China and India Key on Climate, Says Bush," *Financial Times*, July 7, 2008.

80 James Lamont, James Fontanella-Khan, and Daniel Dambey, "India Rebuffs Clinton on Low-Carbon Future," *Financial Times*, July 20, 2009.

81 For a complete analysis of this recent deadline, see Steve Charnovitz, "America's New Climate Unilateralism," *The International Economy* (Fall 2009).

82 Lars G. Josefsson, "The Economics of Climate Change," *The International Economy* (Summer 2008).

83 Agata Antkiewicz and John Whalley, "Recent Chinese Buyout Activity and the Implications for Global Architecture," working paper 12072, National Bureau of Economic Research, March 2006.

84 Nicolas Veron, "Faceoff," *The International Economy* (Fall 2008).

85 David Marchick and Matthew Slaughter, "Ways to Stem the Drift into Protectionism," *Financial Times*, June 26, 2008.

86 For details on such problems, see Agata Antkiewicz and John Whalley, "Recent Chinese Buyout Activity and the Implications for Global Architecture," working paper 12072, National Bureau of Economic Research, March 2006.

87 Much of this bias is catalogued in Nicolas Veron, "Faceoff," *The International Economy* (Fall 2008).

88 Krishna Guha, "Washington and Beijing to Signal Bilateral Investment Treaty Talks," *Financial Times*, June 19, 2008.

89 For a thorough discussion, see Agata Antkiewicz and John Whalley, "Recent Chinese Buyout Activity and the Implications for Global Architecture," working paper 12072, National Bureau of Economic Research, March 2006.

INDEX